Third Editi

A WORLD OF SHORT STORIES

Why Do You Need This New Edition?

If you are wondering why you should buy this new edition of *A World of Short Stories*, here are 7 good reasons!

1. **New stories** from Bessie Head and Kate Chopin have been included to provide additional insights into characters and conflicts and settings and props and irony.

2. The book is now **perforated** so you can work on your studies right next to the story text.

3. The *Contents* and *Intent and/or Tone Contents* have been **arranged to progress** in difficulty. This will assist you in selecting stories to read.

4. The new *Eerie* category has been added to *Intent and/or Tone Contents*, to make for more interesting reading.

5. **New illustrations** offer you graphic insight into each story.

6. The **MLA Works Cited** entries and the parenthetical models have been updated. You will be able to learn and then apply MLA formats correctly for all your literary references.

7. The **Setting and Props** entry has been expanded to help you focus on setting and props as these elements impact each story you read.

PEARSON

Third Edition

A WORLD OF SHORT STORIES

20 SHORT STORIES FROM AROUND THE WORLD

Yvonne Collioud Sisko
Middlesex County College

Illustrations by
John Seymour and Ted Sisko

PEARSON

Boston Columbus Indianapolis New York San Francisco Upper Saddle River
Amsterdam Cape Town Dubai London Madrid Milan Munich Paris Montréal Toronto
Delhi Mexico City São Paulo Sydney Hong Kong Seoul Singapore Taipei Tokyo

Senior Acquisitions Editor: Nancy Blaine
Development Editor: Jamie Fortner
Marketing Manager: Kurt Massey
Production Manager: Maggie Brobeck
Project Coordination, Text Design, and Electronic Page Makeup: Integra Software
  Services, Pvt. Ltd.
Manager, Central Design: Jayne Conte
Cover Designer: Bruce Kenselaar
Cover Art: © Mikael Damkier/Shutterstock
Printer/Binder: Courier Corporation
Cover Printer: Courier Corporation

Credits and acknowledgments borrowed from other sources and reproduced, with
permission, in this textbook appear on page 361.

Library of Congress Cataloging-in-Publication Data
A world of short stories: 20 short stories from around the world/[edited by]
  Yvonne Collioud Sisko.
    p. cm.
Includes index.
ISBN-13: 978-0-205-90230-9
ISBN-10: 0-205-90230-8
1. Short stories, English.   2. Short stories, American.   3. Short stories—
Translations into English.   I. Sisko, Yvonne Collioud.
PN6120.2.W667 2008
808.83'1—dc22

                                              2008021626

5 6 7 8 9 10 V092 15

ISBN-10:   0-205-90230-8
ISBN-13: 978-0-205-90230-9

To Dad and Mom

CONTENTS

Kate Chopin turns marital assumptions upside down with her iconic twist.

Bessie Head presents contrasts in this insightful tale that explores loyalties and relationships.

The children, Mum, and Dad all tangle delightfully in this tale of family relationships

Joseph Bruchac "Bone Girl"   114

There are morals in these eerie ghost stories.

Mark Twain "Strong Temptations—Strategic Movements—The Innocents Beguiled"   129

Told with humor and irony, this is the classic tale of Tom Sawyer whitewashing the fence.

Grace Ogot "The Rain Came"   143

Read to find out if the chief's daughter will be sacrificed for the good of the tribe.

Jialin Peng "What's in a Name?"   160

Specifically influenced by the location and politics of the setting, Jialin Peng portrays his own adoption of a name.

Zora Neale Hurston "Sweat" 236

Chapter 4 IRONY 255

Catherine Lim "Ah Bah's Money" 256

Guy de Maupassant "The Necklace" 269

Intent and/or Tone
CONTENTS

Here is a general listing of stories by themes, although most of these stories do not easily fit into one category or another. For instance, Juan Bosch's "The Beautiful Soul of Don Damian" can as easily be placed in *Triumph of the Spirit*, *Social Commentary*, *Relationships*, or in *Irony*.

TRIUMPH OF THE SPIRIT

These stories inspire and/or offer insight into the human condition.

> *"Cranes"*
> *"Sweat"*
> *"God Sees the Truth, but Waits"*

HUMOR

These stories tickle the reader's funny bone.

> *"The Hockey Sweater"*
> *"It Used to Be Green Once"*
> *"Strong Temptations—Strategic Movements—The Innocents Beguiled"*
> *"The Ransom of Red Chief"*

IRONY

These stories come with unexpected twists.

> *"Trail of the Green Blazer"*
> *"The Madman"*
> *"The Necklace"*
> *"The Adventure of the Speckled Band"*

SOCIAL COMMENTARY

These stories examine social and/or cultural issues.

> *"The Story of an Hour"*
> *"What's in a Name?"*
> *"Jovita"*

RELATIONSHIPS

These stories focus on interpersonal relationships.

EERIE

These stories present mysterious events.

Geographic
CONTENTS

FOREWORD

American 24-Karat Gold grew out of necessity, and *A World of Short Stories* grew out of *24-Karat*. While simultaneously teaching world literature, freshman composition, and developmental studies, I searched for a collection of important short stories to culminate world literature in New World short story genre, to inspire writing, and to answer the question, "But what do they *read* in reading classes?" I found no such collection. Rather, I found monographs (all O. Henry or Twain), ponderous literary anthologies, or shorter collections of esoteric writings by obscure writers. Nowhere was there simply America's best. *24-Karat* was developed to fill that void. After the immediate success of *24-Karat,* we decided to collect the best from around the world and *World* was born.

However, these are not simply collections. Certainly the literature is the core of my books. But to make the literature accessible, each story is surrounded with extensive and consistent student- and teacher-friendly pedagogy that is most carefully designed to support and even maximize student learning, while simultaneously offering the teacher multiple diagnostic and assessment options. Today, *Looking at Literature*, which includes a play and a novel as well as short stories; *Sterling Stories*, which is a collection of very short stories; and the *Longman Annotated Editions*, which are classic novels filled with extensive pedagogy, now join *24-Karat* and *World* in offering both the student and the teacher even more options for learning and teaching. In fact, both reading and writing competencies have dramatically improved for the now over two thousand students who have field-tested these books.

In this new edition, you will find further enhancements. First, there are new and exciting stories. Second, there is the new Eerie category in Intent and/or Tone Contents. Within each chapter, stories have been arranged to progress more accurately in difficulty. Then, the Journal has been extended to expand student focus and learning, and MLA Works Cited format is updated. Finally, How *I* Use this Book offers insights for the teacher.

Of course, in doing these books there are so many to thank for their endless patience and support. First, I deeply thank Lucille Alfieri, Betty Altruda, Jim Bernarducci, Debbie Brady, Santi Buscemi, Wilson Class, Gert Coleman, Jamie Daley, Sallie DelVecchio, Leah Ghiradella, Evelyn and Kristin Honey, Bill and Vernie Jarocki, Jim Keller, Angela Lugo, Jack and JoAnne McWilliams, Ben Marshall, Albert Nicolai, Jerry Olsen, Christine Piscatelli, Renee Price, Ellen Shur, Mat Spano, Helena Swanicke, Shirley Watchtel, Nancy Zavoluk, and Dan Zimmerman, all dear friends and colleagues. Then I thank my cherished mentors—Drs. Bernie Weinstein, Dan O'Day, Bill Evans, Eileen Kennedy, Carla Lord, Carol Kouros-Schaffer, and Howard Didsbury—who ever inspire me. Thank you, Andre Gittens and Liz Oliu, librarians at Middlesex, who always find the impossible for me. Spirited thanks go to Nancy Blaine, my fantastic editor at Pearson Longman, and to wonderful Jamie Fortner, who has become the most extraordinary permissions sleuth. And, of course, deep thanks go to the now over two thousand students who have field-tested this book and who continue to teach me what does and what does not work.

And, of course, loving thanks go to my family. Thank you, sisters Michelle, Dodee, and Alice for understanding my often committed time. Thank you, brother-in-law John, for your highly literary illustrations that light this book. Thank you, George, for asking where and not what is for dinner. Thank you, son-in-law Dave—well, we all thank you for the many technical tantrums from which you and Teddy have saved me. Thank you, new daughter-in-law Jen, for your pedagogical wisdom. And thank you beyond words, Teddy, Laura, and little Alex. Teddy, your laugh and Laura, your sparkle have lit up my life since the day you each were born. And now little Alex—your mom and dad and Uncle Teddy and Aunt Jen and PopPop love you to pieces. For me, you are sheer joy.

And I deeply, deeply thank you for choosing to bring this book to your students. I truly, truly hope you enjoy using this book as much as I have enjoyed creating it.

Yvonne Collioud Sisko
Old Bridge, New Jersey

PREFACE

TO THE STUDENT

It seems that human beings have always loved a good story. In fact, anthropologists tell us that storytelling has been used to teach rules and ideas for millennia.

This book is filled with good stories, or narratives or narrations. Read these stories to gain knowledge about yourself, for a good story offers us some information about ourselves. Most of all, read these stories to enjoy them. Stories have a way of taking us into new worlds, offering universals (feelings we all can understand).

However, the stories in this book are designed to do more than just expose you to each story itself. Each story is surrounded with exercises that will help you better understand each story. Each story includes the following:

- **Vocabulary Exercises**—Vocabulary exercises help you define the words you need to know for the story, before you even read it.
- **Questions**—Questions help guide you through the story.
- **Biography**—A biography of the story's author provides you information about the author's style and other works.
- **Journal**—After reading, you can record and organize your thoughts about the story in a journal.
- **Follow-up Questions**—You can demonstrate what you've learned about the story in follow-up questions.
- **Discussion Questions**—These questions ask you to reach deeper and to react to the story.
- **Writing Ideas**—Writing ideas help guide your own writing.

To understand better how this book works, turn to the Sample Lesson on page 1, and work your way through it. You'll find that you will be actively participating in this book, which will make understanding and appreciating the stories easier and more rewarding for you.

Welcome to *A World of Short Stories!* Read this book, study it, and—most of all—enjoy it.

TO THE TEACHER

The greatest assets of *A World of Short Stories* are its participatory lessons and the many options these lessons offer you. Certainly, the literature is the core of this book, but the pedagogical materials that surround every story require students to actively participate in every story. Simultaneously, these materials offer a choice of multiple, administratively efficient diagnostic and assessment tools. Each story is a self-contained lesson, and all of the stories are consistently formatted, thereby offering students clear expectations and offering you multiple options.

New to this Edition

In the third edition, you will find further enhancements. First, there are new and exciting stories. Second, all stories now have illustrations to encourage discussion. Then, there is the new Eerie category in Intent and/or Tone Contents. Within each chapter, stories have been arranged to progress more accurately in difficulty. Then, the Journal has been extended to expand student focus and learning, and MLA Works Cited format has been updated. And, finally, How *I* Use This Book has been added, offering insights for the teacher.

Sample Lesson

A World of Short Stories starts out with an applied **Sample Lesson**. The Sample Lesson can be used in class *or* it can be assigned as homework. Written in simple and accessible language, this introductory lesson walks students through the basic story format, using Kate Chopin's "Ripe Figs." This lesson, as all lessons, opens with Pre-Reading Vocabulary—Context and Pre-Reading Vocabulary—Structural Attack to help students define important words used in the story. Pre-reading Questions set purpose, and the author's biography supplies relevant background information.

After reading "Ripe Figs," students learn notation strategies that they can then apply to the subsequent readings. With the story completed, students move on to the Journal exercises, which are comprehensive and participatory studies of the story. The Sample Lesson explains the tasks in each Journal section, offers sample answers to get students started, and introduces relevant literary terminology.

With the Journal completed, students now have an active, working understanding of "Ripe Figs." They can then move on to three sets of Follow-up Questions. These questions consistently use multiple assessment formats: (1) ten multiple-choice questions objectively assessing comprehension; (2) five significant quotations subjectively assessing comprehension; and (3) two essay questions subjectively assessing comprehension. Then Discussion Questions ask students to reach deeper, to reflect upon, and to react to each story. Each story ends with Writing suggestions. In the Sample Lesson, students are introduced to pre-writing and outlining strategies. In subsequent stories, students will find multiple writing prompts.

I suggest that you work through the Sample Lesson in class, for it is here that you will find the dynamics and possibilities of this book encapsulated.

Chapter Structure

The stories in *A World of Short Stories* are arranged into four topical chapters, based on and reinforcing the literary terminology the student has already encountered in the Sample Lesson. While all stories contain combinations of these terms and/or elements, each of the chapters focuses on a specific term(s) and/or element(s) by beginning with a restatement of the term(s) and then by presenting the stories that have been specifically chosen to demonstrate the term(s) and/or element(s). Chapter 1 focuses on characters and conflicts, Chapter 2 focuses on setting and props, Chapter 3 focuses on plot and foreshadowing, and Chapter 4 focuses on irony.

Within each chapter, you have many options:

1. You can assign these chapters in any order.
2. You can assign the stories within each chapter in any order. Generally, the stories within each chapter progress from more accessible to more difficult, but the strengths of each class vary, and what may seem more accessible to one group may be more difficult for another.
3. You can assign all of the stories in a chapter or any number of stories you prefer.
4. You can use one of the alternative tables of contents. Selecting from the Intent and/or Tone Contents can make for interesting study. Selecting from Geographic Contents offers different perspectives.
5. You can ignore all of these suggestions and assign any story at your discretion.

Story Structure

Each story in *A World of Short Stories* is set amid carefully designed teaching materials and, because the format is consistent, you will be able to find these materials easily. These materials were discussed generally in the overview of the Sample Lesson on the previous page, but here we look at the materials more closely.

PRE-READING MATERIALS. Each story selection begins with pre-reading materials. The pre-reading materials prepare students for reading stories while offering you insights into their vocabulary mastery and study habits.

1. **Pre-reading Vocabulary—Context** presents words that are crucial to understanding the story. These words have been chosen to make the story accessible to students and may or may not be the most sophisticated words in the story. For more sophisticated study, all potentially troublesome words in any given story are presented in the Instructor's Manual, where you will find words listed in the order in which they appear in the story so that you can easily locate them and identify them for students in the story's text.
2. **Pre-reading Vocabulary—Structural Attack** offers structural analysis exercises. These words have been chosen not for their sophistication, but because they help students apply structural analysis skills. Thus, before students start the story, they have defined at least 20 words in context and 10 to 30 words by structural analysis. The need for distracting glossed words and marginal definitions is thereby eliminated, because students are well prepared by the pre-reading vocabulary to approach the story.

3. **Pre-reading Questions** offer food for thought as students enter the story. The author's **Biography** offers not only biographical background but also additional information about the author's other works.

JOURNAL. After students have read and annotated the story, the **Journal** then draws them into active reflection and participation.

- *MLA Works Cited*—Students record the story in MLA Works Cited entry format, using the generic model provided.
- *Main Characters(s)*—Students separate, describe, and defend the character(s) they have selected as main character(s) (applying and reinforcing the separation of main ideas from supporting details).
- *Supporting Characters*—Students separate, describe, and defend the characters they have selected as supporting characters (applying and reinforcing the separation of main ideas from supporting details).
- *Setting*—Students describe the setting(s) and relevant prop(s) (applying and reinforcing inference skills).
- *Sequence*—Students outline the story's events in order (applying and reinforcing sequencing and outlining skills).
- *Plot*—Students summarize the story's events in no more than three sentences (applying and reinforcing the separation of main ideas from supporting details, as well as summary skills).
- *Conflicts*—Students identify and explain the relevant conflicts (applying and reinforcing inference and judgment skills).
- *Significant Quotations*—Students explain the importance of five quotations that are central to the story (applying and reinforcing inference skills) and learn MLA parenthetical citation format.
- *Literary Elements*—Students identify and explain literary elements (applying and reinforcing inference and judgment skills).
- *Foreshadowing, Irony, and Symbolism*—Students identify and explain examples of foreshadowing, irony, and symbols (applying and reinforcing inference and judgment skills).

The Journal is a comprehensive cognitive workout for students. In the Journal, students reflect on the story, sort out the details, and organize the story's components while applying and/or reinforcing their comprehension skills. You can collect any part or all of the Journal to check on student progress. The wealth of diagnostic information in the Journal will enable you to spot misunderstandings, illogical thinking, and so forth, that may compromise comprehension. Requiring a completed Journal for classroom participation also assures you of students who are prepared to discuss the story.

FOLLOW-UP QUESTIONS. The Journal is followed by three follow-up question formats. The Follow-up Questions are designed for assessment but can also be used for small-group or class discussion. All of these questions are intended to measure comprehension; they purposely avoid literary controversy.

- **10 Short Questions** offer ten multiple-choice questions.

- **5 Significant Quotations** ask students to explain the importance of five quotations that are always central to the story.
- **2 Comprehensive Essay Questions** provide two essay prompts.

The Follow-up Questions offer you multiple, efficient assessment options. You may decide to use some questions for discussion or some for testing. If you are trying to establish standardization, the section of 10 Short Questions is applicable for standardization, measuring comprehension efficiently by psychometrically employing 10 questions (only 6 are needed for accurate measurement) with 3 choices each.

DISCUSSION QUESTIONS. Each story provides two thought-provoking questions. Unlike the Follow-up Questions, Discussion Questions encourage reflection, personal opinion, and/or literary debate. Again, you may choose to have students discuss these or to have students write these answers.

WRITING PROMPTS. Each story concludes with options for **Writing**. Here, two prompts for personal writing are included. Then, under **Further Writing**, you will find prompts for more advanced, research-oriented writing. These prompts may be literary (compare and contrast this story with another in this book, with another by this author, with one by another author, and so forth) or topical research suggestions.

Instructor's Manual

The **Instructor's Manual (IM)** offers valuable resources for teachers. In addition to an overview of the book's pedagogy, the IM offers additional information on each story.

1. The entry for each story starts with a brief overview and suggestions for appropriate readers.
2. Each entry offers an extensive list of all potentially troublesome words in the story, assembled with both the native speaker and the ESL student in mind. Words are listed in the order they appear in the story for easy location.
3. Under plot, each story is condensed to one sentence; you may find these summaries useful in selecting stories for assignment.
4. Suggested answers to the Journal and Follow-up Questions are provided. The suggested answers—suggested because these are, after all, literary pursuits and students' answers will vary—set parameters for correctness. The only areas that have clearly right and/or wrong answers are the MLA Works Cited entry and 10 Short Questions.

To order a copy of the Instructor's Manual, contact your Pearson sales representative and request ISBN: 9780205902316.

Some Final Notes

The materials in *A World of Short Stories*—the context and structural vocabulary exercises, the journal format, the three assessment options, the discussion questions, as well as many of the writing prompts—have been extensively field-tested by over two thousand students. These field tests have taken place in one of the most culturally diverse counties in the nation—Middlesex County, New Jersey. Several results have occurred. First, the story lessons have dramatically improved both reading and writing students' performances. Second, the story lessons have not only increased students' competencies, but they have also come to serve as a basis for acculturation discussions with ESL and/or international students. Third, the pedagogical materials have been streamlined to maximize student learning and administrative efficiency.

It should also be noted that, although copyright restrictions apply, we have elided offensive words wherever feasible.

Last, but certainly not least, we must address the stories themselves. The richness of the literature speaks for itself, and the stories have been carefully chosen to present the best of writers from around the world. This collection sets out to expand the basic literary lexicon of today's entering student.

I sincerely hope you and your students enjoy reading these stories as much as I have enjoyed discovering them, rediscovering them, and working with them.

Yvonne Collioud Sisko
Old Bridge, New Jersey

Third Edition

A WORLD OF SHORT STORIES

A Sample Lesson

RIPE FIGS

BY

KATE CHOPIN

The best way to learn how to use something is to do just that—to use it. This Sample Lesson presents a very short work, "Ripe Figs" by Kate Chopin, to demonstrate how this book works. This Sample Lesson presents all of the materials that surround each chapter. Generally, each story starts with pre-reading activities that are designed to make your reading easier, and ends with a journal, follow-up questions, discussion questions, and writing assignments, all designed to improve your understanding. This Sample Lesson also introduces the elements of a narrative—elements that you will be using throughout this book.

Let's begin.

RIPE FIGS

Kate Chopin

Pre-reading Vocabulary
Context

Use context clues to define these words before reading. Use a dictionary as needed.

> The words that are critical for your understanding of the reading are presented at the beginning of each reading. These are not necessarily the most difficult words. Rather, they are words that you will need to know to understand the reading more easily.
>
> The **Pre-reading Vocabulary—Context** exercises present words in sentences. You should try to define each word by using the context clues in the sentence. Note that the first eight words have been defined as examples for you. Look at sentence 1. The word here is "fig," and the clues let you know that this is something "small" and "purple" that grows "on a tree" and is "delicious." Since "delicious" implies it is something to eat and since fruit grows on a tree, we can define a "fig" as "a small, purple fruit that grows on a tree." Using this same strategy, check the meanings of the next seven words. Then use the clues and define the remaining words.

1. The small, purple *figs* grow on a tree and are delicious. *Fig* means

   a small, purple fruit that grows on a tree   .

2. Some may say "mom" or "mama" for mother, while the French may say

   mère or *maman*. *Mère* or *maman* means _a name for "mother"_   .

3. The campers rowed their boat slowly through the reeds along the side of

   the *bayou*. *Bayou* means _a slow-moving body of water_   .

4. The children licked the long *sugar cane* they found in the field. *Sugar cane*

   means _a stick-like food_   .

5. The elderly person's fingers seemed to cross each other in *gnarled* knots

   from old age and arthritis. *Gnarled* means _knotted and crisscrossed_   .

6. Ted is so *patient*; he doesn't mind if Laura takes two hours to do her hair.

   Patient means _willing to wait_   .

7. There is a stone *statue* of a little boy in the middle of the garden. *Statue* means <u>a carved or sculpted figure</u>.

8. The tiny *humming-bird's* wings moved so quickly that you could not see them. *Humming-bird* means <u>a small bird with rapidly moving wings</u>.

9. Dave was *disconsolate* after he lost the championship game. *Disconsolate* means _____.

10. Kings and queens usually walk in a very upright and *stately* manner. *Stately* means_____.

11. Furniture is often first covered in a simple *muslin* under the fine fabric to protect the fabric. *Muslin* means _____.

12. The haze of color often drawn around a saint's head is called a halo or *aureole*. *Aureole* means _____.

13. In spite of all the upset and confusion, Alex stayed cool and *placid*. *Placid* means _____.

14. The bride's dishes are fine *porcelain* decorated with tiny flowers and trimmed in gold. *Porcelain* means _____.

15. I will go to see my aunt, *Tante* Lena, to celebrate her birthday. *Tante* means _____.

16. I love the large yellow *chrysanthemums* that bloom in a fall garden. *Chrysanthemum* means <u>flower</u>.

PRE-READING VOCABULARY
STRUCTURAL ATTACK

Define these words by solving the parts. Use the Glossary or a dictionary as needed.

The **Pre-reading Vocabulary—Structural Attack** exercises present words that you know but that may look strange or have altered meanings because of added parts. Here you will want to look for and define the **root**, or core, word. Then look for and define the **prefix**, or part added to the front of the word. Finally, look for and define the **suffix**, or part added to the end of the word.

Prefixes (added to the front) and suffixes (added to the end) are called **affixes**. By defining the root and the affixes, you should be able to define each of these words with little trouble. For instance, look at the first vocabulary word. The very simple word "ripe" has two suffixes (-en, -ing) that can be added to it, which change the word's meaning from "ready" or "mature" to "getting ready" or "maturing."

Or look at the fourth vocabulary word. Here two words form a new word. This is called a **compound word**. "Summer" and "time" combine to mean "the warm part of the year."

Using these same strategies, take each word apart, and define it by using the roots and affixes. The first three words are defined for you. Try the last three on your own. See the Glossary (page 355) for affix definitions.

1. ripening   *becoming ripe or maturing*
2. la Madone   *mother or Holy Mother*
3. restless   *active; cannot rest*
4. summertime
5. godmother
6. plumpest

PRE-READING QUESTIONS

Try answering these questions as you read.

Now you have defined words to help you understand the reading. Before reading, it is always helpful to start with a purpose. Use the reading's title and any other relevant information to set up questions to answer while you are reading. Answering these questions will make your reading easier and more efficient, so that you do not have to read and reread to understand the narrative.

Each reading starts with **Pre-reading Questions** to set your purpose. Keep these questions in mind as you read.

Who are the main characters? Supporting characters?

What does Babette want?

What does Maman want?

What does the title mean?

RIPE FIGS

KATE CHOPIN

Before the narrative, a brief **biography** provides some information about the author. In addition to learning about the author's life, you may also pick up information that will help you in reading the narrative. The biography may also list other works by the author, in case you would like to read more by that author.

Read Kate Chopin's biography. It tells you, among other things, that she writes about the people she met in Louisiana and that she likes to use "symbols and images from nature." Both of these pieces of information will come in handy as you read "Ripe Figs."

Kate O'Flaherty Chopin was born in St. Louis in 1851 to an affluent family. Although her father died when she was young, her widowed mother gave young Kate a taste of independence. In 1870 Kate married Oscar Chopin and moved to New Orleans and then Natchitoches Parish. Here she met the Creoles, Acadians, and African Americans she would later write about. However, Oscar died in 1882, and by 1884 she sold the plantation, gathered her five children, and returned home to St. Louis, where she began to write for popular women's magazines. Influenced noticeably by Guy de Maupassant's sense of irony and Henrik Ibsen's social comment, Chopin wrote stories, often touched with rich symbols and images from nature, that question societal assumptions and dictates. *The Awakening* remains her master work, although short stories such as "Desiree's Baby" and "The Kiss" offer Chopin at her most terse. Chopin died in 1904.

Now it is time to turn to the story. As you read, keep the following suggestions in mind. Don't just let your eyes go over words. Instead, *get involved—get out a pen or pencil and highlighters, and use them!*

1. First, *circle the name of each character*, or highlight each in a different color. The first step in understanding a narrative is knowing *whom* it is about.
2. Second, underline or highlight in yet another color all the hints that let you know *where and when the narrative takes place*. The second step in understanding a narrative is knowing *where* and *when* it takes place.
3. Third, *number each event* in the narrative as it occurs. Number these events in the margin or right in the text. The third step in understanding a narrative is knowing what is happening.
4. Fourth, *make notes*—ideas, questions to be answered later, and so on—in the margin. These are ideas you can return to later, and they may help you understand the *how* and/or *why* of the narrative.
5. Fifth, but certainly not least, always *reread the title*. The title often gives you information that is helpful in understanding the narrative.

Maman-Nainaine said that when the figs were ripe Babette might go to visit her cousins down on the Bayou-Lafourche where the sugar cane grows. Not that the ripening of figs had the least thing to do with it, but that is the way Maman-Nainaine was.

2   It seemed to Babette a very long time to wait; for the leaves upon the trees were tender yet, and the figs were like little hard, green marbles.

3   But warm rains came along and plenty of strong sunshine, and though Maman-Nainaine was as patient as the statue of la Madone, and Babette as restless as a humming-bird, the first thing they both knew it was hot summertime. Every day Babette danced out to where the fig-trees were in a long line against the fence. She walked slowly beneath them, carefully peering between the gnarled, spreading branches. But each time she came away disconsolate again. What she saw there finally was something that made her sing and dance the whole day long.

4   When Maman-Nainaine sat down in her stately way to breakfast, the following morning, her muslin cap standing like an aureole around her white, placid face, Babette approached. She bore a dainty porcelain platter, which she set down before her godmother. It contained a dozen purple figs, fringed around with their rich, green leaves.

5   "Ah," said Maman-Nainaine arching her eyebrows, "how early the figs have ripened this year!"

6   "Oh," said Babette. "I think they have ripened very late."

7   "Babette," continued Maman-Nainaine, as she peeled the very plumpest figs with her pointed silver fruit-knife, "you will carry my love to them all down on Bayou-Lafourche. And tell your Tante Frosine I shall look for her at Toussaint—when the chrysanthemums are in bloom."

Now turn to the marked copy of "Ripe Figs" in Figure 1. The first half has already been noted for you. Take out your pen, pencil, and/or highlighters, and using the strategies listed in the last section, complete the notes on "Ripe Figs." Note how effective the notations in Figure 1 are. It's important to know that Chopin uses nature to reflect life, so this is underlined in the biography. The title is "Ripe Figs," so figs (which are a delicate fruit) must somehow relate to the story. Babette and Maman-Nainaine are in the center of the story, and the cousins and Tante Frosine are also involved. Hints like "figs" and "Bayou," as well as information in the biography, all indicate that this story is probably taking place in the South, in Louisiana. The events are numbered in sequence: (1) Babette wants to go visiting, but Maman says not yet; (2) Babette must wait for the figs to ripen; (3) the figs ripen; and (4) Babette now can go and Maman will go in the fall. Now it is easier to see that two things are ripening or maturing here: Babette and the figs. Thus, the ripening figs reflect Babette's maturing. When the figs are ripe, she is also ripe, or mature enough to go visiting. By using the information from the biography and title and combining this information with the story's characters, setting, and events, you can see that as the figs ripen, Babette grows older and becomes ready to travel. Add your own notes in paragraphs 4 through 7.

Ripe Figs

KATE CHOPIN

Kate O'Flaherty Chopin was born in St. Louis in 1851 to an affluent family. Although her father died when she was young, her widowed mother gave young Kate a taste of independence. In 1870 Kate married Oscar Chopin and moved to New Orleans and then Natchitoches Parish. Here she met the Creoles, Acadians, and African Americans she would later write about. However, Oscar died in 1882, and by 1884 she sold the plantation, gathered her five children, and returned home to St. Louis, where she began to write for popular women's magazines. Influenced noticeably by Guy de Maupassant's sense of irony and Henrik Ibsen's social comment, Chopin wrote stories, often touched with rich symbols and images from nature, that question societal assumptions and dictates. Her brief novel *The Awakening* remains her master work, although stories such as "Desiree's Baby" and "The Kiss" offer Chopin at her most terse. Chopin died in 1904.

Maman-Nainaine said that when the figs were ripe Babette might go to visit her cousins down on the Bayou-Lafourche where the sugar cane grows. Not that the ripening of figs had the least thing to do with it, but that is the way Maman-Nainaine was.

1. CAN VISIT WHEN FIGS RIPEN

2   It seemed to Babette a very long time to wait; for the leaves upon the trees were tender yet, and the figs were like little hard, green marbles.

3   But warm rains came along and plenty of strong sunshine, and though Maman-Nainaine was as patient as the statue of la Madone, and Babette as restless as a humming-bird, the first thing they both knew it was hot summertime. Every day Babette danced out to where the fig-trees were in a long line against the fence. She walked slowly beneath them, carefully peering between the gnarled, spreading branches. But each time she came away disconsolate again. What she saw there finally was something that made her sing and dance the whole day long.

2. WAIT FOR FIGS TO GROW

4   When Maman-Nainaine sat down in her stately way to breakfast, the following morning, her muslin cap standing like an aureole around her white, placid face, Babette approached. She bore a dainty porcelain platter, which she set down before her godmother. It contained a dozen purple figs, fringed around with their rich, green leaves.

5   "Ah," said Maman-Nainaine arching her eyebrows, "how early the figs have ripened this year!"

6   "Oh," said Babette. "I think they have ripened very late."

7   "Babette," continued Maman-Nainaine, as she peeled the very plumpest figs with her pointed silver fruit-knife, "you will carry my love to them all down on Bayou-Lafourche. And tell your Tante Frosine I shall look for her at Toussaint—when the chrysanthemums are in bloom."

FIGURE 1   Marked Copy of "Ripe Figs"

RIPE FIGS

Journal

Once you have finished reading and making your notes in the reading, the **Journal** allows you to record and organize all the relevant information. Here you will be able to record, organize, reflect upon, and make sense out of all the details that can make a reading challenging.

1. **MLA Works Cited** *Using this model, record this story here.*

   Author's Last Name, First Name. "Title of the Story." *Title of This Book.* 3rd ed. Ed.

   First Name Last Name. City: Publisher, year. Page number(s) of this story. Print.

Whenever you refer to or use anyone else's words or ideas, you must give that person credit. Failing to give credit is called **plagiarism**. Plagiarism can result in failing an assignment, failing a course, and even being removed from school.

To give credit appropriately, it is helpful to learn the format used to credit works of literature. This format has been created by the Modern Language Association, or MLA. The **MLA Works Cited entry** you use here is the same basic form you will be using in your other English classes.

The MLA entry is really a very simple form. All you have to do is follow the model given. Note that, unlike paragraphs, the first line starts at the left margin and each line *after* that is indented. Try doing this on your own. When you finish, your MLA Works Cited entry for "Ripe Figs" should look like the following.

Chopin, Kate. "Ripe Figs." *A World of Short Stories.* 3rd ed. Ed. Yvonne Sisko. Pearson Longman:

New York, 2014. 7. Print.

2. **Main Character(s)**

Characters are the creatures that create, move, or experience the actions of a narrative. We normally think of characters as alive, animated beings, such as humans or animals who can participate in the action, although some characters will surprise you. A character may also be called an **actor, player, person, personage**, or **persona**.

Characters fall into two categories: **main characters** and **supporting characters**. Generally, a **main character** is central to the action. A **supporting character** may encourage the action and is usually not present as much, or is not as central to the action, as the main character. Sometimes it is difficult to decide if a character is main or supporting. For instance, in a murder mystery, the victim may appear at the beginning or not at all, but the entire narrative is about solving her or his murder. Is the victim a main character because the entire narrative is all about her or him, or is s/he a supporting character because s/he is simply not around much? Both answers may be correct. In literature there are not always so much right or wrong answers as there are explanations, analyses, and debates. The correctness of your answers may depend on how well you explain your choices.

Characters may also be considered protagonists or antagonists. "Pro" means "for," and the **protagonist** is the hero or heroine, the character we **empathize** with or share feelings with, the character we root for. "Anti" means "against," and the **antagonist** is the villain, the enemy of the protagonist, the character we do not like, the character we root against. In "Ripe Figs" our sympathies are with Babette and her longing for adventure; she is the protagonist. Maman, who sets limits on Babette, is the antagonist. Here, these two characters are members of a seemingly close family and love each other, but in other narratives the protagonist and antagonist may not be such close relatives or friends.

Authors speak to us through their characters. When an author writes using "I" or "we," this is called a **first-person narrative**. The first-person makes a story very immediate. The character who tells the story is called the **narrator**. If the author addresses the reader directly using "you," the narrative technique is called a **second-person narrative**. Second-person is not often used today. Finally, if the author uses "he," "she," "it," or "they" to tell the narrative, the narrative technique is called a **third-person narrative**. This is the most common narrative form, with the author seeming to be more of an observer and less of a participant in the story. In "Ripe Figs," both Babette and Maman are observed as "she." The story is thus told in the third-person; the author is the narrator who observes but does not enter the narrative.

With these understandings, turn to the **Main Character(s)** and **Supporting Characters** entries in the Journal. Note that we have already filled in Babette, briefly describing her and noting her important place in the story. Who else should be here? Add an entry in which you describe and defend Maman as a main character.

Note: When discussing literature, always use the **present tense**. Although a narrative may have been written a thousand years ago, each time a narrative is read, the characters and actions come to life and are alive right now, so keep your discussion of the characters and events in the present tense.

Describe each main character, and explain why you think each is a main character.

Babette is a young girl who lives with her godmother and wants to go visit her cousins. She is a main character because the story is about her wants and her godmother's rules.

3. Supporting Characters

Now fill in the **Supporting Characters** entry. This has been started for you. Certainly, the cousins support the action because they are the reason Babette wants to travel. Who else should be here? Add an entry in which you describe and defend Tante Frosine as a supporting character. Remember from your context studies that "tante" means "aunt," so Tante Frosine is probably the cousins' mother.

Describe each supporting character, and explain why you think each is a supporting character.

Babette's cousins are supporting characters. Although we never see them, they are the reason for the story's conflict.

4. Setting and Props

Setting is a catchall term that describes the **time**, **place**, and **surroundings** of a narrative. In a short story, the setting is usually, although not always, limited. The story usually takes place in a shorter amount of time than in a longer work, and fewer places are involved. In a novel, there may be more time and more places.

Props go along with the setting. Props (short for "properties") are the inanimate objects in a narrative. Props sometimes take on the qualities of characters.

Now turn to the **setting** entry. You already have a head start because the place, Louisiana, is described. But you still have several things to do. First, you need to add when the story takes place. Check the biography for when Chopin lived, and remember that traveling seems to be a very big accomplishment in this story, unlike it is in today's world of easy car transportation. Second, think about props and mention the figs, which are certainly part of this story.

Describe the setting(s) and all relevant prop(s).

This must be set in the South because figs are a delicate fruit, because the French words sound like words spoken in Louisiana, and because the biography says that Chopin wrote about the South.

5. Sequence

A narrative is based around a simple skeleton of events called a **plot**. Around this basic plot, a logical order of events or **sequence** occurs that builds tension or, in mysteries, suspense. In narratives we call all the events in the sequence a **story line**. The plot is the bare framework, while the sequence supplies the details that make each narrative unique.

Have you ever gone to the movies and watched the end credits roll while you were still waiting for the movie to get going? You looked at the person sitting next to you, felt cheated, and asked, "What happened?" What happened is that, somewhere along the line, the storyteller failed.

In a well-written narrative, one event logically leads to another, and then to another, and so on, so that each word and action counts and builds tension that carries your interest. The tension peaks at the **climax** and then resolves in the **dénouement**. When any of these pieces are missing, poorly developed, or unbelievable, we are disappointed. (Movie sequels, in fact, purposely stop at the climax and before the dénouement so that we will return for the next episode.) A very simple story line appears in Figure 2.

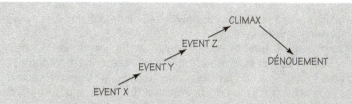

FIGURE 2   Simple Story Line

Use information about sequence and plot in the Journal. In the Sequence entry, you are asked to outline all the events in order. The outline is started for you, with Babette's desire to go visiting and Maman's restriction. Now look at your numbered notes on the story, and complete the outline. Add as many events as you feel are necessary.

Outline the events of the story in order.

I. Babette wants to go visiting, but Maman-Nainaine says she must wait for the figs to ripen.

II.

III.

IV.

6. Plot

Next, in the **Plot** entry, summarize all of these events into one sentence. Summarizing makes you look back over the reading and reflect on what you have read. Remember, this is the bare framework of the narrative, so keep it short.

Tell the story in no more than one sentence.

7. Conflicts

Conflicts are the disagreements between the characters. Conflicts build the tension in a narrative. Many types of conflicts are possible. The conflict may be **human versus human**, as when a character(s) is pitted against another character(s). The conflict may be **human versus society**, as when a character(s) struggles against a group, community, or social structure. The conflict may be **human versus technology**, as when a character(s) vies with the tools of science or machines of her/his society. The conflict may be **human versus nature**, as when a character(s) battles with the forces of nature. The conflict may be **human versus the supernatural**, as when a character(s) vies with God or gods or demons. Finally, the conflict may be **human versus her/himself**, as when a character wrestles with her or his own internal and self-defeating **flaw**. More often than not, a story will contain a combination of these conflicts.

Let's now turn to the **Conflicts** entry. Human versus human, in Babette's struggle with Maman's restriction, is already noted. What other types of conflicts are present in the story? How about human versus nature in Babette's wanting the figs to mature rapidly, and human versus herself in Babette's impatience? Add these and explain them in your Journal entry.

Identify and explain all of the conflicts involved here.

Human versus human applies to Babette wanting to go and Maman-Nainaine stopping her.

8. Significant Quotations

By now, you already understand the narrative well. You have identified the pieces and pulled them together. Now you need to reflect on the narrative. In this section, you will find quotations from key parts of the narrative. By explaining why each quotation is important to the reading, you can deepen your understanding.

First, look up the quotation in the reading text. Underline it and note what is important about this moment in the reading. Then, record the importance of this moment. Tell who is speaking and why this quotation is important to the action in the reading. The first one has been done for you. Now, complete the rest. Record the page number for practice with **MLA parenthetical citation**.

Explain the importance of each of these quotations. Record the page number in the parentheses.

a. "Maman-Nainaine said that when the figs were ripe Babette might go to visit her cousins down on the Bayou-Lafourche where the sugar cane grows" (7).

> This quotation sets the tension in the story between Babette and Maman-Nainaine and between Babette and nature. Babette wants to visit her cousins, but she must wait until the figs—and she—are ripe or mature enough to go.

b. "Every day Babette danced out to where the fig-trees were in a long line against the fence" ( ).

c. "What she saw there finally was something that made her sing and dance the whole day long" (   ).

d. "'Ah,' said Maman-Nainaine arching her eyebrows, 'how early the figs have ripened this year!'" (   ).

e. "'And tell your Tante Frosine I shall look for her at Toussaint—when the chrysanthemums are in bloom'" (   ).

9. Literary Elements

By now, you have become familiar with identifying characters, conflicts, settings, props, sequences, plots, and so forth. These terms or ideas, along with others you will meet, are called **literary elements**. You will see that the chapters in this book stress specific elements. Here you are asked to decide why each story is placed in the chapter in which it appears.

For instance, let's say that "Ripe Figs" had been placed in the *Characters and Conflicts* chapter. "Ripe Figs" not only has characters and conflicts, but also it certainly has a setting and important props, and it certainly has events leading up to a climax. Yet in looking over the whole story, we can see that this story is largely a character study focused on impatient Babette and the conflicts her impatience entails. Thus, here you will want to focus on why characters and conflicts are so important in this story. Likewise, for every other story, you will focus on the chapter's literary element(s) and explain why the element(s) is(are) important to the story. Sometimes you may even disagree with the placement and, if you disagree, explain why you disagree and where else you would place the story. The important thing is that you explain the story in terms of the given element(s). Now, explain why characters and conflicts are so important in "Ripe Figs." Then explain any other chapter(s) in which you feel "Ripe Figs" might also fit.

Look at this chapter's title [here, we are using Characters and Conflicts] and explain why you think this story is placed in this chapter. Explain in which other chapter(s) you might place this story, as relevant to the literary element(s) of the chapter(s).

10. Foreshadowing, Irony, and/or Symbols

Other elements that may enhance a narrative are foreshadowing, irony, and/or symbolism.

Foreshadowing is a technique some authors use to help explain or to predict events to come. The author may sprinkle information or hints throughout the narrative to help predict actions that are yet to happen.

Irony is found in the difference between what *is* and what *should be*. Irony may be bitter—you work and work and work, and someone new, who has done nothing, arrives at your job and gets the promotion you deserve. Irony may be humorous—you wake up late and race around knowing you will be late for class, only to get to school and find out that your class has been canceled. Irony may even be providential—you sleep in and miss your bus, only to find out that the bus was in an accident and you are still safe at home. Think of ironies as unexpected twists in time, places, or events.

Symbols are objects or characters that represent something beyond their face value. For instance, an American flag is really nothing more than pieces of cloth sewn together, but the American flag represents the pride and glory and industry of America. By looking beyond the surface, you may find many symbols in literature.

In **Foreshadowing, Irony, and/or Symbols**, you will be asked to discuss one of these elements. Here, discuss the symbols in this story, and there are several. First and foremost, the figs represent maturity and reflect Babette's growth. Second, the **seasons** are relevant here. Summer is youthful Babette's time, while fall is the older Maman and Tante Frosine's time. In literature, spring may represent birth or rebirth or youth; summer may represent youth or the full blossom of life; fall may represent middle age; and winter may represent the later years. Here Chopin gives us clues to the characters' ages by using the seasons. The chrysanthemums (flowers that bloom in the fall) represent the time for Babette's elders.

Although foreshadowing and irony are not particularly relevant to this story, be aware that Kate Chopin is known for her ironic twists. And, of course, here the ripening figs foreshadow Babette's growth.

Explain examples of foreshadowing, irony, and/or symbols in this story.

FOLLOW-UP QUESTIONS

10 SHORT QUESTIONS

Follow-up Questions are designed to measure your comprehension of each reading. In the first set of questions, you will see multiple-choice entries aimed at measuring your comprehension.

Notice that you are instructed to select "the <u>best</u> answer." In some readings, more than one answer will be correct; it is your job to choose the <u>best</u> answer. The first five have been done for you here.

The answer to question 1 is "a" because Babette is the younger of the two. We know this because Babette's actions and the information from the story—*Maman* means "mother" and Maman is Babette's godmother—imply that Babette is younger and Maman is older. The answer to question 2 is "b" for the same reasons listed in the answer to question 1. The answer to question 3 is "c" because we are clearly told that Maman is the godmother. The cousins are in Babette's age group and are whom she wants to visit; there is no mention of a sister in the story. The answer to question 4 is "a" because, as the story implies, figs need a warm summer and rain to grow; neither "cold" nor "desert" fits the story's setting. The answer to question 5 is "c" because we are clearly told about Babette's "restlessness" as opposed to Maman's "patience."

Now complete questions 6 through 10 on your own. The correct answers appear on page 20.

What is the <u>best</u> answer for each?

<u>a</u> 1. Babette is
   a. younger than Maman.
   b. older than Maman.
   c. the same age as Maman.

<u>b</u> 2. Maman-Nainaine is
   a. younger than Babette.
   b. older than Babette.
   c. the same age as Babette.

<u>c</u> 3. Maman-Nainaine is Babette's
   a. sister.
   b. cousin.
   c. godmother.

<u>a</u> 4. "Ripe Figs" is probably set in
   a. a warm climate.
   b. a cold climate.
   c. a desert climate.

<u>c</u> 5. Babette
   a. does not wait for the figs.
   b. waits calmly for the figs.
   c. waits impatiently for the figs.

____ 6. Maman
   a. does not wait for the figs.
   b. waits calmly for the figs.
   c. waits impatiently for the figs.

____ 7. The figs symbolize
   a. Maman's maturing.
   b. Babette's maturing.
   c. Babette's cousins' maturing.

____ 8. We can infer that Maman is relatively
  a. poor.
  b. middle class.
  c. well off.

____ 9. We can infer that the cousins live
  a. nearby.
  b. a distance away.
  c. very, very far away.

____ 10. The chrysanthemums tell us that Maman is
  a. very young.
  b. very old.
  c. in her middle years.

5 SIGNIFICANT QUOTATIONS

Approach these **5 Significant Quotations** by reflecting on the reading. The quotations are important and central to the reading. Remember that you are demonstrating how well you have understood the reading, so explain why each quotation is important as completely as you can.

The first quotation here has already been done for you. Now, explain the significance of the remaining four. (The answers are on page 20.)

What is the importance of each of these quotations?

1. "Maman-Nainaine said that when the figs were ripe Babette might go to visit her cousins down on the Bayou-Lafourche where the sugar cane grows."

   This sentence sets the tension in the story between Babette and Maman-Nainaine and between Babette and nature. Babette wants to visit her cousins, but she must wait until the figs—and she—are ripe or mature enough.

2. "It seemed to Babette a very long time to wait […]."

3. "But warm rains came along and plenty of strong sunshine, and though Maman-Nainaine was as patient as the statue of la Madone, and Babette as restless as a humming-bird, the first thing they knew it was hot summertime."

4. "It [the platter] contained a dozen purple figs, fringed around with their rich, green leaves."

5. "'Babette,' continued Maman-Nainaine, as she peeled the very plumpest figs with her pointed silver fruit-knife, 'you will carry my love to them all down on Bayou-LaFourche.'"

2 COMPREHENSION ESSAY QUESTIONS

The **2 Comprehension Essay Questions** offer opportunities for extended essays. Your teacher may assign one or both for individual assignment or for group discussion. Gather your thoughts and respond, demonstrating what you have learned from the reading. Note that none of these questions asks how well you liked the reading or even if you liked it at all. The intention here is very simply to find out what you have understood in the reading.

Note that the directions ask you to "use specific details and information from the story." This does not mean that you have to memorize the reading, but it does mean that you should know the characters and events in the reading. Look at question 1. It asks you to explain the title, so for this essay question, you will want to review the story's events and the relevance of the figs. Now look at question 2. It asks you to focus on the ages involved in the story, and for this you will want to discuss the ages of Babette and her cousins as opposed to those of Maman and Tante Frosine, remembering the references to summer and fall in the story.

Use specific details and information from the story to answer these questions as completely as possible.

1. How does the title relate to the story? Explain the significance of the title, using specific details and information from the story.

2. What is the relevance of age in this story? Use specific details and information from the story to support your explanation.

DISCUSSION QUESTIONS

Now that you have read and studied the narrative, **Discussion Questions** are questions that are always focused on the narrative and designed to help you think about the narrative. Here, you may be asked to share your opinions or reactions to elements in the narrative. Notice that you are instructed to "be prepared to discuss these in class." Although your teacher may ask you to discuss these questions as a class or to write the answers independently, your thoughtful answers should reflect what you have learned about the narrative. The first one has been started for you.

Here, you need to reflect on the story and on your own youth. You need to identify and explain what characteristics you think Babette possesses that are youthful. Of course, when one thinks of youth, one thinks of energy, and you might want to discuss Babette's activities that require lots of energy, such as being physically busy and active, surrounding oneself with busy friends, and so forth. Related to energy, one thinks of impatience when one thinks of youth, and you may want to discuss Babette's impatience with the figs and Maman and traveling. Finally, the curiosity to explore, or in this case to travel, may also be a sign of youth, and you may want to discuss Babette's desire to travel. Think of anything else you might want to add to question 1.

Then, reflect on the story and relate it to your own observations of mature people. Complete question 2.

Be prepared to discuss these questions in class.

1. What characteristics mark Babette's youth?

    One characteristic of youth is having lots of energy. Babette is continually in motion, expending a great deal of physical energy. She is also looking forward to visiting with her cousins, and visiting also requires a great deal of energy. With all this energy, another characteristic of youth is impatience. Babette is impatient with Maman, wanting to speed the ripening of the figs to suit Maman's rules. Babette is also impatient with the figs themselves, as she spends much time and energy checking and wishing them into ripening. And Babette is impatient to travel. Curiosity and inquisitiveness are often associated with the young, and Babette has both the energy and the curiosity to look forward to this trip.

2. What characteristics mark Maman's maturity?

WRITING

Each reading ends with a final section of **Writing** prompts. The first set of prompts offer suggestions for personal writing. The prompts under **Further Writing** are designed with research in mind. These may suggest comparing and contrasting the reading with other narratives in this book or with other narratives the author or another author has written, or they may suggest other research topics. Your teacher will guide you through the writing process.

   At this point, a few words about the writing process are in order. Writing does not start with a pen or pencil; it starts with ideas. Before you start writing, jot down ideas, and then organize them. Here are two **pre-writing strategies** to get the ideas flowing:

1. On a clean sheet of paper, write one key word based on the topic you plan to write about. Now look at the key word, and start listing every word that this key word brings to mind. Avoid sentences or even phrases, which take longer to write and can break your train of thought. Just write words—lots of words; the more the merrier. When you run out of words, look back at the key word, and write more words. When you finish, you will have a whole list of ideas to start thinking about for your essay. This process is called **free associating** or **brainstorming.**

2. On a clean sheet of paper, draw a circle. Inside that circle, write one key word from the topic you plan to write about. Now look at the key word, and start tagging related words onto the circle. Then tag words onto the tag words, and so on. When you get stuck, look back at the key word, and add more words. When you finish, you will have groups of words—ideas—to start thinking about for your essay. This process is called **grouping, networking,** or **clustering.**

Once you have the ideas—and you should have plenty from either of these pre-writing strategies—the next step is to organize them into an **outline.** Do not worry about Roman numerals at this stage. Rather, develop logical groupings of these ideas into a working outline. You may find that there are words/ideas in your pre-write that you do not want to use. Cross these out. You may also find ideas in your outline that are out of place. Number and renumber the groups to make them work for you. (Your instructor may want you to formalize your outline later, but at this point the important thing is to find an organization that works for you.)

Look at the first writing idea. It asks you, first, to discuss one specific maturing process you have experienced and, second, to relate this process to a reflective image, much like the figs in our story. In Figure 3 both a cluster and an outline on the topic "Getting a License are demonstrated, but you may want to try "Learning to Ride a Bike" or "Graduating from High School" or any other maturing process you prefer.

To prepare the pre-writing cluster and outline shown in Figure 3, we first tagged ideas onto "License" and then tagged ideas onto ideas. Second, we looked for a logical order and numbered and renumbered the cluster. Third, we transferred these numbers into the informal, working outline. Finally, we looked back over what we had and decided that getting a license was like attending high school, because of all the preparation and responsibility involved in getting a license. With these ideas initiated and organized, we are now ready to write an intelligent and orderly essay.

Now try your hand at the other writing prompts.

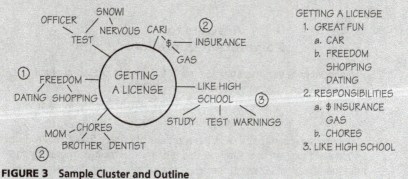

FIGURE 3   Sample Cluster and Outline

Use each of these ideas for writing an essay.

1. We all go through maturing processes. Think of a specific process you have experienced. Then think of something that reflects your process, much like the figs reflect Babette's growth. Write an essay on your growing-up process, relating it to a continuing symbol.

2. Age has an effect on all of us. Write about a specific incident when age affected you or someone you know.

Further Writing

1. Read Kate Chopin's "The Storm" (available in a library), and compare and contrast the images of nature in "The Storm" to those in "Ripe Figs."

2. Read Kate Chopin's "The Kiss" (available in a library), and compare the women in "The Kiss" with those in "The Storm."

Answers to
10 Short Questions

6. b. We are clearly told Maman is "patient" and not "impatient."

7. b. We know Babette is the one growing and "maturing."

8. c. Their genteel life, her leisurely breakfast, and the "silver fruit-knife" all imply wealth.

9. b. Bayou-Lafourche, in Louisiana, and Maman's reluctance to let Babette go at all both imply that this is, on the one hand, not "near by" and, on the other hand, not "very, very far away." The middle choice is the *best* choice here.

10. c. Again, we have discussed literary seasons, and the middle choice is the *best* choice here. Spring or summer would refer to youth, and winter would refer to old age. Chrysanthemums are fall, and fall is middle age.

Answers to
5 Significant Quotations

2. You should note that this sets up the central tension of Babette having to wait for the figs to ripen so that she can go visiting.

3. You should comment on Babette's "restlessness" and Maman's patience. This is not an easy wait for Babette.

4. You should explain that this is the moment of climax. The figs are ripe. You should explain that the ripe figs represent Babette's maturing and that she now is old enough/mature enough/ripe enough to travel to see her cousins.

5. You should note that this is the story's resolution, the dénouement. Babette may now travel.

Characters and Conflicts

Characters are the creatures that create, move, and experience the actions of a story. We normally think of characters as alive, animated beings, such as humans or animals, who can participate in the action. A character may also be called an **actor, player, person, persona,** or **personage**.

Characters fall into two categories: main characters and supporting characters. Generally, a **main character** is central to the action. A **supporting character** may encourage the action and is usually not present as much, or as central to the action, as the main character. Sometimes, it is difficult to decide if a character is main or supporting. For instance, in a murder mystery the victim may only appear at the beginning of the story or not at all, but the entire story is about solving her or his murder. Is the victim a main character because the story is about her or him, or is s/he a supporting character because s/he simply is not present? Both answers may be correct. In literature there are not always so much right or wrong answers as there are explanations, analyses, and debates. The correctness of your answer may depend on how well you explain your choices.

The author speaks to us through her or his characters. When an author writes using "I" or "we," this is called **first-person narration**. The first-person makes a story very immediate. The character who tells the story is called the **narrator**. If the author addresses the reader directly using "you" or "thou," this narrative technique is called **second-person narration**. The second-person is not used very often today. Finally, if the author uses "he," "she," "it," or "they" to tell the story, this narrative technique is called **third-person narration**. This is the most common narrative form, with the author seeming to be more of an observer and less of a participant. In this chapter, all the stories are told in the third-person. Notice how immediate and how different stories in the first-person are.

Characters may also be considered to be protagonists or antagonists. "Pro" means "for," and the **protagonist** is the hero or heroine, the character we **empathize** with, or share feelings with, the character we root for. "Anti" means "against," and the **antagonist** is the villain, the enemy of the protagonist, the character we do not like, the character we root against. Be aware that some authors like to play with these roles. You may be sympathetic to one character and then find that the author turns things upside down and you no longer like the character.

When we talk about protagonists and antagonists, we need to talk about conflicts. **Conflicts** are the disagreements and even struggles between characters. Conflicts build tension in a story. Several types of conflicts are possible. The conflict may be **human versus human**, as when a character(s) is pitted against another character(s). Notice the personal conflicts between the characters in "The Beautiful Soul of Don Damian." The conflict may be **human versus society**, as when a character(s) struggles against a group, community, or social structures. All the main characters in this chapter struggle against societal roles or norms. The conflict may be **human versus technology**, as when a character(s) vies with the tools of science or the machines in her or his society. Conflicts with technology are at the very base of the children's struggles in "It Used to Be Green Once." The conflict may be **human versus nature**, as when a character(s) battles with the forces of nature. Mrs. Mallard's heart, Don Damian's failing health, and Jovita's gender—let alone the children's rotting fruit—are all battles with nature. The conflict may be **human versus the supernatural**, as when a character(s) vies with God or gods or demons. Don Damian's hovering soul may be a struggle with the beyond-life supernatural. Finally, the conflict may be **human versus herself/himself**, as when a character wrestles with her or his own self-defeating **flaw**. Mrs. Mallard's nonconformity, Neo's arrogance, the children's embarrassment, Don Damian's self-serving image, and Jovita's determination are all internal struggles.

Stories in this chapter focus on characters and are called **character studies**. In a character study, the emphasis is on getting to know each character, and the action is used to help you understand each character better. Kate Chopin delivers swift irony as we get to know Mrs. Mallard, while Bessie Head presents Neo's determination. Patricia Grace lays bare the children's embarrassment, and Juan Bosch presents the soul's increasing awareness, while Dinah Silveira de Queiroz walks us through Jovita's personal disappointments. In each of these stories, we look beyond the mere events and into the thoughts and feelings of each of these characters.

Now it is time to turn to the stories. Enjoy the characters you meet.

THE STORY OF AN HOUR
Kate Chopin

Pre-reading Vocabulary
Context

Use context clues to define these words before reading. Use a dictionary as needed.

1. Kara was *afflicted* with headaches that caused her constant pain. *Afflicted* means _____.

2. The horrible earthquake caused a major *disaster,* with gas explosions and buildings collapsing, that resulted in injuries and deaths. *Disaster* means _____.

3. Before there were telephones, in order to send news to his family Sung Yu had to go to an office and send a *telegram. Telegram* means

_____.

4. Vernie tried to *hasten* Stephanie so that she could get to school on time. *Hasten* means _____.

5. After the children lost their beloved dog, they suffered much *grief* and cried for days. *Grief* means _____.

6. The little leaves were all *aquiver* as the breeze blew through the tree. *Aquiver* means _____.

7. Some people are never allowed to laugh; they suffer severe *repression* when they see something funny. *Repression* means

_____.

8. When Rob did not understand the directions, his face became *vacant* and without expression. *Vacant* means _____.

9. The puppy had a *keen* sense of smell and could scent a hamburger a mile away. *Keen* means _____.

10. Blood *pulses* through our veins with a steady beat. *Pulse* means

    _____.

11. The king held the most *exalted* position in the realm. *Exalted* means

    _____.

12. In the Macy's *procession*, colorful floats followed one after another

    after another. *Procession* means _____.

13. The host opened the door and warmly *welcomed* each guest as he

    or she arrived. *Welcome* means _____.

14. Without thinking about it, Kirk followed his *impulse* and suddenly

    bet all his chips on red. *Impulse* means _____.

15. When Bill thinks he is right, he answers with enough confidence

    and *self-assertion* to convince others he is correct. *Self-assertion*

    means _____.

16. Nancy *implored* the builder to start her deck as soon as possible before

    the rains came. *Implore* means _____.

17. A substance that can change base metals into gold, that can make one

    live forever, or that allows one to taste the very best of life is called

    an *elixir*. *Elixir* means _____.

18. Daren *shuddered* at the thought of having to take another algebra test.

    Shudder means _____.

19. The Cougars yelled, screamed, and jumped in *triumph* when they won

    the game. *Triumph* means _____.

20. Margaret was absolutely *amazed* when she won the ten-million-dollar

    lottery. *Amazed* means _____.

Pre-reading Vocabulary
Structural Attack

Define these words by solving the parts. Use the Glossary or a dictionary as needed.

1. inability
2. bespoke
3. fearfully
4. powerless
5. fellow-creatures

6. illumination
7. keyhole
8. feverish
9. latchkey
10. travel-stained

Pre-reading Questions

Try answering these questions as you read.

What happens to Mr. Mallard?

How does Mrs. Mallard feel?

What happens to Mrs. Mallard?

What is ironic in the story?

THE STORY OF AN HOUR

KATE CHOPIN

Kate O'Flaherty Chopin was born in St. Louis, Missouri, in 1851 to an affluent family. Although her father died when she was young, her widowed mother gave young Kate a taste of female independence. In 1870 Kate married Oscar Chopin and moved to New Orleans and then Natchitoches Parish. Here she met the Creoles, Acadians, and African Americans she would later write about. However, Oscar died in 1882, and by 1884 she sold the plantation, gathered her five children, and returned home to St. Louis, where she began to write for popular women's magazines. Influenced noticeably by Guy de Maupassant's sense of irony and Henrik Ibsen's social comment, Chopin wrote stories, often touched with rich symbols and images of nature, that question societal assumptions and dictates. *The Awakening* remains her masterwork, although short stories offer Chopin at her most terse. Chopin died in 1904.

Knowing that Mrs. Mallard was afflicted with a heart trouble, great care was taken to break to her as gently as possible the news of her husband's death.

2   It was her sister Josephine who told her, in broken sentences; veiled hints that revealed in half concealing. Her husband's friend Richards was there, too, near her. It was he who had been in the newspaper office when intelligence of the railroad disaster was received, with Brently Mallard's name leading the list of "killed." He had only taken the time to assure himself of its truth by a second telegram, and had hastened to forestall any less careful, less tender friend in bearing the sad message.

3   She did not hear the story as many women have heard the same, with a paralyzed inability to accept its significance. She wept at once, with sudden, wild abandonment, in her sister's arms. When the storm of grief had spent itself she went away to her room alone. She would have no one follow her.

4   There stood, facing the open window, a comfortable, roomy armchair. Into this she sank, pressed down by a physical exhaustion that haunted her body and seemed to reach into her soul.

5   She could see in the open square before her house the tops of trees that were all aquiver with the new spring life. The delicious breath of rain was in the air. In the street below a peddler was crying his wares. The notes of a distant song which some one was singing reached her faintly, and countless sparrows were twittering in the eaves.

6   There were patches of blue sky showing here and there through the clouds that had met and piled one above the other in the west facing her window.

7   She sat with her head thrown back upon the cushion of the chair, quite motionless, except when a sob came up into her throat and shook her, as a child who has cried itself to sleep continues to sob in its dreams.

8   She was young, with a fair, calm face, whose lines bespoke repression and even a certain strength. But now there was a dull stare in her eyes, whose gaze was fixed away off yonder on one of those patches of blue sky. It was not a glance of reflection, but rather indicated a suspension of intelligent thought.

9   There was something coming to her and she was waiting for it, fearfully. What was it? She did not know; it was too subtle and elusive to name. But she felt it, creeping out of the sky, reaching toward her through the sounds, the scents, the color that filled the air.

10   Now her bosom rose and fell tumultuously. She was beginning to recognize this thing that was approaching to possess her, and she was striving to beat it back with her will—as powerless as her two white slender hands would have been.

11   When she abandoned herself a little whispered word escaped her slightly parted lips. She said it over and over under her breath: "free, free, free!" The vacant stare and the look of terror that had followed it went from her eyes. They stayed keen and bright. Her pulses beat fast, and the coursing blood warmed and relaxed every inch of her body.

12   She did not stop to ask if it were or were not a monstrous joy that held her. A clear and exalted perception enabled her to dismiss the suggestion as trivial.

13   She knew that she would weep again when she saw the kind, tender hands folded in death; the face that had never looked save

with love upon her, fixed and gray and dead. But she saw beyond that bitter moment a long procession of years to come that would belong to her absolutely. And she opened and spread her arms out to them in welcome.

14   There would be no one to live for her during those coming years; she would live for herself. There would be no powerful will bending hers in that blind persistence with which men and women believe they have a right to impose a private will upon a fellow-creature. A kind intention or a cruel intention made the act seem no less a crime as she looked upon it in that brief moment of illumination.

15   And yet she had loved him—sometimes. Often she had not. What did it matter! What could love, the unsolved mystery, count for in the face of this possession of self-assertion which she suddenly recognized as the strongest impulse of her being!

16   "Free! Body and soul free!" she kept whispering.

17   Josephine was kneeling before the closed door with her lips to the keyhole, imploring for admission. "Louise, open the door! I beg; open the door—you will make yourself ill. What are you doing, Louise? For heaven's sake open the door."

18   "Go away. I am not making myself ill." No; she was drinking in a very elixir of life through that open window.

19   Her fancy was running riot along those days ahead of her. Spring days, and summer days, and all sorts of days that would be her own. She breathed a quick prayer that life might be long. It was only yesterday she had thought with a shudder that life might be long.

20   She arose at length and opened the door to her sister's importunities. There was a feverish triumph in her eyes, and she carried herself unwittingly like a goddess of Victory. She clasped her sister's waist, and together they descended the stairs. Richards stood waiting for them at the bottom.

21   Someone was opening the front door with a latchkey. It was Brently Mallard who entered, a little travel-stained, composedly carrying his grip-sack and umbrella. He had been far from the scene of the accident, and did not even know there had been one. He stood amazed at Josephine's piercing cry; at Richards' quick motion to screen him from the view of his wife.

22   But Richards was too late.

23   When the doctors came they said she had died of heart disease—of joy that kills.

THE STORY OF AN HOUR

JOURNAL

1. **MLA Works Cited**   *Using this model, record this story here.*

   Author's Last Name, First Name. "Title of the Story." *Title of the Book.* 3rd ed. Ed.

   First Name Last Name. City: Publisher, year. Page number(s) of this story. Print.

2. **Main Character(s)**   *Describe each main character, and explain why you think each is a main character.*

3. **Supporting Characters**   *Describe each supporting character, and explain why you think each is a supporting character.*

4. **Setting and Props**   *Describe the setting(s) and all relevant prop(s).*

5. Sequence   *Outline the events of the story in order.*

6. Plot   *Tell the story in no more than two sentences.*

7. Conflicts   *Identify and explain all the conflicts involved here.*

8. Significant Quotations   *Explain the importance of each of these quotations. Record the page number in the parentheses.*

a. "Knowing that Mrs. Mallard was afflicted with a heart trouble, great care was taken to break to her as gently as possible the news of her husband's death" ( ).

b. "When the storm of grief had spent itself she went away to her room alone" ( ).

c. "She could see in the open square before her house the tops of trees that were all aquiver with the new spring life" ( ).

d. "When she abandoned herself a little whispered word escaped her slightly parted lips. She said it over and over under her breath: 'free, free, free!' " ( ).

e. "Someone was opening the door with a latchkey" ( ).

9. **Literary Elements**   *Look at this chapter's title and explain why you think this story is placed in this chapter. Explain in which other chapter(s) you might place this story, as relevant to the literary element(s) of the chapter(s).*

10. **Foreshadowing, Irony, and/or Symbolism**   *Explain examples of foreshadowing, irony, and/or symbolism in this story.*

FOLLOW-UP QUESTIONS

10 SHORT QUESTIONS

What is the __best__ answer for each?

_____ 1. The person to first hear the news of the accident is
   a. Mrs. Mallard.
   b. Josephine.
   c. Richards.

_____ 2. S/he hears the news
   a. at the railroad station.
   b. at the newspaper office.
   c. at home.

_____ 3. Josephine and Richards are at the Mallard house
   a. to awaken Mrs. Mallard.
   b. to have lunch with Mrs. Mallard.
   c. to tell Mrs. Mallard about the accident.

_____ 4. Mrs. Mallard is immediately
   a. overwhelmed.
   b. overjoyed.
   c. unimpressed.

_____ 5. Mrs. Mallard
   a. goes to her room.
   b. stays with her sister.
   c. makes lunch.

_____ 6. Mrs. Mallard slowly
   a. cries.
   b. faints.
   c. whispers "free."

_____ 7. Mrs. Mallard
   a. always loved Brently Mallard.
   b. did not always love Brently Mallard.
   c. was looking forward to Brently Mallard's return.

_____ 8. Brently Mallard
   a. was at home all the time.
   b. was in the accident.
   c. was not in the accident.

_____ 9. Brently Mallard
   a. does come home.
   b. does not come home.
   c. is dead.

_____ 10. Mrs. Mallard is
   a. delighted by his return.
   b. unmoved by his return.
   c. destroyed by his return.

5 SIGNIFICANT QUOTATIONS

What is the importance of each of these quotations?

1. "Knowing that Mrs. Mallard was afflicted with a heart condition, great care was taken to break to her as gently as possible the news of her husband's death."

2. "She wept at once, with sudden, wild abandonment, in her sister's arms."

3. "There was something coming to her and she was waiting for it, fearfully."

4. "She breathed a quick prayer that life might be long. It was only yesterday she had thought with a shudder that life might be long."

5. "When the doctors came they said she had died of heart disease—of joy that kills."

2 COMPREHENSION ESSAY QUESTIONS

Use specific details and information from the story to answer these questions as completely as possible.

1. How does the title relate to the story? Explain the significance of the title using specific details and information from the story.

2. What does the phrase "of joy that kills" mean? Use specific details and information from the story in your explanation.

DISCUSSION QUESTIONS

Be prepared to discuss these questions in class.

1. What does this story tell you about assumptions concerning husbands and wives? Use specific details from the story to support your ideas.

2. For which character do you feel more sympathy? Why?

WRITING

Use each of these ideas for writing an essay.

1. We have all tried to cover up our feelings at one time or another. Tell the story of a time you or someone you know used pleasure or sorrow to cover up real feelings about a situation or event. Pay special attention in your narrative to the reactions of others.

2. We have all made mistakes about how we think others feel. Sometimes these misunderstandings are quite humorous. Describe a time when you or someone you know assumed the wrong thing about someone else's feelings.

Further Writing

1. Discuss the similarities between Mrs. Mallard in this story and Calixta in Kate Chopin's "The Storm" (available in a library).

2. Discuss the similarities between Mrs. Mallard in this story and Nathalie in Kate Chopin's "The Kiss" (available in a library).

3. Discuss the similarities between Mrs. Mallard in this story and Mrs. Alving in Henrik Ibsen's *Ghosts* (available in a library).

SNAPSHOTS OF A WEDDING
Bessie Head

Pre-reading Vocabulary
Context

Use context clues to define these words before reading. Use a dictionary as needed.

1. When Paul and Tricia decided to get married, they planned a beautiful *wedding* party. *Wedding* means _____.

2. They invited all their *relatives*, including their parents, sisters, brothers, aunts, uncles, and cousins. *Relatives* means

    _____.

3. When their team was losing, the men *ululated* a loud, howling kind of noise. *Ululate* means _____.

4. John prefers very new, *modern* furniture in his home to older, more dated furniture. *Modern* means _____.

5. Judy prefers the older, more *traditional* furniture that her grandmother left to her. *Traditional* means _____.

6. When he graduated from college, Mukendi received his diploma at the very formal and beautiful graduation *ceremony*. *Ceremony* means

    _____.

7. After Carlo won the science fair, he became *haughty and arrogant* and acted as if he were better than everyone else. *Haughty and arrogant* means

    _____.

8. Jim and Barry look on each other as *rivals* and try to outdo each other all the time. *Rival* means _____.

9. The boss treated his employees in a very *patronizing* manner, always talking down to them as if they were stupid. *Patronizing* means

    _____.

I ♥ Michael

10. Cheryl had terrible *anxieties* before her final exam because she was so afraid of failing the test. *Anxiety* means

_____.

11. Lusumba worked very hard at *securing* a job in the bank and made sure he did well in all his accounting courses. *Secure* means

_____.

12. Laura became a *wife* when she formally married Dave in a beautiful wedding ceremony in Orlando. *Wife* means

_____.

13. Ted became a *husband* when he formally married Jen in the beautiful wedding ceremony in Soho. *Husband* means

_____.

14. Laura asked her godmother who is her *aunt*, her mother's sister, to present the gifts at the ceremony. *Aunt* means

_____.

15. Marriage, uniting two people as partners for life, is an *ancient rite* dating back several thousand years. *Ancient rite* means

_____.

16. Sean had to teach his dog to *obey* Sean's commands so the dog would not jump on people and run in the street. *Obey* means

_____.

17. The farmer used a *plough and hoe* in his fields to make ruts in the ground so he could plant the seeds. *Plough and hoe* means

_____.

18. In Alex's kindergarten classroom, the teacher put a *mat* on the floor so the children could sit comfortably on the floor. *Mat* means

_____.

19. After the evening air turned cool, Blair wrapped a lovely, lacy woolen

    shawl around her shoulders. *Shawl* means

    _____.

20. Dodee tied a triangular *kerchief* around her head, because her hair

    was still wet and it had started to snow outside. *Kerchief* means

    _____.

PRE-READING VOCABULARY
STRUCTURAL ATTACK

Define these words by solving the parts. Use the Glossary or a dictionary as needed.

1. magical
2. shimmering
3. bestirred
4. unearthly
5. watery
6. bridegroom
7. melodiously
8. appalling
9. illiterate
10. bemused
11. disliked

12. uneducated
13. housemaid
14. showered
15. money-earners
16. disrespect
17. precariously
18. maternal
19. expressionless
20. formation
21. married
22. immobile

PRE-READING QUESTIONS

Try answering these questions as you read.

What is Neo like?

What is Mathata like?

What does Kegoletile have to decide?

SNAPSHOTS OF A WEDDING

Bessie Head

> **Bessie Head's** troubled life was marked with much internal conflict. She was born in South Africa in 1937 to an originally unidentified black father and a mentally institutionalized, white mother. At first placed with a white family, she was then sent to a school for colored children. She later married and then divorced, taking her young son with her to Botswana. She rarely seemed to feel comfortable in her own surroundings. Trained as a teacher, she turned to writing to explore her own inner conflicts, writing both novels and short stories. This story, in fact, examines the conflicts between old and new and explores the condescension she perceived in the roles of wife and of mother. Bessie Head died in 1986.

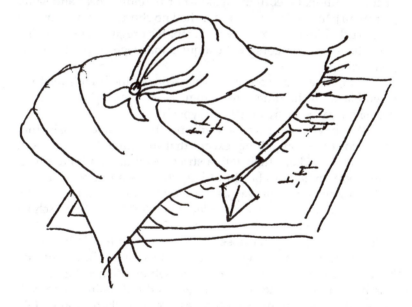

Wedding days always started at the haunting magical hour of early dawn when there was only a pale crack of light on the horizon. For those who were awake, it took the earth hours to adjust to daylight. The cool and damp of the night slowly arose in shimmering waves like water and even the forms of the people who bestirred themselves at this unearthly hour were distorted in the haze; they appeared to be dancers in slow motion, with fluid, watery forms. In the dim light, four men, the relatives of the bridegroom, Kegoletile, slowly herded an ox before them toward the yard of MmaKhudu, where the bride, Neo, lived. People were already astir in MmaKhudu's yard, yet for a while they all came and peered closely at the distorted fluid forms that approached, to ascertain if it were indeed the relatives of the bridegroom. Then the ox, who was a rather stupid fellow and unaware of his sudden and impending end as meat for the wedding feast, bellowed casually his early morning yawn. At this, the beautiful ululating of the women rose and swelled over the air like water bubbling rapidly and melodiously over the stones of a clear, sparkling stream. In between ululating all the while, the women began to weave about the yard in the wedding dance; now and then they bent over and shook their buttocks in the air. As they handed over the ox, one of the bridegroom's relatives joked:

2   "This is going to be a modern wedding." He meant that a lot of the traditional courtesies had been left out of the planning for the wedding day; no one had been awake all night preparing diphiri or the traditional wedding breakfast of pounded meat and samp [cornflour]; the bridegroom said he had no church and did not care about such things; the bride was six months pregnant and showing it, so there was just going to be a quick marriage ceremony at the police camp.

3   "Oh, we all have our own ways," one of the bride's relatives joked back. "If the times are changing, we keep up with them." And she weaved away ululating joyously.

4   Whenever there was a wedding the talk and gossip that preceded it were appalling, except that this time the relatives of the bride, Neo, kept their talk a strict secret among themselves. They were anxious to be rid of her; she was an impossible girl with haughty, arrogant ways. Of all her family and relatives, she was the only one who had completed her "O" levels [high school diploma exams] and she never failed to rub in this fact. She walked around with her nose in the air; illiterate relatives were beneath her greeting—it was done in a clever way, she just turned her head to one side and smiled to herself or when she greeted it was like an insult; she stretched her hand out, palm outspread, swung it down laughing with a gesture that plainly said: "Oh, that's you!" Only her mother seemed bemused by her education. At her own home Neo was waited on hand and foot. Outside her home nasty remarks were passed. People bitterly disliked conceit and pride.

5   "That girl has no manners!" the relatives would remark. "What's the good of education if it goes to someone's head so badly they have no respect for the people? Oh, she is not a person."

6   Then they would nod their heads in that fatal way, with predictions that one day life would bring her down. Actually, life had treated Neo rather nicely. Two months after completing her "O" levels she became pregnant by Kegoletile with their first child. It

soon became known that another girl, Mathata, was also pregnant by Kegoletile. The difference between the two girls was that Mathata was completely uneducated; the only work she would ever do was that of a housemaid, while Neo had endless opportunities before her—typist, bookkeeper, or secretary. So Neo merely smiled; Mathata was no rival. It was as though the decision had been worked out by circumstance because when the families converged on Kegoletile at the birth of the children—he was rich in cattle and they wanted to see what they could get—he of course immediately proposed marriage to Neo; and for Mathata, he agreed to a court order to pay a maintenance of R10.00 a month until the child was twenty years old. Mathata merely smiled too. Girls like her offered no resistance to the approaches of men; when they lost them, they just let things ride.

7 "He is of course just running after the education and not the manners," Neo's relatives commented, to show they were not fooled by human nature. "He thinks that since she is as educated as he is they will both get good jobs and be rich in no time..."

8 Educated as he was, Kegoletile seemed to go through a secret conflict during that year he prepared a yard for his future married life with Neo. He spent most of his free time in the yard of Mathata. His behaviour there wasn't too alarming but he showered Mathata with gifts of all kinds—food, fancy dresses, shoes, and underwear. Each time he came, he brought a gift and each time Mathata would burst out laughing and comment: "Ow, Kegoletile, how can I wear all these dresses? It's just a waste of money! Besides, I manage quite well with the R10.00 you give every month for the child..."

9 She was a very pretty girl with black eyes like stars; she was always smiling and happy; immediately and always her own natural self. He knew what he was marrying—something quite the opposite, a new kind of girl with false postures and acquired, grand-madame ways. And yet, it didn't pay a man these days to look too closely into his heart. They all wanted as wives, women who were big money-earners and they were so ruthless about it! And yet it was as though the society itself stamped each of its individuals with its own particular brand of wealth and Kegoletile had not yet escaped it; he had about him an engaging humility and eagerness to help and please that made him loved and respected by all who knew him. During those times he sat in Mathata's yard, he communicated nothing of the conflict he felt but he would sit on a chair with his arms spread out across its back, turn his head sideways and stare at what seemed to be an empty space beside him. Then he would smile, stand up, and walk away. Nothing dramatic. During the year he prepared the huts in his new yard, he frequently slept at the home of Neo.

10   Relatives on both sides watched this division of interest between the two yards and one day when Neo walked patronizingly into the yard of an aunt, the aunt decided to frighten her a little.

11   "Well aunt," she said, with the familiar careless disrespect which went with her so-called, educated, status. "Will you make me some tea? And how's things?"

12   The aunt spoke very quietly.

13   "You may not know it, my girl, but you are hated by everyone around here. The debate we have going is whether a nice young man like Kegoletile should marry bad-mannered rubbish like you. He would be far better off if he married a girl like Mathata, who though uneducated, still treats people with respect."

14   The shock the silly girl received made her stare for a terrified moment at her aunt. Then she stood up and ran out of the house. It wiped the superior smile off her face and brought her down a little. She developed an anxiety to greet people and also an anxiety about securing Kegoletile as a husband—that was why she became pregnant six months before the marriage could take place. In spite of this, her own relatives still disliked her and right up to the day of the wedding they were still debating whether Neo was a suitable wife for any man. No one would have guessed it though with all the dancing, ululating, and happiness expressed in the yard and streams of guests gaily ululated themselves along the pathways with wedding gifts precariously balanced on their heads. Neo's maternal aunts, all sedately decked up in shawls, sat in a select group by themselves in a corner of the yard. They sat on the bare ground with their legs stretched out before them but they were served like queens the whole day long. Trays of tea, dry white bread, plates of meat, rice, and salad were constantly placed before them. Their important task was to formally hand over the bride to Kegoletile's maternal aunts when they approached the yard at sunset. So they sat the whole day with still, expressionless faces, waiting to fulfill this ancient rite.

15   Equally still and expressionless were the faces of the long column of women, Kegoletile's maternal aunts, who appeared outside the yard just as the sun sank low. They walked slowly into the yard indifferent to the ululating that greeted them and seated themselves in a group opposite Neo's maternal aunts. The yard became very silent while each group made its report. Kegoletile had provided all the food for the wedding feast and a maternal aunt from his side first asked:

16   "Is there any complaint? Has all gone well?"

17   "We have no complaint," the opposite party replied.

18   "We have come to ask for water," Kegoletile's side said, meaning that from times past the bride was supposed to carry water at her in-law's home.

19   "It is agreed to," the opposite party replied.

20   Neo's maternal aunts then turned to the bridegroom and counselled him: "Son, you must plough and supply us with corn each year."

21   Then Kegoletile's maternal aunts turned to the bride and counselled her: "Daughter, you must carry water for your husband. Beware, that at all times, he is the owner of the house and must be obeyed. Do not mind if he stops now and then and talks to other ladies. Let him feel free to come and go as he likes…"

22   The formalities over, it was now time for Kegoletile's maternal aunts to get up, ululate and weave and dance about the yard. Then, still dancing and ululating, accompanied by the bride and groom they slowly wound their way to the yard of Kegoletile where another feast had been prepared. As they approached his yard, an old woman suddenly dashed out and chopped at the ground with a hoe. It was all only a formality. Neo would never be the kind of wife who went to the lands to plough. She already had a well-paid job in an office as a secretary. Following on this another old woman took the bride by the hand and led her to a smeared and decorated courtyard wherein had been placed a traditional animal skin Tswana mat. She was made to sit on the mat and a shawl and kerchief were placed before her. The shawl was ceremonially wrapped around her shoulders; the kerchief tied around her head—the symbols that she was now a married woman.

23   Guests quietly moved forward to greet the bride. Then two girls started to ululate and dance in front of the bride. As they both turned and bent over to shake their buttocks in the air, they bumped into each other and toppled over. The wedding guests roared with laughter. Neo, who had all this time been stiff, immobile, and rigid, bent forward and her shoulders shook with laughter.

24   The hoe, the mat, the shawl, the kerchief, the beautiful flute-like ululating of the women seemed in itself a blessing on the marriage but all the guests were deeply moved when out of the crowd, a woman of majestic, regal bearing slowly approached the bride. It was the aunt who had scolded Neo for her bad manners and modern ways. She dropped to her knees before the bride, clenched her fists together and pounded the ground hard with each clenched fist on either side of the bride's legs. As she pounded her fists she said loudly:

25   "Be a good wife! Be a good wife!"

● ●

SNAPSHOTS OF A WEDDING

Journal

1. **Works Cited**   *Using this model, record this story here.*

   Author's Last Name, First Name. "Title of the Story." *Title of the Book.* 3rd ed. Ed.

   First Name Last Name. City: Publisher, year. Page number(s) of this story. Print.

2. **Main Character(s)**   *Describe each main character, and explain why you think each is a main character.*

3. **Supporting Characters**   *Describe each supporting character, and explain why you think each is a supporting character.*

4. **Setting and Props**   *Describe the setting(s) and all relevant prop(s).*

5. Sequence   *Outline the events of the story in order.*

6. Plot   *Tell the story in no more than two sentences.*

7. Conflicts   *Identify and explain all conflicts involved here.*

8. Significant Quotations   *Explain the importance of each quotation completely. Record the page number in the parentheses.*

a. "In between ululating all the while, the women began to weave about the yard in the wedding dance;[...]" (   ).

b. " 'That girl has no manners!' the relatives would remark" (   ).

    c. "Educated as he was, Kegoletile seemed to go through a secret conflict during that year he prepared a yard for his future married life with Neo" ( ).

    d. " 'Be aware, that at all times, he is the owner of the house and must be obeyed'" ( ).

    e. "The shawl was ceremonially wrapped around her shoulders; the kerchief tied around her head—symbols that she was now a married woman" ( ).

9. **Literary Elements**   *Look at this chapter's title and explain why you think this story is placed in this chapter. Explain in which other chapter(s) you might place this story, as relevant to the literary element(s) of the chapter(s).*

10. **Foreshadowing, Irony, and/or Symbols**   *Explain examples of foreshadowing, irony, and/or symbols in this story.*

FOLLOW-UP QUESTIONS

10 SHORT QUESTIONS

What is the __best__ answer for each?

_____ 1. The town feels this is
   a. a new, modern wedding.
   b. an old, traditional wedding.
   c. not a wedding.

_____ 2. In fact, the marriage takes place in
   a. a temple.
   b. a church.
   c. a yard.

_____ 3. In fact, the marriage uses
   a. no formalities.
   b. the aunts' collective approvals.
   c. a minister.

_____ 4. In fact, the wedding requires
   a. a gown.
   b. a veil.
   c. a mat, shawl, and kerchief.

_____ 5. The above facts infer this is
   a. a new, modern wedding.
   b. a traditional wedding.
   c. a little old and a little new.

_____ 6. Neo is considered to be
   a. uneducated.
   b. well educated.
   c. kind and friendly.

_____ 7. Mathata is considered to be
   a. kind and friendly.
   b. arrogant.
   c. well educated.

_____ 8. The aunts' collective approvals seem
   a. necessary for the marriage.
   b. unnecessary for the marriage.
   c. of no relevance to the marriage.

_____ 9. Kegoletile seems to
   a. be marrying strictly for love.
   b. have doubts about his marriage.
   c. have little wealth.

_____ 10. Neo probably will want
   a. to take care of crops.
   b. to carry water.
   c. not to take care of crops.

5 SIGNIFICANT QUOTATIONS

What is the importance of each of these quotations?

1. "This is going to be a modern wedding" ( ).

2. "They were anxious to be rid of her; she was an impossible girl with haughty, arrogant ways" ( ).

3. "His behaviour there wasn't too alarming but he showered Mathata with gifts of all kinds—[…]" ( ).

4. "Then Kegoletile's maternal aunts turned to the bride and counselled her: 'Daughter, you must carry water for your husband'" ( ).

5. "Be a good wife! Be a good wife!" ( ).

2 Comprehension Essay Questions

Use specific detail and information from the story to answer these questions as completely as possible.

1. How would Mathata feel about this wedding? Tell this story from her point of view, using specific details and information from the story to substantiate your ideas.

2. What is Kegoletile's "secret conflict"? Explain his conflicted feelings using specific details and information from the story.

Discussion Questions

Be prepared to discuss these questions in class.

1. Do you think Kegoletlle will be loyal to Neo? Use specific details and information from the story to substantiate your thinking.

2. Do you think Kegoletile will maintain his promise to Mathata? Do you think her trust is wise or unwise? Use specific details and information from the story to substantiate your opinions.

Writing

Use each of these ideas for writing an essay.

1. Think of a family or community tradition that you have wanted to change. Discuss the tradition and the changes you would make.

2. Kegoletile has a "secret conflict." Think of a personal conflict you or someone you know has experienced. Discuss the conflict and the resolution.

Further Writing

1. Research important rituals (naming ceremonies, rites of passage ceremonies, marriage ceremonies, burial ceremonies, and so forth) in a culture different from your own. Compare and contrast the similarities and the differences in these rituals.

2. Research Bessie Head's life and the influences her life had on her writing and her thinking.

IT USED TO BE GREEN ONCE

Patricia Grace

PRE-READING VOCABULARY
CONTEXT

Use context clues to define these words before reading. Use a dictionary as needed.

1. Hital was *ashamed* of her behavior after she ranted and raved and threw a juvenile tantrum. *Ashamed* means _____.

2. When the socks got a hole in them, instead of throwing them away Mom *darned* up the hole and used the socks again. *Darn* means

   _____.

3. Mom went shopping to buy all kinds of new *togs*—shirts, sweaters, pants—so the children could go to school. *Togs* means

   _____.

4. In Australia, it is common for one to call one's friend a *mate*. *Mate* means

   _____.

5. When the bedspreads were marked down ninety percent, Jennifer was able to buy one for a very *cheap* price. *Cheap* means

   _____.

6. After Keith yelled and screamed like a brat, his mother took him aside and gave him a good *hiding* on his behind. *Hiding* means

   _____.

7. In order to get the car to move more quickly, Dad pushed down on the *accelerator*. *Accelerator* means

   _____.

8. In order to get the car to slow down, Dad pushed down on the *brake* pedal. *Brake* means _____.

9. When the ship was sinking, the captain ordered all the people to sail away in the small *dinghy*. *Dinghy* means _____.

10. Tom *skited* to all that would listen that he was the greatest and the smartest guy in the world. *Skited* means _____.

11. The Sebring *convertible*, with its roof that effortlessly goes up and down, is the most desired car of its kind in America. *Convertible* means

    _____.

12. When Jennifer redid her kitchen flooring, she decided to use a sheet of continuous *lino* instead of individual ceramic tiles. *Lino* means

    _____.

13. At dinner, Bernie served all kinds of *kai*, including ham, chicken, potatoes, and beans. *Kai* means _____.

14. When the rain waters started to rise, Mark put on rubber *galoshes* over his shoes to keep his shoes dry. *Galoshes* means

    _____.

15. In order to drive a car in America, Anthony took a written and a road test so he could get a driver's *license*. *License* means

    _____.

16. When Geri wanted to make mashed potatoes for dinner, she went to the supermarket to buy a bag of *spuds*. *Spuds* means

    _____.

17. Bob decided to serve *mutton* at the dinner party and went to the butcher to see if he had any fresh sheep. *Mutton* means

    _____.

18. Robert was *astonished* and *amazed* when the audience grew to hundreds and thunderously applauded his music. *Astonished* and *amazed* mean

    _____.

19. After Rose put the ice on her sore, the aching stopped and she couldn't feel anything because the area was *numb. Numb* means

_____.

20. When David bought a ladder that stuck out of his trunk, he used a *rope* to tie the trunk down. *Rope* means

_____.

PRE-READING VOCABULARY
STRUCTURAL ATTACK

Define these words by solving the parts. Use the Glossary or a dictionary as needed.

1. backside
2. holey
3. over-ripe
4. wheelbarrow

5. cowshed
6. handbrake
7. sunhat
8. modernized

PRE-READING QUESTIONS

Try answering these questions as you read.

What does the car mean to the kids?
What does the car mean to Mum?

IT USED TO BE GREEN ONCE

Patricia Grace

> **Patricia Grace** was born in Welling, New Zealand, of Maori lineage in 1937. Grace originally taught in a convent, and then continuing on to St. Mary's College, she became a teacher and writer. Combining her formal education with her Maori heritage, Grace's writing reflects everyday glimpses of, and insights into, Maori culture. Her writings can be found in novels and short story collections.

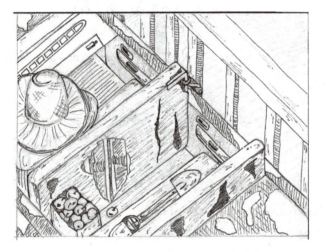

We were all ashamed of our mother. Our mother always did things to shame us. Like putting red darns in our clothes, and cutting up old swimming togs and making two—girl's togs from the top half for my sister, and boy's togs from the bottom half for my brother. Peti and Raana both cried when Mum made them take the togs to school. Peti sat down on the road by our gate and yelled out she wasn't going to school. She wasn't going swimming. I didn't blame my sister because the togs were thirty-eight chest and Peti was only ten.

2   But Mum knew how to get her up off the road. She yelled loudly, "Get up off that road my girl. There's nothing wrong with those togs. I didn't have any togs when I was a kid and I had to swim in my nothings. Get up off your backside and get to school." Mum's got a loud voice and she knew how to shame us. We all dragged Peti up off the road before our mates came along and heard Mum. We pushed Peti into the school bus so Mum wouldn't come yelling up the drive.

3   We never minded our holey fruit at first. Dad used to pick up the cases of over-ripe apples or pears from town that he got cheap.

Mum would dig out the rotten bits, and then give them to us to take for play-lunch. We didn't notice much at first, not until Reweti from down the road yelled out to us one morning, "Hey you fullas. Who shot your pears?" We didn't have anywhere to hide our lunch because we weren't allowed school bags until we got to high school. Mum said she wasn't buying fourteen school bags. When we went to high school we could have shoes too. The whole lot of us gave Reweti a good hiding after school.

4   However, this story is mainly about the car, and about Mum and how she shamed us all the time. The shame of rainbow darns and cut-up togs and holey fruit was nothing to what we suffered because of the car. Uncle Raz gave us the car because he couldn't fix it up any more, and he'd been fined because he lived in Auckland. He gave the car to Dad so we could drive our cream cans up to the road instead of pushing them up by wheelbarrow.

5   It didn't matter about the car not having brakes because the drive from our cowshed goes down in a dip then up to the gate. Put the car in its first gear, run it down from the shed, pick up a bit of speed, up the other side, turn it round by the cream stand so that it's pointing down the drive again, foot off the accelerator and slam on the handbrake. Dad pegged a board there to make sure it stopped. Then when we'd lifted the cans out on to the stand he'd back up a little and slide off down the drive—with all of us throwing ourselves in over the sides as if it were a dinghy that had just been pushed out into the sea.

6   The car had been red once because you could still see some patches of red paint here and there. And it used to have a top too, that you could put down or up. Our uncle told us that when he gave it to Dad. We were all proud about the car having had a top once. Some of the younger kids skited to their mates about our convertible and its top that went up and down. But that was before our mother started shaming us by driving the car to the shop.

7   We growled at Mum and we cried but it made no difference. "You kids always howl when I tell you to get our shopping," she said.

8   "We'll get it Mum. We won't cry."

9   "We won't cry Mum. We'll carry the sack of potatoes."

10   "And the flour."

11   "And the bag of sugar."

12   "And the rolled oats."

13   "And the tin of treacle."

14   "We'll do the shopping Mum."

15   But Mum would say, "Never mind, I'll do it myself." And after that she wouldn't listen any more.

16   How we hated Wednesdays. We always tried to be sick on Wednesdays, or to miss the bus. But Mum would be up early

yelling at us to get out of bed. If we didn't get up when we were told she'd drag us out and pull down our pajama pants and set our bums on the cold lino. Mum was cruel to us.

17   Whoever was helping with the milking had to be back quickly from the shed for breakfast, and we'd all have to rush through our kai and get to school. Wednesday was Mum's day for shopping.

18   As soon as she had everything tidy she'd change into her good purple dress that she'd made from a Japanese bedspread, pull on her floppy brimmed blue sunhat and her slippers and galoshes, and go out and start up the car.

19   We tried everything to stop her shaming us all.

20   "You've got no license Mum."

21   "What do I want a license for? I can drive can't I? I don't need the proof."

22   "You got no warrant."

23   "Warrant? What's warrant?"

24   "The traffic man'll get you Mum."

25   "That rat. He won't come near me after what he did to my niece. I'll hit him right over his smart head with a bag of riwais [potatoes] and I'll hit him somewhere else as well." We never could win an argument with Mum.

26   Off she'd go on a Wednesday morning, and once out on the road she'd start tooting the horn. This didn't sound like a horn at all but like a flock of ducks coming in for a feed. The reason for the horn was to let all her mates and relations along the way know she was coming. And as she passed each one's house, if they wanted anything they'd have to run out and call it out loud. Mum couldn't stop because of not having any brakes. "E Kiri," each would call. "*Mauria mai he riwai,*" if they wanted spuds; "*Mauria mai he paraoa,*" if they wanted bread. "*Mauria mai he tarau, penei te kaita,*" hand spread to show the size of the pants they wanted Mum to get. She would call out to each one and wave to them to show she'd understood. And when she neared the store she'd switch the motor off, run into the kerbing [curb] and pull on the handbrake. I don't know how she remembered all the things she had to buy—I only know that by the time she'd finished, every space in that car was filled and it was a squeeze for her to get into the driver's seat. But she had everything there, all ready to throw out on the way back.

27   As soon as she'd left the store she'd begin hooting again, to let the whole district know she was on her way. Everybody would be out on the road to get their shopping thrown at them, or just to watch our mother go chuffing past. We always hid if we heard her coming.

28   The first time Mum's car and the school bus met was when they were both approaching a one-way bridge from opposite directions. We had to ask the driver to stop and give way to Mum

because she had no brakes. We were all ashamed. But everyone soon got to know Mum and her car and they always stopped whenever they saw her coming. And you know, Mum never ever had an accident in her car, except for once when she threw a side of mutton out to Uncle Peta and it knocked him over and broke his leg.

29   After a while we started walking home from school on Wednesdays to give Mum a good chance of getting home before us, and so we wouldn't be in the bus when it had to stop and let her pass. The boys didn't like having to walk home but we girls didn't mind because Mr. Hadley walked home too. He was a new teacher at our school and he stayed not far from where we lived. We girls thought he was really neat.

30   But one day, it had to happen. When I heard the honking and tooting behind me I wished that a hole would appear in the ground and that I would fall in it and disappear for ever. As Mum came near she started smiling and waving and yelling her head off. "Whoever wants a ride," she yelled, "they'll have to run and jump in."

31   We all turned our heads the other way and hoped Mr. Hadley wouldn't notice the car with our mother in it, and her yelling and tooting, and the brim of her hat jumping up and down. But instead, Mr. Hadley took off after the car and leapt in over the back seat on top of the shopping. Oh the shame.

32   But then one day something happened that changed everything. We arrived home to find Dad in his best clothes, walking round and grinning, and not doing anything like getting the cows in, or mending a gate, or digging a drain. We said, "What are you laughing at Dad?" "What are you dressed up for? Hey Mum what's the matter with Dad?"

33   "Your Dad's a rich man," she said. "Your Dad, he's just won fifty thousand dollars in a lottery."

34   At first we couldn't believe it. We couldn't believe it. Then we all began running round and laughing and yelling and hugging Dad and Mum. "We can have shoes and bags," we said. "New clothes and swimming togs, and proper apples and pears." Then do you know what Dad said? Dad said, "Mum can have a new car." This really astounded and amazed us. We went numb with excitement for five minutes then began hooting and shouting again, and knocking Mum over.

35   "A new car!"
36   "A new car?"
37   "Get us a Packard Mum."
38   "Or a De Soto. Yes, yes."
39   Get this, get that....
40   Well Mum bought a big shiny green Chevrolet, and Dad got a new cowshed with everything modernized and water gushing

everywhere. We all got our new clothes—shoes, bags, togs—and we even started taking posh lunches to school. Sandwiches cut in triangles, bottles of cordial, crisp apples and pears, and yellow bananas.

41   And somehow all of us kids changed. We started acting like we were somebody instead of ordinary like before. We used to whine to Dad for money to spend and he'd always give it to us. Every week we'd nag Mum into taking us to the pictures, or if she was tired we'd go ourselves by taxi. We got flash bedspreads and a piano and we really thought we were neat.

42   As for the old car—we made Dad take it to the dump. We never wanted to see it again. We all cheered when he took it away, except for Mum. Mum stayed inside where she couldn't watch, but we all stood outside and cheered.

43   We all changed, as though we were really somebody, but there was one thing I noticed. Mum didn't change at all, and neither did Dad. Mum had a new car all right, and a couple of new dresses, and a new pair of galoshes to put over her slippers. And Dad had a new modern milking shed and a tractor, and some other gadgets for the farm. But Mum and Dad didn't change. They were the same as always.

44   Mum still went shopping every Wednesday. But instead of having to do all the shopping herself she was able to take all her friends and relations with her. She had to start out earlier so she'd have time to pick everyone up on the way. How angry we used to be when Mum went past with her same old sunhat and her heap of friends and relations, and them all waving and calling out to us.

45   Mum sometimes forgot that the new car had brakes, especially when she was approaching the old bridge and we were coming the opposite way in the school bus. She would start tooting and the bus would have to pull over and let her through. That's when all our aunties and uncles and friends would start waving and calling out. But some of them couldn't wave because they were too squashed by people and shopping, they'd just yell. How shaming.

46   There were always ropes everywhere over Mum's new car holding bags of things and shovel handles to the roof and sides. The boot [trunk] was always hanging open because it was too full to close—things used to drop out on to the road all the time. And the new car—it used to be green once, because if you look closely you can still see some patches of green paint here and there.

IT USED TO BE GREEN ONCE

Journal

1. **MLA Works Cited**   *Using this model, record this story here.*

   Author's Last Name, First Name. "Title of the Story." *Title of the Book.* 3rd ed. Ed.

   First Name Last Name. City: Publisher, year. Page number(s) of this story. Print.

2. **Main Character(s)**   *Describe each main character, and explain why you think each is a main character.*

3. **Supporting Characters**   *Describe each supporting character, and explain why you think each is a supporting character.*

4. **Setting and Props**   *Describe the setting(s) and all relevant prop(s).*

5. Sequence   *Outline the events of the story in order.*

6. Plot   *Tell the story in no more than three sentences.*

7. Conflicts   *Identify and explain all the conflicts involved here.*

8. Significant Quotations   *Explain the importance of each quotation completely. Record the page number in the parentheses.*

a. "The shame of rainbow darns and cut-up togs and holey fruit was nothing to what we suffered because of the car" (   ).

b. "The car had been red once because you could still see some patches of red paint here and there" (   ).

c. "As soon as she'd left the store she'd begin hooting again, to let the whole district know she was on her way. [...]. We always hid if we heard her coming" ( ).

d. " 'Your Dad, he's just won fifty thousand dollars in a lottery'" ( ).

e. "And the new car—it used to be green once, because if you look closely you can still see some patches of green paint here and there" ( ).

9. **Literary Elements**   *Look at this chapter's title and explain why you think this story is placed in this chapter. Explain in which other chapter(s) you might place this story, as relevant to the literary element(s) of the chapter(s).*

10. **Foreshadowing, Irony, and/or Symbols**   *Explain examples of foreshadowing, irony, and/or symbols in this story.*

Follow-up Questions

10 Short Questions

What is the best answer for each?

_____ 1. The family is probably
   a. very poor.
   b. very rich.
   c. middle class.

_____ 2. The family probably lives
   a. in a city or town.
   b. outside a city or town.
   c. far away from a city or town.

_____ 3. The children seem to
   a. not mind wearing the left-over clothes.
   b. resent the left-over clothes.
   c. always wear new clothes.

_____ 4. The children seem to
   a. accept the over-ripe fruit.
   b. not take the over-ripe fruit.
   c. be embarrassed by the over-ripe fruit.

_____ 5. Mum
   a. does not mind the left-over clothes.
   b. is embarrassed by the left-over clothes.
   c. only uses new clothes.

_____ 6. Mum
   a. is embarrassed by the over-ripe fruit.
   b. sees nothing wrong with the over-ripe fruit.
   c. throws the over-ripe fruit away.

_____ 7. Mum seems to
   a. enjoy the left-over car.
   b. hide the left-over car.
   c. be embarrassed by the left-over car.

_____ 8. Life changes for the family when
   a. the car has an accident.
   b. Mum stops driving.
   c. Dad wins the lottery.

_____ 9. Then, the kids get
   a. new clothes.
   b. a new car.
   c. a new cowshed.

_____ 10. Mum's new car
   a. stays new.
   b. gets removed.
   c. gets old like the other car.

5 Significant Quotations

What is the importance of each of these quotations?

1. "Like putting red darns in our clothes, and cutting up old swimming togs and making two—girl's togs from the top half for my sister, and boy's togs from the bottom half for my brother."

2. "We didn't notice much at first, not until Reweti from down the road yelled out to us one morning, 'Hey you fullas. Who shot your pears?'"

3. "The reason for the horn was to let all her mates and relations along the way know she was coming."

4. "Well Mum bought a big shiny green Chevrolet, and Dad got a new cowshed with everything modernized and water gushing everywhere."

5. "There were always ropes everywhere over Mum's new car holding bags of things and shovel handles to the roof and sides."

2 COMPREHENSION ESSAY QUESTIONS

Use specific details and information from the story to answer these questions as completely as possible.

1. What is the role of the car in this story? Use specific details and information from the story to support your answer.

2. What do Mum and the children differ on in this story? Use specific details and information from the story to support your contrasts.

DISCUSSION QUESTIONS

Be prepared to discuss these questions in class.

1. What does the car mean to Mum? To the children?

2. What statements or events are humorous in this story? What makes them humorous?

WRITING

Use each of these ideas for writing an essay.

1. This story is all about embarrassment. Think of a time you or someone you know has been embarrassed. Write about the embarrassment and what effect this had on the people involved.

2. This story is also about change, or the lack of it. Think of a change you or someone you know has experienced. Write about the change, contrasting the before and the after.

Further Writing

1. Compare and contrast Mum in this story with the mother in "Ah Bah's Money" (page 259).

2. Contrast Mum in this story with Matilda Loisel in "The Necklace" (page 272).

THE BEAUTIFUL SOUL OF DON DAMIAN

JUAN BOSCH

PRE-READING VOCABULARY
CONTEXT

Use context clues to define these words before reading. Use a dictionary as needed.

1. One has a body, which is physical, and one has a mind, which is mental, but that which lives on is the *soul*. *Soul* means

   _____.

2. *Don* Domingo is a great man who leads his town with fairness and who is greatly respected by all. *Don* means _____.

3. After Clyde had a heart attack, he was in a *coma* and was unconscious and did not know what was happening around him. *Coma* means

   _____.

4. The octopus had a round body and slender, arm-like *tentacles* that reached out from the body in all directions. *Tentacle* means

   _____.

5. When the sun came up at *dawn*, Joann knew it was a new day and time to feed the chickens. *Dawn* means _____.

6. In order to *escape* the ordeal of sitting in rush hour traffic, George decided to take a little-used side street. *Escape* means

   _____.

7. Teddy was greatly impressed with the *luxurious* hotel that featured elegant marble lobbies and mahogany sitting rooms. *Luxurious* means

   _____.

8. When Dave married Laura, Laura's mother, Yvonne, became Dave's *mother-in-law*. *Mother-in-law* means

   _____.

9. In some cultures, sad people cry and scream and *wail* at funeral services for the dead. *Wail* means _____.

10. After Carlo died, his family had his *corpse* removed from his home by the funeral home. *Corpse* means

   _____.

11. Frank suffered much sorrow and *grief* when his cat wandered off and he could not find it. *Grief* means _____.

12. Theodore felt great *jealousy* when Tom hit a hole-in-one and won the golf tournament and the grand prize. *Jealousy* means

   _____.

13. When people are confused, they may go to a church and discuss their problems with a *priest*. *Priest* means _____.

14. People sometimes review their conscience and tell the things they've done wrong to a priest in *confession*. *Confession* means

   _____.

15. Pedro had a *suspicion* that Maria was planning a surprise trip when he found a pair of airline tickets. *Suspicion* means

   _____.

16. When Carol felt upset, she would go to church and pray for *divine* comfort, hoping God would help her feel better. *Divine* means

   _____.

17. When Edgar had a headache and fever, the doctor told him that he had the *symptoms* of the flu. *Symptom* means

   _____.

18. Don found his friends to be *hypocrites* when they said they liked everyone and then thought they were too good to talk to anyone. *Hypocrite* means _____.

19. Angela was *lamenting* her harsh words when she saw her sister cry because of her unkind words. *Lamenting* means

_____.

20. Mary thought it was a *miracle* when her flowers survived the frost that killed everything else around them. *Miracle* means

_____.

PRE-READING VOCABULARY
STRUCTURAL ATTACK

Define these words by solving the parts. Use the Glossary or a dictionary as needed.

1. beautifully
2. uncomfortable
3. innumerable
4. deathly
5. invisible
6. housemaid
7. forearm
8. shamelessly
9. skillful
10. disagreeable
11. unpleasant
12. well-to-do
13. gentleman
14. debtor
15. tearful
16. noiselessly
17. weightless
18. powerless
19. tiptoed

PRE-READING QUESTIONS

Try answering these questions as you read.

What has happened to Don Damian?
Who is loyal to Don Damian?
Who is disloyal to Don Damian?

THE BEAUTIFUL SOUL OF DON DAMIAN

Juan Bosch

Juan Bosch was born in the Dominican Republic in 1909. Although poor farmers in the fertile area of the Cibao, his family stressed the importance of reading and of music. Bosch became an able student and started writing stories as a child. In time, he became involved in politics and, when Rafael Lemidos Trujillo took power, Bosch was forced to leave the Dominican Republic. After being in exile for over twenty years and with the assassination of Trujillo, Bosch returned to the Dominican Republic and became president for a short time, until he was unseated by the military. He continued to teach politics and to write on, and to advocate for, the poor of his country. His writings can be found in essay and short story collections. Bosch died in 2001.

Don Damian, with a temperature of almost 104, passed into a coma. His soul felt extremely uncomfortable, almost as if it were being roasted alive; therefore it began to withdraw, gathering itself into his heart. The soul had an infinite number of tentacles, like an octopus with innumerable feet, some of them in the veins and others, very thin, in the smaller blood vessels. Little by little it pulled out those feet, with the result that Don Damian turned cold and pallid. His hands grew cold first, then his arms and legs, while his face became so deathly white that the change was observed by the people who stood around his bed. The nurse, alarmed, said it was time to send for the doctor. The soul heard her, and thought: "I'll have to hurry, or the doctor will make me stay in here till I burn to a crisp."

2   It was dawn. A faint trickle of light came in through the window to announce the birth of a new day. The soul, peering out of Don Damian's mouth, which was partly open to let in a little air, noticed the light and told itself that if it hoped to escape it would have to act promptly, because in a few minutes somebody would see it and prevent it from leaving its master's body. The soul of Don Damian was quite ignorant about certain matters: for instance, it had no idea that once free it would be completely invisible.

3   There was a rustling of skirts around the patient's luxurious bed, and a murmur of voices which the soul had to ignore, occupied as it was in escaping from its prison. The nurse came back into the room with a hypodermic syringe in her hand.

4   "Dear God, dear God," the old housemaid cried, "don't let it be too late!"

5   It was too late. At the precise moment that the needle punctured Don Damian's forearm, the soul drew its last tentacles out of his mouth, reflecting as it did so that the injection would be a waste of money. An instant later there were cries and running footsteps, and as somebody—no doubt the housemaid, since it could hardly have been Don Damian's wife or mother-in-law—began to wail at the bedside, the soul leaped into the air, straight up to the Bohemian glass lamp that hung in the middle of the ceiling. There it collected its wits and looked down: Don Damian's corpse was now a spoiled yellow, with features almost as hard and transparent as the Bohemian glass; the bones of his face seemed to have grown, and his skin had taken on a ghastly sheen. His wife, his mother-in-law, and the nurse fluttered around him, while the housemaid sobbed with her gray head buried in the covers. The soul knew exactly what each one of them was thinking and feeling, but it did not want to waste time observing them. The light was growing brighter every moment, and it was afraid it would be noticed up there on its perch. Suddenly the mother-in-law took her daughter by the arm and led her out into the hall, to talk to her in a low voice. The soul heard her say, "Don't behave so shamelessly. You've got to show some grief."

6   "When people start coming, Mama," the daughter whispered.

7   "No, Right now. Don't forget the nurse—she'll tell everybody everything that happens."

8   The new widow ran to the bed as if mad with grief. "Oh Damian, Damian!" she cried. "Damian, my dearest, how can I live without you?"

9   A different, less worldly soul would have been astounded, but Don Damian's merely admired the way she was playing the

part. Don Damian himself had done some skillful acting on occasion, especially when it was necessary to act—as he put it—"in defense of my interests." His wife was now "defending her interests." She was still young and attractive, whereas Don Damian was well past sixty. She had had a lover when he first knew her, and his soul had suffered some very disagreeable moments because of its late master's jealousy. The soul recalled an episode of a few months earlier, when the wife had declared, "You can't stop me from seeing him. You know perfectly well I married you for your money."

10   To which Don Damian had replied that with his money he had purchased the right not to be made ridiculous. It was a thoroughly unpleasant scene—the mother-in-law had interfered, as usual, and there were threats of a divorce—but it was made even more unpleasant by the fact that the discussion had to be cut short when some important guests arrived. Both husband and wife greeted the company with charming smiles and exquisite manners, which only the soul could appreciate at their true value.

11   The soul was still up there on the lamp, recalling these events, when the priest arrived almost at a run. Nobody could imagine why he should appear at that hour, because the sun was scarcely up and anyhow he had visited the sick man during the night. He attempted to explain.

12   "I had a premonition. I was afraid Don Damian would pass away without confessing."

13   The mother-in-law was suspicious. "But, Father, didn't he confess last night?"

14   She was referring to the fact that the priest had been alone with Don Damian, behind a closed door, for nearly an hour. Everybody assumed that the sick man had confessed, but that was not what took place. The soul knew it was not, of course; it also knew why the priest had arrived at such a strange time. The theme of that long conference had been rather arid, spiritually: the priest wanted Don Damian to leave a large sum of money toward the new church being built in the city, while Don Damian wanted to leave an even larger sum than that which the priest was seeking—but to a hospital. They could not agree, the priest left, and when he returned to his room he discovered that his watch was missing.

15   The soul overwhelmed by its new power, now it was free, to know things that had taken place in its absence, and to divine what people were thinking or were about to do. It was aware that the priest had said to himself: "I remember I took out my watch at Don Damian's house, to see what time it was. I must have left it there." Hence it was also aware that his return visit had nothing to do with the Kingdom of Heaven.

16   "No, he didn't confess," the priest said, looking straight at the mother-in-law. "We didn't get around to a confession last night, so we decided I would come back the first thing in the morning, to hear confession and perhaps"—his voice grew solemn—"to administer the last rites. Unfortunately I've come too late." He glanced toward the gilt tables on either side of the bed in hopes of seeing his watch on one or the other.

17   The old housemaid, who had served Don Damian for more than forty years, looked up with streaming eyes.

18   "It doesn't make any difference," she said, "God forgive me for saying so. He had such a beautiful soul he didn't need to confess." She nodded her head. "Don Damian had a very beautiful soul."

19   Hell, now, that was something! The soul had never even dreamed that it was beautiful. Its master had done some rather rare things in his day, of course, and since he had always been a fine example of a well-to-do gentleman, perfectly dressed and exceedingly shrewd in his dealings with the bank, his soul had not had time to think about its beauty or its possible ugliness. It remembered, for instance, how its master had commanded it to feel at ease after he and his lawyer found a way to take possession of a debtor's house, although the debtor had nowhere else to live; or when, with the help of jewels and hard cash (this last for her education, or her sick mother), he persuaded a lovely young girl from the poorer sector to visit him in the sumptuous apartment he maintained. But was it beautiful, or was it ugly?

20   The soul was quite sure that only a few moments had passed since it withdrew from its master's veins; and probably even less time had passed than it imagined, because everything had happened so quickly and in so much confusion. The doctor had said as he left, well before midnight: "The fever is likely to rise toward morning. If it does, watch him carefully, and send for me if anything happens."

21   Was the soul to let itself be roasted to death? Its vital center, if that is the proper term, had been located close to Don Damian's intestines, which were radiating fire, and if it had stayed in his body it would have perished like a broiled chicken. But actually how much time had passed since it left? Very little, certainly, for it still felt hot, in spite of the faint coolness in the dawn air. The soul decided that the change in climate between the innards of its late master and the Bohemian glass of the lamp had been very slight. But change or no change, what about that statement by the old housemaid? "Beautiful," she said...and she was a truthful woman who loved her master because she loved him, not because he was rich or generous or important. The soul found rather less sincerity in the remarks that followed.

22   "Why, of course he had a beautiful soul," the priest said.

23   "'Beautiful' doesn't begin to describe it," the mother-in-law asserted.

24   The soul turned to look at her and saw that as she spoke she was signaling to her daughter with her eyes. They contained both a command and scolding, as if to say: "Start crying again, you idiot. Do you want the priest to say you were happy your husband died?" The daughter understood the signal, and broke out into tearful wailing.

25   "Nobody ever had such a beautiful soul! Damian, how much I loved you!"

26   The soul could not stand any more: it wanted to know for certain, without losing another moment, whether or not it was truly beautiful, and it wanted to get away from those hypocrites. It leaped in the direction of the bathroom, where there was a full-length mirror, calculating the distance so as to fall noiselessly on the rug. It did not know it was weightless as well as invisible. It was delighted to find that nobody noticed it, and ran quickly to look at itself in front of the mirror.

27   But good God, what had happened? In the first place, it had been accustomed, during more than sixty years, to look out through the eyes of Don Damian, and those eyes were over five feet from the ground; also, it was accustomed to seeing his lively face, his clear eyes, his shining gray hair, the arrogance that puffed out his chest and lifted his head, the expensive clothes in which he dressed. What it saw now was nothing at all like that, but a strange figure hardly a foot tall, pale, cloud-gray, with no definite form. Where it should have had two legs and two feet like the body of Don Damian, it was a hideous cluster of tentacles like those of an octopus, but irregular, some shorter than others, some thinner, and all of them seemingly made of dirty smoke, of some impalpable mud that looked transparent but was not; they were limp and drooping and powerless, and stupendously ugly. The soul of Don Damian felt lost. Nevertheless, it got up the courage to look higher. It had no waist. In fact, it had no body, no neck, nothing: where the tentacles joined there was merely a sort of ear sticking out on one side, looking like a bit of rotten apple peel, and a clump of rough hairs on the other side, some twisted, some straight. But that was not the worst, and neither was the strange grayish-yellow light it gave off: the worst was the fact that its mouth was a shapeless cavity like a hole poked in a rotten fruit, a horrible and sickening thing…and in the depths of this hole an eye shone, its only eye, staring out of the shadows with an expression of terror and treachery! Yet the women and the priest in the next room, around the bed in which Don Damian's corpse lay, had said he had a beautiful soul!

28   "How can I go out in the street looking like this?" it asked itself, groping in a black tunnel of confusion.

29   What should it do? The doorbell rang. Then the nurse said: "It's the doctor, ma'am. I'll let him in."

30   Don Damian's wife promptly began to wail again, invoking her dead husband and lamenting the cruel solitude in which he had left her.

31   The soul, paralyzed in front of its true image, knew it was lost. It had been used to hiding in its refuge in the tall body of Don Damian; it had been used to everything, including the obnoxious smell of the intestines, the heat of the stomach, the annoyance of chills and fevers. Then it heard the doctor's greeting and the mother-in-law's voice crying: "Oh, Doctor, what a tragedy it is!"

32   "Come, now, let's get a grip on ourselves."

33   The soul peeped into the dead man's room. The women were gathered around the bed, and the priest was praying at its foot. The soul measured the distance and jumped, with a facility it had not known it had, landing on the pillow like a thing of air or like a strange animal that could move noiselessly and invisibly. Don Damian's mouth was still partly open. It was cold as ice, but that was not important. The soul tumbled inside and began to thrust its tentacles into place. It was still settling in when it heard the doctor say to the mother-in-law: "Just one moment, please."

34   The soul could still see the doctor, though not clearly. He approached the body of Don Damian, took his wrist, seemed to grow excited, put his ear to his chest and left it there a moment. Then he opened his bag and took out a stethoscope. With great deliberation he fitted the knobs into his ears and placed the button on the spot where Don Damian's heart was. He grew even more excited, put away the stethoscope, and took out a hypodermic syringe. He told the nurse to fill it, while he himself fastened a small rubber tube around Don Damian's arm above the elbow, working with the air of a magician who is about to perform a sensational trick. Apparently these preparations alarmed the old housemaid.

35   "But why are you doing all that if the poor thing is dead?"

36   The doctor stared at her loftily, and what he said was intended not only for her but for everybody.

37   "Science is science, and my obligation is to do whatever I can to bring Don Damian back to life. You don't find souls as beautiful as his just anywhere, and I can't let him die until we've tried absolutely everything."

38   This brief speech, spoken so calmly and grandly, upset the wife. It was not difficult to note a cold glitter in her eyes and a certain quaver in her voice.

39   "But...but isn't he dead?"

40   The soul was almost back in its body again, and only three tentacles still groped for the old veins they had inhabited for so many years. The attention with which it directed these tentacles

into their right places did not prevent it from hearing that worried question.

41   The doctor did not answer. He took Don Damian's forearm and began to chafe it with his hand. The soul felt the warmth of life surrounding it, penetrating it, filling the veins it had abandoned to escape from burning up. At the same moment, the doctor jabbed the needle into a vein in the arm, untied the ligature above the elbow, and began to push the plunger. Little by little, in soft surges, the warmth of life rose to Don Damian's skin.

42   "A miracle," the priest murmured. Suddenly he turned pale and let his imagination run wild. The contribution to the new church would now be a sure thing. He would point out to Don Damian, during his convalescence, how he had returned from the dead because of the prayers he had said for him. He would tell him. "The Lord heard me, Don Damian, and gave you back to us." How could he deny the contribution after that?

43   The wife, just as suddenly, felt that her brain had gone blank. She looked nervously at her husband's face and turned toward her mother. They were both stunned, mute, almost terrified.

44   The doctor, however, was smiling. He was thoroughly satisfied with himself, although he attempted not to show it.

45   "He's saved, he's saved," the old housemaid cried, "thanks to God and you." She was weeping and clutching the doctor's hands. "He's saved, he's alive again. Don Damian can never pay you for what you've done."

46   The doctor was thinking that Don Damian had more than enough money to pay him, but that is not what he said. What he said was: "I'd have done the same thing even if he didn't have a penny. It was my duty, my duty to society, to save a soul as beautiful as his."

47   He was speaking to the housemaid, but again his words were intended for the others, in the hope they would repeat them to the sick man as soon as he was well enough to act on them.

48   The soul of Don Damian, tired of so many lies, decided to sleep. A moment later, Don Damian sighed weakly and moved his head on the pillow.

49   "He'll sleep for hours now," the doctor said. "He must have absolute quiet."

50   And to set a good example, he tiptoed out of the room.

• •

THE BEAUTIFUL SOUL OF DON DAMIAN

JOURNAL

1. **MLA Works Cited**   *Using this model, record this story here.*

   Author's Last Name, First Name. "Title of the Story." *Title of the Book.* 3rd ed. Ed.

   First Name Last Name. City: Publisher, year. Page number(s) of this story. Print.

2. **Main Character(s)**   *Describe each main character, and explain why you think each is a main character.*

3. **Supporting Characters**   *Describe each supporting character, and explain why you think each is a supporting character.*

4. **Setting and Props**   *Describe the setting(s) and all relevant prop(s).*

5. Sequence   *Outline the events of the story in order.*

6. Plot   *Tell the story in no more than two sentences.*

7. Conflicts   *Identify and explain all the conflicts involved here.*

8. Significant Quotations   *Explain the importance of each quotation completely. Record the page number in the parentheses.*

   a. "The soul of Don Damian was quite ignorant about certain matters; for instance, it had no idea that once free it would be completely invisible" ( ).

   b. "A different, less worldly soul would have been astounded, but Don Damian's merely admired the way she was playing the part" ( ).

c. "The old housemaid, who had served Don Damian for more than forty years, looked up with streaming eyes" ( ).

d. "It remembered, for instance, how its master had commanded it to feel at ease after he and his lawyer found a way to take possession of a debtor's house, [...] or when, with the help of jewels and hard cash [...], he persuaded a lovely young girl from the poorer sector to visit him [...]" ( ).

e. "The doctor was thinking that Don Damian had more than enough money to pay him, but that is not what he said" ( ).

9. **Literary Elements**   *Look at this chapter's title and explain why you think this story is placed in this chapter. Explain in which other chapter(s) you might place this story, as relevant to the literary element(s) of the chapter(s).*

10. **Foreshadowing, Irony, and/or Symbols**   *Explain examples of foreshadowing, irony, and/or symbols in this story.*

FOLLOW-UP QUESTIONS

10 SHORT QUESTIONS

What is the <u>best</u> answer for each?

_____ 1. Don Damian is
   a. an elderly and stately man.
   b. a young and shriveled man.
   c. of unknown description.

_____ 2. Don Damian's soul
   a. looks like his body.
   b. is a form unto itself.
   c. is the same as his body.

_____ 3. The person who seems honesty to love Don Damian is
   a. his wife.
   b. the priest.
   c. the maid.

_____ 4. Don Damian's wife and mother-in-law seem to
   a. honestly love Don Damian.
   b. keep back tears of sadness.
   c. like Don Damian for his money.

_____ 5. The priest seems to
   a. honestly care about Don Damian.
   b. be interested in Don Damian's money.
   c. care about Don Damian's soul.

_____ 6. The doctor seems
   a. to be interested in Don Damian's money.
   b. honestly to care about Don Damian.
   c. about to kill Don Damian.

_____ 7. Don Damian
   a. has always been a kind man.
   b. has always been a generous man.
   c. has not always been a kind man.

_____ 8. The people in Don Damian's room
   a. think he is dying.
   b. can see his soul.
   c. talk to his soul.

_____ 9. Don Damian's soul
   a. is the same as his body.
   b. is separate from this body.
   c. cannot see or hear the people.

_____ 10. At the end, Don Damian seems to
   a. be alive.
   b. be dead.
   c. be unchanged.

5 SIGNIFICANT QUOTATIONS

What is the importance of each of these quotations?

1. "The soul knew exactly what each one of them was thinking and feeling, but it did not want to waste time observing them."

2. "Suddenly the mother-in-law took her daughter by the arm and led her out into the hall, to talk to her in a low voice. The soul heard her say, 'Don't behave so shamelessly. You've got to show some grief.'"

3. "The theme of that long conference had been rather arid, spiritually: the priest wanted Don Damian to leave a large sum of money toward the new church being built in the city, while Don Damian wanted to leave an even larger sum than that which the priest was seeking—but to a hospital."

4. "She [the housemaid] nodded her head. 'Don Damian had a very beautiful soul.'"

5. "What he [the doctor] said was: 'I'd have done the same thing even if he didn't have a penny.'"

2 Comprehension Essay Questions

Use specific details and information from the story to answer these questions as completely as possible.

1. How would you describe the "soul" of Don Damian? Use specific details and information from the story to support your description.

2. How are the sincere people different from the insincere people in this story? Use specific details and information from the story to support your contrasts.

Discussion Questions

Be prepared to discuss these questions in class.

1. Is the soul of Don Damian beautiful or ugly? Use specific details and information from the story to support your answer.

2. Did Don Damian suspect the mourners before his coma? Use specific details and information from the story to support your answer.

Writing

Use each of these ideas for writing an essay.

1. We all know people who are truly kind and loyal friends. Focus on a specific example of loyalty and describe a truly kind and loyal friend you have.

2. We also all know of people who are insincere. Tell about someone whom you thought of as a sincere friend who turned out to be insincere. Use specific examples of insincerity.

Further Writing

1. Compare and contrast the characters in Saki's "Tobermory" (available in a library) with those in "The Beautiful Soul of Don Damian."

2. Examples of after-death experiences are continually being recorded. Compare selected after-death examples with Don Damian's experience.

JOVITA
Dinah Silveira de Queiroz

Pre-reading Vocabulary
Context

Use context clues to define these words before reading. Use a dictionary as needed.

1. Murder is a most *grave* crime and can be punished with life imprisonment or death. *Grave* means _____.

2. The Army sent trained advisors to try to get new *recruits* to join the Army. *Recruit* means _____.

3. Being embarrassed to death in front of all of your friends can be a most *humiliating* experience. *Humiliating* means _____.

4. John offered to *volunteer* his time and energy free of charge to help rebuild the poor people's house. *Volunteer* means

   _____.

5. In a colorful celebration of *patriotism* for their country, Americans fly flags and join parades on the Fourth of July. *Patriotism* means

   _____.

6. Alice was very discouraged when the men she hired to fix her kitchen turned out to be lazy, do-nothing *louts*. *Lout* means

   _____.

7. The leader of the country suddenly started putting innocent people in jail and became a true *tyrant*. *Tyrant* means

   _____.

8. The small china dolls were so *fragile* that we were all afraid that they would break when we moved them. *Fragile* means

   _____.

9. Being named the best in your class is a great *honor* and gives you great respect. *Honor* means _____.

10. Allison watched in *astonishment*, her mouth wide open, as the principal named her prom queen. *Astonishment* means

    _____.

11. In his gun collection, Rich took special pride in the long, shiny *rifle* he had found from the Revolutionary War. *Rifle* means

    _____.

12. José was extremely angry after his team lost the championship and went into a *rage* over the loss. *Rage* means

    _____.

13. Dave became Laura's *fiancé* when they became engaged to be married. *Fiancé* means _____.

14. The Navy gave the new sailors identical white *uniforms* that they always had to wear on the ship. *Uniform* means

    _____.

15. Maria was truly a *heroine* when she risked her life to race in and save the people from the fire. *Heroine* means _____.

16. The artist painted a beautiful *portrait* of the woman and her two children, which they hung where everyone could see it. *Portrait* means _____.

17. Because of his musical talent and the many songs he has written, Mike Love has become a *legend*. *Legend* means

    _____.

18. After the football team won the championship, the fans were thrilled and broke into joyous *pandemonium*. *Pandemonium* means

    _____.

19. After breaking his mother's favorite vase and ruining her birthday, Luis felt true *remorse* and sorrow. *Remorse* means

    _____.

20. JoAnne and Jack met the priest at the church and asked the good *vicar* to marry them. *Vicar* means _____.

PRE-READING VOCABULARY
STRUCTURAL ATTACK

Define these words by solving the parts. Use the Glossary or a dictionary as needed.

1. precaution
2. governmental
3. vigorously
4. weak-kneed
5. miserably
6. disgrace
7. madman
8. bystander
9. dismount
10. good-for-nothing
11. ennobled
12. defenseless
13. tyranny
14. metallic
15. sympathized
16. passionately
17. fiery
18. antipathy
19. baptismal
20. uproar
21. scheming
22. behalf
23. courageous
24. irreclaimable
25. forgiveness
26. fabricated
27. inexperienced

PRE-READING QUESTIONS

Try answering these questions as you read.

Who is Jovita?

What does Jovita want to do?

What does Jovita do?

JOVITA

Dinah Silveira de Queiroz

Dinah Silveira de Queiroz was born in São Paulo, Brazil, in 1911. At the age of 26, she published her first story, "Coreio Paulittano," which later appeared in America in *Mademoiselle*. Two years later, she published *Blossoms on the Mountain*, which later inspired a movie and television series. In her writing, Silveira de Queiroz has explored many forms of literature and themes. She received many awards, including the Machado de Assis Prize. She died in 1982, one year after being elected to the Brazilian Academy of Letters. Her writings can be found in novels and short story collections.

From his window up above, the Governor saw the town square and surroundings move up and down as he went back and forth in his rocking chair. Sufficiently accustomed to the malicious stares from behind neighboring shutters, he had taken precautions on that damp, warm afternoon: he had put a coat over his large nightshirt so that whoever looked at him from outside would see him dressed to the waist in perfect governmental dignity.

It was four o'clock in the afternoon and the town square was beginning to come alive. People were leaving their houses

2

to take their afternoon refreshments. Slaves loaned out for hire strolled among the groups of people selling orangeade and lemonade. A beggar dressed up as a saint, who took advantage of the moments of collective good humor following dinner time, leaned against the Church door dressed as St. Roque, with his tunic, dog, and staff. Someone in the Church was rehearsing a vigorously sung litany dedicated to the Virgin Mary. The Governor looked at all this and thought: "Shameless land! No one would ever think we were at war."

3   The movement of his rocking blew air up his nightshirt, shaping it like a barrel; and yet, despite the fact that he was only half-dressed, His Excellency began thinking grave thoughts. He supposed it was the paltry number of recruits sent by his State to fight in the Paraguayan War that had motivated the most humiliating letter he had ever received in his whole life. It had been sent to him by a Senator:

4   *It appears that Your Excellency has still not awakened: our State is the disgrace of the North. I went to the docks to wait for the volunteers. I saw a half-dozen yellowish blacks and a few weak-kneed whites come off the ship. Three had fever, but the doctor told me it wasn't because they were sick—they had put garlic in their armpits to make their temperatures rise. They're making fun of me at Court. I live miserably, like a rat afraid to come out of its hole. Excellency, isn't there some way of stirring up these people's patriotism? Haven't even the most recent echoes of battle found their way there? I know very well that the Brazilian sertão is rich with proud men. Why hasn't the Governor followed the example of the other state leaders and dispatched people he can trust to round up volunteers?*

5   The Governor mulled over this extremely grave matter as his traveling eye went up and down, taking in different portions of the square. Over there, two young women were talking, showing off their lively embroidered shawls as they sipped their orangeade. They laughed, then whispered to one another and to the young men who were gathered in a corner, watching the people pass by.

6   "A disgrace!" the Governor murmured to himself. "So many louts around here, sighing, serenading, and reciting poems, when they're not flirting in the square...and we're at war—a sacred war against the tyrant López!"

7   At that point in his sad meditation, the Governor saw that something extraordinary was going on below, at the far end of the square. A strange band of ragged men came into the street alongside the Church. One of them cried out in despair, looking like a madman. People went running; the group stopped, and one man,

who was on horseback accompanying the group, began gesturing and shouting to the people as the street grew more and more crowded with curious by-standers.

8   The Governor got up out of his chair and watched as the angry man on horseback whipped the crazy-looking fellow, who was crying out in desperation. Shortly thereafter, the leader prodded the human agglomerate forward and positioned it in front of the Palace. It was then that the Governor recognized the man on horseback as his friend, Captain Jonas, who had gone into the interior in search of volunteers.

9   Excited, he called to a slave and quickly began to dress. A few minutes later, he was going down the Palace steps. Captain Jonas greeted him effusively as he dismounted and began showing him the men he had brought:

10   "Governor, forgive me. *This* was all there was, all I was able to round up. Only God knows with what difficulty! Look here, these ten are slaves; these twenty, here, came because they wanted to come—and more than half of them regretted it on the way. You know that in order to travel seventy-two leagues, a man has to be a man! Seriously speaking, there's only one, this young fellow here, who's a real man. If it's not too much to ask of you, shake his hand as an example to the others!"

11   "But he's not a young fellow…he's a child!"

12   "By your leave, sir, I ain't no child. I already turned seventeen!"

13   As the small recruit answered on behalf of Captain Jonas, the Governor took in the whole of the fellow's fragile body and was amazed:

14   "Come up here on the sidewalk, my son. All these people need to see what a patriot looks like. You sir," the Governor said in a loud voice, "are invited to stay at the Palace. I want everyone to admire your courage."

15   At that moment, one of the recruits fell to the ground. It was the same one who had shouted as he came into the square.

16   "I can't take any more, have pity!…"

17   Captain Jonas snorted:

18   "There's nothing wrong with this good-for-nothing. He's pretending just so he won't have to ship out."

19   To which the young fellow responded, with a sympathetic smile that showed his teeth filed to a point:

20   "Governor, this man's so scared of war he cut off his little toe. Take a look there. Tell him to take off the bandage."

21   The sign of cowardice was laid bare. The recruit had used a knife to cut off his little toe, and once the sandal was removed and the rags were unwrapped, the mutilation was exposed.

22   "Have pity on a poor wretch," he said to the Governor, "have pity on a wretch who tripped over a rock and pulled out his toe! For the love of God, have pity on me!"

23   The Governor had no doubts about what he should do in the face of this depressing scene. He launched into a energetic speech to the people of his city about the bravery of the recruits from all over Brazil. Then, he added:

24   "Thank God that some of them salvaged the honor of our land. I present these few for veneration by this city, which is redeemed by these brave men and ennobled by the act of this young fellow here, who fearlessly traveled seventy-two leagues to come here and embark on a ship to go to war!"

25   Addressing himself to the lad, whom the young women and men looked upon with admiration, he asked like a proud schoolmaster:

26   "Son, tell these people why you want to fight!"

27   With a singing, childlike voice, the young fellow responded:

28   "I'm going to defend the honor of the Brazilian women!"

29   The Governor kindly spoke up:

30   "You mean... the honor of all Brazilians, don't you?"

31   "No, sir. I mean the *Brazilian women*. I curse those Paraguayans who're goin' around insultin' the young women of Brazil. In the *sertão* there's a whole lot of stories bein' told and by people who don't lie. What I'm really gonna do is defend the honor of Brazilian women!"

32   "Wonderful!" exclaimed the Governor, who was moved. "That's a fine reason that all men"—and he shot a heated look at the group of young men—"should hear. The honor of the Brazilian woman has been trampled by our enemy, who sacks cities and violates defenseless young women from way over in Mato Grosso, whose brothers are fighting for the cause of freedom against tyranny."

33   An emotional moment followed. The young fellow had said something far more important than the Governor's haranguing. Everyone thought about the young man's words; saddened, forgetting the pleasant peacefulness of the square, they were shaken to their very souls and brought closer to the war, which, just a little while ago, had been insignificant.

34   Suddenly the woman schoolteacher, who also carried out the duties of midwife and had attended the noblest ladies in the place, strode up the sidewalk and, grabbing the youth by the shoulders, proclaimed:

35   "Governor, look for someone else to serve as your hero. I doubt if this recruit will because... this one has a pierced ear! It's a girl... not a man." (Then, she pinched the chest of the recruit.) "Governor, let the truth be told. This is no man, no sir!"

36   The youth raised a hand to his face. The schoolteacher went on in her metallic voice:

37   "I swear it's the truth; you can order an examination. It's a young lady...."

38   A wave of astonishment spread over the square. Even the beggar dressed up as a saint, pretending he was crazy, prodded his dog; and with lucid, piercing eyes, he approached the sidewalk where a great confusion had broken out. In the midst of the hubbub, a redheaded woman yelled out:

39   "This is really shameful! The hussy wants to be right in with the men...."

40   But the girl, who was trying to find a way to escape the public's curiosity and was already slipping away, was struck still by the insult and turned to confront the situation:

41   "Captain Jonas," she said in a loud voice. "Gimme your rifle." Defying the curious onlookers and the woman who had offended her, she insisted as Captain Jonas looked on half-perplexed. "Gimme your rifle, Captain!"

42   Captain Jonas didn't wait for permission from the Governor. Confounded by the situation, he pulled his weapon out of his saddle and handed it to the young woman. Throughout the trip he had deeply admired this youth, who had been so reserved, so stalwart and firm. Trembling with rage, her eyes shining wet and dark, the girl took the gun and shouted, spitting in her rage:

43   "Get outta the way, people, I'm gonna shoot!"

44   A clearing suddenly appeared in the square. Looking at the shocked Governor, who was about to call in the police to take control of the situation, she said:

45   "Pick out some branch over there, on the other side of the square. Where you want me to aim?"

46   The trembling in the Governor's legs was replaced by a general feeling of ease. He now sympathized with the brave young woman and said:

47   "Look, I want a difficult target. Do you see that dried branch, there, on the right? Look closely. Is that all right?"

48   Just as the last women were racing away, screaming, the *cabocla* raised the rifle to her shoulder, took aim, and rapidly fired in the direction of the trees. She hit the target. Then she handed the gun to Captain Jonas, saying in a loud voice:

49   "I just wanted to show that freckle-faced redhead what I wanna do in the war!"

50   Then she made another attempt to flee from the crowd, but it was the Governor himself who stopped her:

51   "Come here, my child." The crowd blocked her way. She had to make peace with the Governor.

52   "Your Excellency ain't gonna arrest me, are you?"

53   "Because you wanted to pass for a man?"

54   "But if I'd dressed in a skirt, they wouldn't have let me go to war. A soldier even told me so."

55   Once again, the circle of people began to close in tighter around the girl. At this point, the police had to intervene. Some of the women shouted. Others said harsh words in defense of the girl. The men were quiet. The Governor finally managed to raise his voice above the noise:

56   "Go back to your homes," he said. And to the soldiers, "Look over there! Keep an eye on those recruits, they're getting away!" He took the girl's hand, paternally. "I stand behind what I said: you are my guest at the Palace!"

57   It was a hectic night. Jovita—which was the young woman's name—had difficulty sitting at the table and taking part in the dinner. She didn't know how to use a fork. Finally she declared:

58   "There's no way I'm eatin' with this stick, no sir."

59   The Governor made her feel at ease. He told her he had a daughter her age, who was with her mother in Rio de Janeiro. Jovita could sleep in her room, he said. With considerable skill, Jovita formed little mounds of food on her plate and quickly raised them to her mouth. She talked about how the idea for the trip came about:

60   "I got boilin' mad. I called my older brother—we're orphans—and said: 'It's about time you got your things together and paid the bill at the store.' My brother pretended he didn't know what for. That got me mad. But because my older brother is, to my way of thinkin', second to the Lord Our Father, I told him what he already knew: 'It's time to go to war; all the good men have left!' Then he began a long speech: 'And who'll take care of my goat house? And who'll keep an eye on my vegetables? And who'll take care of the newborn calves?' I said: 'Your sister. Me. The one you're lookin' at....' But he wasn't satisfied with that and began tryin' to make excuses. I wasn't rude to him 'cause I owe him respect, but I said to him real calm: 'Captain Jonas'll be back here in ten days; either you go or...' 'Or what?' he asked, in a louder voice. '...or then I'll leave. You'll never set eyes on your sister again!' "

61   Jovita carefully formed a little ball of food with her fingers and swallowed it. Then she finished the story:

62   "That's it, Governor. My brother's probably hightailin' here after me."

63   "You didn't have anyone else, a fiancé? You're just about at the marrying age."

64   "Properly speaking, I don't have a fiancé; but there's a fella who lives near me by the name of Pedro, who I know likes me. All the girls are crazy about him. I don't mean to offend you, but he was always wantin' to put his arms around me. Then one afternoon he stopped me on the road and said some things to me in a low voice. But I'm a bit contrary and I threw water on his fire: 'Go put your arms around your grandmother. Next time you come lookin' for me, you best be wearin' a uniform....'"

65   They had reached this point in the conversation when a group of women asked to enter the dining room. The Governor got up to go to another room, but the ladies rushed in, the most important one exclaiming as she spied Jovita:

66   "We came to make amends with our heroine!"

67   Jovita looked all around her, curious, in search of someone. What had the ladies come there to do? This strange talk couldn't have anything to do with her. The spokeswoman, followed by the other ladies, proclaimed to the Governor:

68   "We're here to ask in the name of all the women in this country, who are against the invader, that Your Excellency allow this courageous young woman to follow her destiny and defend us since the men from this place haven't shown themselves to be up to their role. We also wish to say that we are in solidarity with this brave young girl, that we are proud of our sex, and that we deplore the attitude of certain ladies in the square today."

69   The women began talking all at the same time. They spoke not only with words, but with fluttery gestures and the rustlings of their skirts and shawls. They smelled of jasmine and nervous perspiration.

70   Jovita only vaguely understood what was happening. She got up from the table:

71   "Governor, sir, you wanna tell me what these ladies are talkin' about?"

72   "They're honoring you; they came to ask me to allow you to go with the other recruits."

73   "Well, Governor...I'm just a poor Christian—as you can see—and these ladies here ain't no poor folk. But you ain't goin' let me go, are you?"

74   It suddenly occurred to the politician, who had suffered so much because of the troop situation, that this young woman could very well become a symbol of patriotic pride. He affably designated places for his visitors to sit down at the table, and then he said, vehemently:

75   "Jovita doesn't want to go any longer. She's going to return home tomorrow."

76   The little *cabocla* jumped up, passionately:

77   "Governor, sir, is it so, you wanna send me back?"

78   The Governor subtly provoked the girl:

79   "No woman is going to war. Since you don't have a mother or father, I should watch out for you and send you home tomorrow."

80   Her eyes welling with tears, the little *cabocla* said:

81   "You don't have to take care of me. There's somebody greater than you who'll take care of me."

82   The ladies thought she was referring to God, but the *cabocla* surprised them:

83   "The Emperor'll take care of me! If he goes to war...I'll go too. I'll dress up like a man, I'll wear a skirt...don't interfere, sir, I'm goin' no matter what!"

84   At that point, the Governor's voice grew louder:

85   "My child, I was just testing to see how far your courage to fight went." He chuckled affably in the direction of the ladies:

86   "Our State is going to teach a lesson to those who don't know how to be good Brazilians. This girl is going to leave tomorrow on the ship, and when she does, she'll be wearing a sergeant's uniform."

87   And that's just how she shipped out: wearing a sergeant's uniform. The troopship was supposed to leave at two in the afternoon, but it didn't depart until five. An emotional revolution shook the little city. The Governor made fiery speeches. Something unexpected happened: six young men from the area joined the recruits. Away they went, waving goodbye, still dressed in their civilian clothes, which varied from the doctor's coat to the stripped outfit of the baker's assistant. Women wept profusely; children threw flowers at Jovita, who was stunned. Later they saw her, half-lost in her uniform and with her tanned cheeks shaded by her cap, take a seat in the last boat heading out toward the ship that had cast anchor in the distance. And everyone cried when the band from the Theater struck up the Anthem. Finally, the ship turned around, slowly heading south on its way to war.

88   There had never been anyone whose absence created such a voice in a city as Jovita. When she was gone, they painted an embellished portrait of her, in which she was no longer the little *cabocla* but a fair girl with rosy cheeks, and they presented it to the Governor. A young poet wrote the lyrics of a song entitled "Jovita," which was quickly set to music by the band conductor and sung throughout the city.

89   Two weeks later, workers building the new annex to the Church could be heard whistling the tune.

90   And young girls at home would sing the rousing creation:

91   *Who inspires us to bravery?*
Jovita!
Who in uniform is the prettiest?
Jovita!
Who is blessed by the Country?
Jovita! Jovita!

92   The Governor was happy. This girl had been sent by his guardian angel. A wave of civic pride inundated the little city; the young men enlisted; there was even the beginning—and in just a few days!—of antipathy toward those who, able to leave, sent their slaves instead. The square had turned into a sadder place, but at night, meetings were held; the women smiled and wept and the men were moved when anyone spoke of Jovita.

93   Two more ships had left with volunteers when the Governor received a troubling letter from his friend, the Senator:

94   *Jovita is a guest in our home; she is unable to accompany the battalion; she's waiting for permission to embark. She called upon the Marquis of Caxias, but until today we haven't received a response. But Your Excellency need not mention this to the people of our land; she was at the dock to see our courageous volunteers off—they made a wonderful impression here. Jovita unexpectedly met up with her brother and her fiancé. It was an emotional scene. Your Excellency, think about the consequences if word reached there that Jovita didn't set off with the soldiers....*

95   He read the letter two or three times, then he tore it up. That day he restationed himself at his observation post—his rocking chair. He thought about the brave girl and about his own role. The Emperor had left for the war. The Governor felt ill at ease, unprotected.

96   From the heights of his observatory, where he was dressed in his coat and nightshirt, he let the breeze and the comings and goings of the rocking chair cool his concern. "There must be a solution," he said. "As they say, there's a solution for everything."

97   At night, instead of sending a public employee to announce the war news, as he normally did on a daily basis, he himself ascended the small bandstand and gave enthusiastic reports. He ended by saying that Jovita had been cheered by crowds of people in Rio de Janeiro; he read an article from the *Jornal do Comércio,* which praised the young woman's civic virtues. The townspeople's hearts were set on fire, and at ten o'clock when they dispersed, they spontaneously began to sing "Jovita."

98   Months passed and new letters from the Senator arrived at the Governor's Palace. They no longer praised Jovita so much. Because of the difficulties she'd encountered, the girl had become ill-tempered.

99   *I'm very unhappy: if I send Jovita back, I fear what might happen in our land. If I don't, I displease my wife, who, if you'll pardon me, Your Excellency, thinks that Jovita's a bit off in the head....*

100   This letter was like a stab in the Governor's heart; he remained still in his chair for a long time, lacking the courage even to rock. At times he linked his longing for his daughter to a curious longing for the little *cabocla*. He almost confessed to himself: "I was a rascal! I knew she couldn't go." But he didn't have the courage to tell himself the truth. He sent Jovita one hundred *mil réis* that afternoon by way of Captain Jonas, who had finally departed with the last of the territory's recruits. His most pressing problem was finding a way to announce Jovita's return. The poor girl couldn't be kept waiting indefinitely in Rio. He even prayed to the Virgin Mary, his baptismal godmother. Jovita's case represented a political crisis about to explode and— who knows?—affect the prestige of his party, bring about the Ministry's collapse. This "national heroine" he had created could end up toppling him.

101   The Governor spent two sleepless nights; the newspaper accounts and the enthusiastic references to Jovita no longer had the same effect. She was having difficulty leaving; but the legend of Jovita was by now so powerful that it seemed the very moment she arrived on the battlefield, the war would be won. All the city's hopes rested on her youth and grace highlighted in the pictures they drew of her.

102   The Governor finally received a letter:

101   *I'm taking the liberty of sending Jovita back on the 10th.* By the time the Governor read it, Jovita was already on her way back to his land. He was moved by the Setnator's words: *She is resigned to waiting there for the response to the letter she sent by way of my intermediary to the Marquis of Caxias. She hopes he will be her protector and that he will understand what the others don't want to understand.*

104   The Governor took a dose of chloral in order to sleep and, on the following day, he announced to the people:

105   "I bring you glorious news: We've won the most extraordinary field battle...Brazil has won in Tuiuti!"

106   Applause and shouts burst forth. The Governor let the wave of cheers dry up and said:

107   "I bring you other news, equally good. It has to do with our beloved Jovita." And without giving them time to ask "Has she gotten off to war?" he rapidly continued: "The heroine of our land has set out…to raise the spirits of those who still lack the will to fight, who don't have our civic pride and aren't making any effort on behalf of our Country!" Then, raising his voice in order to hide, with sheer volume, the deception he felt aching inside of him like the threat of a heart attack:

108   "Our Jovita, the modern-day Joan of Arc, is traveling from port to port, from city to city, raising spirits and sowing enthusiasm. In this way, she'll be helping in our Country's last effort toward a decisive victory over the infamous López!"

109   There was a moment of silence. The Governor held his breath with the anguishing expectation that, at the very least, someone would ask him questions difficult to answer, or that one or another person might loudly voice their disappointment and contaminate the populace with a dangerous pessimism. He might even be insulted. And…if he were? But suddenly a woman's voice shouted out: "Viva Jovita!" Then a mute and unintelligible uproar gave way, which spread around the square. Soon it was pandemonium. Orators followed orators, and they began to prepare for Jovita's arrival. The joy of receiving her was combined with celebration of the victory won. With steady legs, the Governor made his way to the Palace.

110   It rained that night and he slept peacefully, something he hadn't done for a long time.

111   Jovita finally arrived. She was received like a conqueror, but she was no longer a slight young girl; she had matured and was somber. The Governor went to meet her on board ship. He was amazed how his scheme had come true. Wherever Jovita went, she was greeted with a fiery enthusiasm, a frenzied popularity.

112   It was difficult to convince her to accept the presents they offered her; in vain, the Governor asked her to smile at the people who happily welcomed her. She was downcast, suspicious—her eyes sunken in her drawn face. But she hadn't lost her hope of leaving. She felt the Marquis of Caxias had to oppose the order from General Headquarters, which was explained to her at length by the Senator…*As a woman, you can accompany the troops but not fight in battle; that is, your services need to be compatible with the nature of your sex.* A pretty and polished way of being denied…but what good were nice words when the attitude was condescending?

113   Accompanied by an enormous crowd, Jovita walked alongside the man who had made her believe in her own dreams. She

couldn't bring herself to tell the multitude that she hadn't been commissioned to make speeches in order to seduce people and that she was simply waiting for the Marquis of Caxias to answer her letter.

114   The Governor was disturbed; he now felt a deep remorse. As much as he tried, he couldn't carry out this painful farce. The ladies accompanying the "heroine" had given her a gold necklace with a cross, which was to protect her in battle. The more Jovita's popularity grew, the more distressing the potential end of all this scheming seemed to the Governor.

115   At his request, they were left alone in the large hall of the Palace. He showed her the enormous portrait adorned with garlands of flowers.

116   "Who's that girl?" asked Jovita, whose eyes smarted from the light.

117   "It's you."

118   "But I'm not pretty like that."

119   "You are to the people, my child."

120   She continued to look without understanding, staring at the lofty figure that looked back at her, dressed in a beautiful ceremonial uniform. She couldn't find any explanation for so much pageantry and so many presents. She said to the Governor:

121   "I only ask that you lend me a horse. I wanna wait for the Marquis of Caxias's letter back home. I got faith in God that I, a young virgin maiden, might still avenge the honor of the Brazilian women."

122   "Of course," said the Governor. "I'll do as you ask. I'll even provide you with an escort. The new vicar from your parish; but first, let's eat dinner."

123   The two of them dined almost in silence. Jovita spent a long time arranging little mounds of dried beef, beans, and manioc on her plate, but she ate very little. The Governor didn't eat either because of the lump in his throat that prevented him from swallowing. The letter from the Marquis of Caxias had arrived on the same boat in which Jovita had traveled.

124   At the end of the dinner, the cheers of "Jovita! Jovita!" burst forth from under the window.

125   "Jesus!" she said. "This'll never end!"

126   "Be patient just this one time. Come say goodbye from the window."

127   And the city voraciously took hold of her in her guise as a youth dressed up in his father's uniform. She took off her cap, waved it in the air, and without wanting to, as if frightened, she let it drop. Many people ran at once to pick it up.

128   She murmured:

129   "These people're crazy.... I can't take it no more. Please...."

130   They went back inside. A slave closed the window; the cheers were muted. Then, putting some courage into his weakened heart, the Governor took a deep breath and finally said:

131   "There arrived...a present for you from the Marquis of Caxias."

132   Jovita's lips turned white:

133   "A present...for me? I knew he was gonna help me...that he's not just brave, but he understands too. He's good to all the soldiers...."

134   "Yes...yes...a present for you that you'll receive on behalf of your brother. A medal for bravery...that was conferred upon him in Tuiuti!"

135   "Holy Virgin!" Jovita said at last. Her eyes filled with tears. Pounding the table with her fists in an attempt to subdue a wave of emotion, she tore the painful words out of herself:

136   "You mean to say my brother, who didn't wanna go...was a real man...."

137   "Your brother was a hero!"

138   She made an enormous effort to understand. She knew this wasn't good news. She knew...and she didn't have the courage to ask: If the Marquis of Caxias sent the medal, was it because my brother died?

139   The Governor rushed through what he had to say. And with a furrowed brow, he confronted and overcame his final hesitation:

140   "You are courageous like a good soldier and you ought to know.... Your brother died!"

141   But his sad mission still wasn't over. He saw the little *cabocla*, who looked like a stubborn child with her lost gaze welling up with tears, strike the table with her fist, rebelling against her own fear of the cries that begged to pour forth. Jovita clenched her teeth, believing that she was a good soldier.

142   He couldn't stop now. He'd have to be merciless to the end.

143   "On the list of those killed in combat in Tuiuti, there also appears another acquaintance of yours...."

144   "Pedro?"

145   "Yes."

146   She went limp, no longer concerned with balling her fists or struggling against the weakness. She sat down and remained quiet. She recalled a day long ago, when the cheerful Pedro had caressed her, saying words of love. She moved her hand over her arm, feeling the thick fabric of the uniform, and inside her flesh trembled as she remembered that irreclaimable day when Pedro's fingers had touched her.

147   "Can I go, Governor?"

148   "We're waiting for the vicar, my child. I said he'd accompany you. Don't you remember? But before he arrives, I'm going to read the Marquis of Caxia's response."

147   *Though I have nothing but complete admiration for such a noble, unselfish gesture as yours, nevertheless, the Brazilian Army's laws are rigorous. So that you will not be downcast by this denial, which we issue with the greatest feeling of sorrow, let us remind our fearless comrade that, thanks to God, Brazil has enough soldiers to defend it and lead it to a final victory. We pray to God that He give you long life; we are grateful and wish to reward you because of your lofty expression of patriotism, which elevates and dignifies the women of our land....*

150   Jovita didn't want to understand. She stammered:

151   "Does this mean the Marquis...says no?"

152   The Governor let all his anxiety out in a long sigh. Unburdening himself, he announced:

153   "It means no. He sent an award; some money to reimburse your trip...."

154   Emerging from the silence that had fallen over her like an absolute inertia, the young woman felt a vehement desire:

155   "Governor, will you loan me some clothes from one of your slaves? I don't deserve this uniform."

156   The Governor called for the black housemaid and ordered her to give Jovita one of his daughter's dresses. He wanted to thank this worn-out, wretched girl, who had barely heard the order given to the slave and dragged herself in the direction of his daughter's room with the feeble steps of an old woman. He wanted her to stay; he wanted to ask for her forgiveness; but he did nothing. When the priest arrived, a half-hour later, Jovita asked:

157   "I wanna go out through the slave quarters. Gimme permission, Governor; I don't want 'em to see me."

158   The weather turned cold at the moment of her departure. He let her pass through the large door that led to the kitchen and from there to the slave quarters; he didn't detain her any longer. He no longer thought about political complications. He no longer cared about what might happen tomorrow when everyone found out that the fabricated heroine had not been allowed to go to war, would never be allowed to go, and that everything was nothing more than a petty, stupid scheme. Jovita had been nothing more than a means to an end.

159   The new vicar, who had donned a cassock just the month before, rode silently behind Jovita. She was riding sidesaddle, and her wide flannel skirt undulated to the rhythm of the horse's gait.

It was already dark, the day having ended suddenly in one of those rapid, equatorial nightfalls. The priest had been filled in quickly by the Governor. He felt so sorry for this poor young girl that he fabricated ingenious plans to console her. If she had a good voice, he'd arrange for her to sing in the Church choir.

160   Just as the sudden and thick cover of night descended upon them, the riders came to a crossroads. Jovita hesitated, moved to the priest's side, and the two of them began discussing which road to take.

161   At that point they heard a far-off singing that was growing louder, bursting with enthusiasm. They noticed some white shapes in the distance; they were new recruits coming from the *sertão* on their way to war.

162   Now the shapes could be distinguished one from the other. A few sang and then others responded with the refrain:

163   *Who is blessed by the Country?*
Jovita! Jovita!

164   Passing by so close that their horses' breathing could be heard, one of the young men asked, coming up to Jovita and studying her in the light of the lamp:

165   "Praise be Our Lord Jesus Christ! Is this the road to the city?"

166   The road along which the men had come was the road to the *sertão*, there was no longer any doubt.

167   As the priest and Jovita headed in the direction of the *sertão*, he answered the fellow:

168   "The road to the city is over there."

169   When the riders withdrew, once again singing the song about Jovita, one man who had seen her up close and illuminated by the lamp fell back, distracted, and didn't enter the chorus. He said to his companion:

170   "That girl's the spittin' image of Jovita."

171   The other one laughed:

172   "Whoever heard of Jovita wearin' a skirt?"

173   Immersed as they were in the darkness—before the moonlight could illuminate the endless road of return—the priest nonetheless knew Jovita was crying. Her body was shaking and giving sudden little jerks; she desperately struggled against her own sobs, pressing her mouth closed, squeezing her eyes shut, lashing at herself. She would never again see her brother, who loved her as well as everything God had given them. He must be rotting away in that far-off, foreign land by now. Never again would she see Pedro.

174   "I'm dyin' of shame. Please, Father, gimme absolution, I sinned for being proud. I lost my brother...and I lost the one who loved me, but they went on to the very end. They avenged

the Brazilian women, and here I am. In a little while, everyone'll be makin' fun of me.... The people on the streets called me a *heroine*. Such a pretty name, it's killin' me now."

175   With infinite caution, the priest searched for words. This would be his first job as a pastor, with his first lamb. An inexperienced young fellow, he didn't know how to talk to Jovita. He spoke half ingenuously to the night, to the clearing, there, at the end of the road where the full moon, rising, was revealed:

176   "Heroine or hero, female or male saint, you don't need to do great things. Saints were always defeated by the battles they waged in the world. What remains of them is so very much, yet they did almost nothing: a gesture, an example."

177   A little while later, the moon defied the sad, wartime night. Bloodred moon of the dead, bountiful moon of the glorious light of the living that travel toward victory.

178   The priest and the young girl went deeper and deeper down the road, disappearing on the moonlit ribbon that uncurled up to the horizon.

179   Farewell, Jovita. Jovita, farewell.

JOVITA

Journal

1. **MLA Works Cited**   *Using this model, record this story here.*

   Author's Last Name, First Name. "Title of the Story." *Title of the Book.* 3rd ed. Ed.

   First Name Last Name. City: Publisher, year. Page number(s) of this story. Print.

2. **Main Character(s)**   *Describe each main character, and explain why you think each is a main character.*

3. **Supporting Characters**   *Describe each supporting character, and explain why you think each is a supporting character.*

4. **Setting and Props**   *Describe the setting(s) and all relevant prop(s).*

5. Sequence   *Outline the events of the story in order.*

6. Plot   *Tell the story in no more than two sentences.*

7. Conflicts   *Identify and explain all the conflicts involved here.*

8. Significant Quotations   *Explain the importance of each quotation completely. Record the page number in the parentheses.*

a. "He supposed it was the paltry number of recruits sent by his State to fight in the Paraguayan War that had motivated the most humiliating letter he had ever received in his whole life" ( ).

b. "'Captain Jonas,' she said in a loud voice. 'Gimme your rifle'" ( ).

c. "Our Jovita, the modern-day Joan of Arc, is traveling from port to port, from city to city, raising spirits and sowing enthusiasm" ( ).

d. "You mean to say my brother, who didn't wanna go…was a real man…" ( ).

e. "Immersed as they were in the darkness—before the moonlight could illuminate the endless road of return—the priest nonetheless knew Jovita was crying" ( ).

9. **Literary Elements**   *Look at this chapter's title and explain why you think this story is placed in this chapter. Explain in which other chapter(s) you might place this story, as relevant to the literary element(s) of the chapter(s).*

10. **Foreshadowing, Irony, and/or Symbols**   *Explain examples of foreshadowing, irony, and/or symbols in this story.*

FOLLOW-UP QUESTIONS

10 SHORT QUESTIONS

What is the <u>best</u> answer for each?

_____ 1. At first, Jovita
   a. poses as a man.
   b. poses as a woman.
   c. states from the beginning she is a woman.

_____ 2. She does this so that
   a. she can inspire others.
   b. she can go to war.
   c. she will not have to go to war.

_____ 3. She is revealed to be
   a. a soldier.
   b. a woman.
   c. a man.

_____ 4. She proves her ability
   a. by shooting at a branch.
   b. by striding into town.
   c. by overcoming the governor.

_____ 5. Then, the governor
   a. sends her back home
   b. calls her forward.
   c. dismisses her.

_____ 6. The governor then
   a. uses Jovita to inspire others.
   b. hides Jovita.
   c. ignores Jovita.

_____ 7. Because of Jovita
   a. many men volunteer.
   b. many women volunteer.
   c. no one volunteers.

_____ 8. Her brother and Pedro
   a. stay at home.
   b. join her.
   c. go to war.

_____ 9. Her brother and Pedro
   a. become heroes.
   b. die.
   c. die and become heroes.

_____10. Ultimately, Jovita
   a. goes to war.
   b. dies.
   c. returns home brokenhearted.

5 SIGNIFICANT QUOTATIONS

What is the importance of each of these quotations?

1. " 'A disgrace!' the Governor murmured to himself. 'So many louts around here […] and we're at war—a sacred war against the tyrant López!'"

2. "I swear it's the truth; you can order an examination. It's a young lady.…"

3. "And that's just how she shipped out: wearing a sergeant's uniform. […]. And everyone cried when the band from the Theater struck up the Anthem."

4. "The Governor was happy. This girl had been sent by his guardian angel. A wave of civic pride inundated the little city; the young men enlisted; there was even the beginning—and in just a few days!—of antipathy toward those who, able to leave, sent their slaves instead."

5. "Does this mean the Marquis...says no?"

2 COMPREHENSION ESSAY QUESTIONS

Use specific details and information from the story to answer these questions as completely as possible.

1. What role does gender play in this story? Use specific details and information from the story to support your answer.

2. What are the Governor's actions and how does he change in the story? Use specific details and information from the story to support your answer.

DISCUSSION QUESTIONS

Be prepared to discuss these questions in class.

1. What emotions does Jovita inspire in you? Why?

2. What do you feel is fair or unfair in this story? Use specific details from the story to support your observations.

WRITING

Use each of these ideas for writing an essay.

1. Here, Jovita appears to be a man and is really a woman. Compare and contrast someone or something that you thought to be one way and that turned out to be another.

2. Jovita wants to be a soldier, yet her sex limits her. Women and men are often treated differently, even in our own families. Contrast specific ways males and females are treated differently within your own family or your own community.

Further Writing

1. Compare Jovita with Mulan in the story *Mulan* by Maxine Hong Kingston (available in a library or a video store).

2. Research the life of St. Joan of Arc. Compare and contrast Jovita with St. Joan.

NOTES

Setting and Props

Setting is the catch all term that describes the time, place, and surroundings of a story. The surroundings include the mood and/or tone of the story and even the inanimate objects that support the actions of the story. In a short story, the setting is usually, although not always, limited. The story usually takes place in a shorter amount of time than in a longer work, and fewer places are involved.

The **time** during which a story takes place may be a historical period, such as the ancient, medieval, or modern period, or it may be an era, such as the Roaring Twenties, the Depression, or a world war. The time period may be a season—spring, summer, winter, or fall—or it may be a rainy, sunny, planting, or harvesting period, or part of a day, such as daytime or nighttime. "Strong Temptations—Strategic Movements—The Innocents Beguiled," for instance, will make more sense to you if you know that it takes place on a beautiful day.

Place is the location where a story is set. That "The Hockey Sweater" is set in Canada where hockey is *the* national pastime and where there are difficulties between the French- and English-speaking people, that "Bone Girl" takes place on a reservation, and that "What's in a Name?" is set in China, where name selection is different from other places, are all important to the events of each story.

Mood and **tone** set the general feeling of the story. A bright setting that is filled with sunlight and gentle breezes sets a much different mood or tone than a decaying, haunted house. Think of setting *Pet Sematary* on a bright, sun-filled beach; it would not work. Notice in "The Hockey Sweater," "Bone Girl," "Strong Temptations—The Innocents Beguiled—Strategic Movements," and "What's in a Name?" the authors use humor and a lighter touch. In "The Rain Came," the author uses a more serious tone to create drama.

Props (short for "properties") are the inanimate objects in a story. Props are important to recognize and sometimes even take on the qualities of characters. In "The Hockey Sweater," the sweater takes on a life of its own as its effects swirl around the narrator. In "Bone Girl," the lights in the cemetery and the flowing hair are as essential as the fence in "Strong Temptations—Strategic Movements—The Innocents Beguiled." In "The Rain Came," the camouflage is crucial and in "What's in a Name?" the abstraction of name itself immediately initiates the actions. Later in this book, "The Necklace" (page 272) is a classic example of a prop being at the core of a story.

Enjoy the times and places to which these stories take you.

THE HOCKEY SWEATER

Roch Carrier

Pre-reading Vocabulary
Context

Use context clues to define these words before reading. Use a dictionary as needed.

1. *Hockey* is a game played on ice between two teams that each try to hit a small puck into a net. *Hockey* means _____.

2. For some winter fun, the children took their skates and went to the *skating-rink* to slide on the ice. *Skating-rink* means

   _____.

3. After the criminal robbed the bank, the judge told him he would have to go to prison as *punishment. Punishment* means

   _____.

4. The team members all agreed to wear the same clothes in their games, so they all ordered white *uniforms. Uniform* means

   _____.

5. Pierre rooted for the *Montreal Canadiens* because they play in his city of Montreal and because they have been hockey champions. *Montreal Canadiens* means

   _____.

6. When Rich became a *referee*, he had to be on the field for every game and he had to call all of the penalties. *Referee* means

   _____.

7. Ellen gave Matty a *whistle* that he could put in his mouth and blow each time there was a penalty. *Whistle* means

   _____.

8. In hockey, the object of the game is to hit the small, hard, black *puck* into the net to score a goal. *Puck* means

_____.

9. Dodee took out the J.C. Penney *catalogue* and looked at all of the pictures to decide what shoes to order. *Catalogue* means

_____.

10. When Lori is in America she shops at Macy's, but when she is in Canada she shops at *Eaton's*. *Eaton's* means

_____.

11. After planting the fields, Scott went to the *general store* to buy milk, seeds, a sweater, and a blanket. *General store* means

_____.

12. Avani cried and felt much *sorrow* when she learned that her pet cat had died. *Sorrow* means

_____.

13. The *Toronto Maple Leafs* is the hockey team that wears the maple leaf that symbolizes the non-French part of Canada. *Toronto Maple Leafs* means_____.

14. Andy's team *trounced* the other team by winning with a score of 65 to 1. *Trounce* means_____.

15. Blowing one's nose in a napkin and burping and belching after dinner is *abominable* behavior. *Abominable* means

_____.

16. In Canada, some people speak English and some speak French; French speakers refer to English speakers as *Anglais*. *Anglais* means

_____.

17. Cheryl, who is a hard worker, felt deeply *insulted* when the consultant told her that she is lazy. *Insulted* means

_____.

18. Early Christians suffered great *persecution* under the Romans and were often tortured or killed. *Persecution* means

_____.

19. Our *vicar*, or pastor, offers religious services at our church every Sunday morning. *Vicar* means

_____.

20. The white *moth*, a relative of the butterfly, flew around the light and looked for a wool blanket to lay its eggs in. *Moth* means

_____.

PRE-READING VOCABULARY
STRUCTURAL ATTACK

Define these words by solving the parts. Use the Glossary or a dictionary as needed.

1. daydream
2. schoolteacher
3. disappointment
4. triumphant

PRE-READING QUESTIONS

Try answering these questions as you read.

What does the narrator love to do?

What happens to his old sweater?

What happens because of his new sweater?

THE HOCKEY SWEATER

Roch Carrier

Roch Carrier was born in 1937. Carrier uses his humor to portray societal tensions in Quebec, Canada. The people of Quebec Province are largely French-speaking, while much of the remaining population of Canada is largely English-speaking. Over the years, the differences in language and cultural heritage have led to various societal tensions and conflicts. In this story, Carrier uses an innocuous piece of clothing to contrast the child's needs with the misunderstandings of the institutions around him. Carrier's masterwork is *La Guerre, Yes Sir!*

The winters of my childhood were long, long seasons. We lived in three places—the school, the church and the skating-rink—but our real life was on the skating-rink. Real battles were won on the skating-rink. Real strength appeared on the skating-rink. The real leaders showed themselves on the skating-rink. School was a sort of punishment. Parents always want to punish children and school is their most natural way of punishing us. However, school was also a quiet place where we could prepare for the next hockey game, lay out our next strategies. As for church, we found there the tranquility of God: there we forgot school and dreamed about the next hockey game. Through our daydreams it might happen that we would recite a prayer: we would ask God to help us play as well as Maurice Richard.

2   We all wore the same uniform as he, the red, white and blue uniform of the Montreal Canadiens, the best hockey team in the world; we all combed our hair in the same style as Maurice Richard, and to keep it in place we used a sort of glue—a great deal of glue. We laced our skates like Maurice Richard, we taped our sticks like Maurice Richard. We cut all his pictures out of the papers. Truly, we knew everything about him.

3   On the ice, when the referee blew his whistle the two teams would rush at the puck; we were five Maurice Richards taking it away from five other Maurice Richards; we were ten players, all of us wearing with the same blazing enthusiasm the uniform of the Montreal Canadiens. On our backs, we all wore the famous number 9.

4   One day, my Montreal Canadiens sweater had become too small; then it got torn and had holes in it. My mother said: "If you wear that old sweater people are going to think we're poor!" Then she did what she did whenever we needed new clothes. She started to leaf through the catalogue the Eaton company sent us in the mail every year. My mother was proud. She didn't want to buy our clothes at the general store; the only things that were good enough for us were the latest styles from Eaton's catalogue. My mother didn't like the order forms included with the catalogue; they were written in English and she didn't understand a word of it. To order my hockey sweater, she did as she usually did; she took out her writing paper and wrote in her gentle schoolteacher's hand: "Cher Monsieur Eaton, Would you be kind enough to send me a Canadiens' sweater for my son who is ten years old and a little too tall for his age and Docteur Robitaille thinks he's a little too thin? I'm sending you three dollars and please send me what's left if there's anything left. I hope your wrapping will be better than last time."

5   Monsieur Eaton was quick to answer my mother's letter. Two weeks later we received the sweater. That day I had one of the greatest disappointments of my life! I would even say that on that day I experienced a very great sorrow. Instead of the red, white and blue Montreal Canadiens sweater, Monsieur Eaton had sent us a blue and white sweater with a maple leaf on the front—the sweater of the Toronto Maple Leafs. I'd always worn the red, white and blue Montreal Canadiens sweater; all my friends wore the red, white and blue sweater; never had anyone in my village ever worn the Toronto sweater, never had we even seen a Toronto Maple Leafs sweater. Besides, the Toronto team was regularly trounced by the triumphant Canadiens. With tears in my eyes, I found the strength to say:

6   "I'll never wear that uniform."

7   "My boy, first you're going to try it on! If you make up your mind about things before you try, my boy, you won't go very far in this life."

8   My mother had pulled the blue and white Toronto Maple Leafs sweater over my shoulders and already my arms were inside the sleeves. She pulled the sweater down and carefully smoothed all the creases in the abominable maple leaf on which, right in the middle of my chest, were written the words "Toronto Maple Leafs." I wept.

9   "I'll never wear it."

10   "Why not? This sweater fits you…like a glove."

11   "Maurice Richard would never put it on his back."

12   "You aren't Maurice Richard. Anyway, it isn't what's on your back that counts, it's what you've got inside your head."

13   "You'll never put it in my head to wear a Toronto Maple Leafs sweater."

14   My mother sighed in despair and explained to me:

15   "If you don't keep this sweater which fits you perfectly I'll have to write to Monsieur Eaton and explain that you don't want to wear the Toronto sweater. Monsieur Eaton's an *Anglais*. He'll be insulted because he likes the Maple Leafs. And if he's insulted do you think he'll be in a hurry to answer us? Spring will be here and you won't have played a single game, just because you didn't want to wear that perfectly nice blue sweater."

16   So I was obliged to wear the Maple Leafs sweater. When I arrived on the rink, all the Maurice Richards in red, white and blue came up, one by one, to take a look. When the referee blew his whistle I went to take my usual position. The captain came and warned me I'd be better to stay on the forward line. A few minutes later the second line was called; I jumped onto the ice. The Maple Leafs sweater weighed on my shoulders like a mountain. The captain came and told me to wait; he'd need me later, on defense. By the third period I still hadn't played; one of the defensemen was hit in the nose with a stick and it was bleeding. I jumped on the ice: my moment had come! The referee blew his whistle; he gave me a penalty. He claimed I'd jumped on the ice when there were already five players. That was too much! It was unfair! It was persecution! It was because of my blue sweater! I struck my stick against the ice so hard it broke. Relieved, I bent down to pick up the debris. As I straightened up I saw the young vicar, on skates, before me.

17   "My child," he said, "just because you're wearing a new Toronto Maple Leafs sweater unlike the others, it doesn't mean you're going to make the laws around here. A proper young man doesn't lose his temper. Now take off your skates and go to the church and ask God to forgive you."

18   Wearing my Maple Leafs sweater I went to the church, where I prayed to God; I asked Him to send, as quickly as possible, moths that would eat up my Toronto Maple Leafs sweater.

● ●

THE HOCKEY SWEATER

Journal

1. MLA Works Cited   *Using this model, record this story here.*

Author's Last Name, First Name. "Title of the Story." *Title of the Book.* 3rd ed. Ed.

First Name Last Name. City: Publisher, year. Page number(s) of this story. Print.

2. Main Character(s)   *Describe each main character, and explain why you think each is a main character.*

3. Supporting Characters   *Describe each supporting character, and explain why you think each is a supporting character.*

4. Setting and Props   *Describe the setting(s) and all relevant prop(s).*

5. Sequence   *Outline the events of the story in order.*

6. Plot   *Tell the story in no more than two sentences.*

7. Conflicts   *Identify and explain all the conflicts involved here.*

8. Significant Quotations   *Explain the importance of each quotation completely. Record the page number in the parentheses.*

a.   "Real battles were won on the skating-rink" (   ).

b.   "On the ice, when the referee blew his whistle the two teams would rush at the puck; [...] we were ten players, all of us wearing with the same blazing enthusiasm the uniform of the Montreal Canadiens" (   ).

c.   "One day, my Montreal Canadiens sweater had become too small; then it got torn and had holes in it" (   ).

d. "That day I had one of the greatest disappointments of my life!" ( ).

e. "The captain came and told me to wait; he'd need me later, on defense" ( ).

9. **Literary Elements**   *Look at this chapter's title and explain why you think this story is placed in this chapter. Explain in which other chapter(s) you might place this story, as relevant to the literary element(s) of the chapter(s).*

10. **Foreshadowing, Irony, and/or Symbols**   *Explain examples of foreshadowing, irony, and/or symbols in this story.*

FOLLOW-UP QUESTIONS

10 SHORT QUESTIONS

What is the <u>best</u> answer for each?

_____ 1. The most important place in the narrator's world is
   a. school.
   b. church.
   c. the skating-rink.

_____ 2. Church is a place where
   a. the narrator prays for peace.
   b. the narrator prays for wisdom.
   c. the narrator prays for hockey victories.

_____ 3. The narrator
   a. gets sick of his old sweater.
   b. wears out his old sweater.
   c. loses his old sweater.

_____ 4. The maple leaf symbolizes
   a. Toronto.
   b. Montreal.
   c. Quebec.

_____ 5. The narrator roots for
   a. the Montreal Canadiens.
   b. the Toronto Maple Leafs.
   c. the Montreal Maple Leafs.

_____ 6. To get the new sweater
   a. the narrator's mother goes to Eaton's.
   b. the narrator's mother writes to Eaton.
   c. the narrator goes to Eaton's.

_____ 7. When the new sweater arrives, the narrator is
   a. delighted.
   b. distressed.
   c. unconcerned.

_____ 8. The narrator is upset because
   a. it is the wrong team's sweater.
   b. it is too new.
   c. it is too big.

_____ 9. Mom feels the new sweater
   a. is too big.
   b. is just right.
   c. is the wrong team's sweater.

_____ 10. As a result of the new sweater, the narrator
   a. has problems.
   b. is respected by his friends.
   c. wins the game.

5 SIGNIFICANT QUOTATIONS

What is the importance of each of these quotations?

1. "We lived in three places—the school, the church and the skating-rink—[…]."

2. "We all wore the same uniform as he, the red, white and blue uniform of the Montreal Canadiens […]."

3. "She started to leaf through the catalogue the Eaton company sent us in the mail every year."

4. "Monsieur Eaton was quick to answer my mother's letter. Two weeks later we received the sweater."

5. "The referee blew his whistle; he gave me a penalty."

2 Comprehension Essay Questions

Use specific details and information from the story to answer these as completely as possible.

1. How is the sweater central to the story? Use specific details and information from the story to support your answer.

2. What are three specific statements or events that are funny in this story? Use specific details and information from the story to support your answer.

Discussion Questions

Be prepared to discuss these questions in class.

1. What is your favorite team? How would you feel about wearing a rival team's uniform?

2. What are specific statements or events in this story that are funny?

Writing

Use each of these ideas for writing an essay.

1. Tell about a time you or someone you know has worn the wrong thing, done the wrong thing, or said the wrong thing. Demonstrate the humor and/or discomfort and the consequences of this wrong act.

2. Discuss a team you root for and your feelings for your team. Compare, or contrast, your feelings with those of the narrator.

Further Writing

1. French-speaking Quebec and the remainder of English-speaking Canada have not always agreed. Research recent developments in Canada.

2. Team loyalty can become a problem when fans get carried away. Research recent violence at games, notably European and/or Latin American soccer matches.

BONE GIRL

Joseph Bruchac

PRE-READING VOCABULARY
CONTEXT

Use context clues to define these words before reading. Use a dictionary as needed.

1. The miners dug a big ditch into the ground that became the *quarry* where they would mine for ore. *Quarry* means _____.

2. The government set aside specific land for the Native Americans to settle on and build their town in this *reservation* or, as they called it, "the *res*." *Reservation* or *res* means _____.

3. Little Mike is sometimes afraid of ghosts or *spirits* and becomes scared on Halloween. *Spirit* means _____.

4. The murderer was *condemned* to spend the rest of his life in jail, alone, with no hope of freedom. *Condemned* means

   _____.

5. Native Americans are also referred to as *Indians*, a name that supposedly comes from Columbus's belief that he had found the water passage to India. *Indian* means _____.

6. When people die, they are normally taken to the *graveyard* or cemetery to be buried with others who have died. *Graveyard* means _____.

7. A particularly ugly or mean ghost may be referred to as a *ghoul*. *Ghoul* means _____.

8. Alice's *ancestors* came to America over two hundred years ago and settled in New Jersey. *Ancestor* means _____.

9. Missy *dreaded* going to her boss's office because she was always afraid she would say the wrong thing. *Dread* means _____.

10. Michelle is very *familiar* with everyone in her family because she knows them all well and sees them often. *Familiar* means

    _____.

11. Patrice is a real *neurotic* about her soap opera; she almost seems to think the characters are real. *Neurotic* means _____.

12. Allison has beautiful *blond* hair that is the color of pale yellow roses. *Blond* means _____.

13. In order to get across the river, John had to get in traffic and drive over the *bridge*. *Bridge* means _____.

14. Sarah was a very *shy* child who seemed afraid to speak to anyone, but now she talks to everyone. *Shy* means _____.

15. Tom thought he would create *romance* and invited his fiancée, Jacky, out for a candlelit dinner under the stars. *Romance* means

    _____.

16. Jake is no *fool*; he studies carefully and is completely aware of all the people and events around him. *Fool* means

    _____.

17. Arjay loves *spooky* movies and enjoys reading ghost and horror stories. *Spooky* means _____.

18. A full *moon* lights the night sky with its reflection, even if it is hidden behind clouds. *Moon* means _____.

19. Laura has an exquisitely beautiful *face*; her eyes sparkle above her delicately shaped nose and bright smile. *Face* means

    _____.

20. After the skin and muscles had rotted away, all that was left of the corpse's head was the *skull. Skull* means _____.

PRE-READING VOCABULARY
STRUCTURAL ATTACK

Define these words by solving the parts. Use the Glossary or a dictionary as needed.

1. outsiders	7. development
2. international	8. flickering
3. drainage	9. goofing
4. resurfaced	10. staggering
5. homeless	11. old-fashioned
6. disconnected	12. high-buttoned

PRE-READING QUESTIONS

Try answering these questions as you read.

Where does the narrator live?

How does the narrator feel about spirits?

What happens to the narrator?

BONE GIRL

Joseph Bruchac

> **Joseph Bruchac** is of Abenaki heritage. He shares his heritage in his many writings and in his role of the storyteller, a role and revered position that is absolutely essential to the transmission of culture within a tribe or community. He has told his stories around the world. Some of his other writings are *The Dawn Land* and *Turtle Meat*.

The Storyteller - Hopi Statuette

There is this one old abandoned quarry on the reservation where she is often seen. Always late, late at night when there is a full moon. The kind of moon that is as white as bone.

2   Are ghosts outsiders? That is the way most white people seem to view them. Spirits who are condemned to wander for eternity. Ectoplasmic remnants of people whose violent deaths left their spirits trapped between the worlds. You know what I mean. I'm sure. I bet we've seen the same movies and TV shows. Vengeful apparitions. Those are real popular. And then there is this one: scary noises in the background, the lights get dim, and a hushed voice saying "But what they didn't know was that the house had been built on an *Indian graveyard!*" And the soundtrack fills with muted tomtoms. Bum-bum-bum-bum, bum-bum-bum-bum.

3   Indian graveyards. White people seem to love to talk about them. They're this continent's equivalent of King Tut's tomb.

On the one hand, I wish some white people in particular really were more afraid of them than they are—those people that some call "pot hunters," though I think the good old English word "ghoul" applies pretty well. There's a big international trade in Indian grave goods dug up and sold. And protecting them and getting back the bones of our ancestors who've been dug up and stolen and taken to museums, that is real important to us. I can tell you more about that, but that is another tale to tell another time. I'd better finish this story first.

4   Indian graveyards, you see, mean something different to me than places of dread. Maybe it's because I've spent a lot of time around real Indian graveyards, not the ones in the movies. Like the one the kids on our res walk by on their way to school—just like I used to. That cemetery is an old one, placed right in the middle of the town. It's a lot older than the oldest marker stones in it. In the old days, my people used to bury those who died right under the foundation of the lodge. No marker stones then. Just the house and your relatives continued to live there. That was record enough of the life you'd had. It was different from one part of the country to another, I know. Different Indian people have different ways of dealing with death. In a lot of places it still isn't regarded as the right thing to do to say the names of those who've died after their bodies have gone back into the earth. But, even with that, I don't think that Indian ghosts *are* outsiders. They're still with us and part of us. No farther away from us than the other side of a leaf that has fallen. I think Chief Cornplanter of the Seneca people said that. But he wasn't the only one to say it. Indian ghosts are, well, familiar, family. And when you're family, you care for each other. In a lot of different ways.

5   Being in my sixties, now, it gives me the right to say a few things. I want to say them better, which is why I have taken this extension course in creative writing. Why I have read the books assigned for this class. But when I put my name on something I have written, when you see the name Russell Painter on it, I would like it to be something I am proud of. I worked building roads for a good many years and I was always proud that I could lay out a road just so. The crest was right and the shoulders were right and that road was even and the turns banked and the drainage good so that ice didn't build up. Roads eventually wear away and have to be resurfaced and all that, but if you make a road right then you can use it to get somewhere. So I would like to write in the same way. I would like any story I tell to get somewhere and not be a dead end or so poorly made that it is full of holes and maybe even throws someone off it into the ditch. This is called an extended metaphor.

6   You may note that I am not writing in the style which I have begun to call "cute Indian." There is this one Canadian who pretends to be an Indian when he writes and his Indians are very cute and he has a narrator telling his stories who is doing what I am doing, taking a creative writing course. My writing instructor is a good enough guy. My writing instructor would like me to get cuter. That is why he has had me read some books that can furnish me, as he put it, with some good "boilerplate models." But I think I have enough models just by looking at the people around me and trying to understand the lessons they've taught me. Like I said, as I said, being in my sixties and retired gives me the right to say some things. Not that I didn't have the right to say them before. Just that now I may actually be listened to when I start talking.

7   Like about Indian ghosts. Most of the real ghost stories I have heard from people in the towns around the res don't seem to have a point to them. It's always someone hearing a strange noise or seeing a light or the furniture moving or windows shutting or strange shapes walking down a hallway. Then they may find out later that someone died in that house a long time ago and that the spirit of that person is probably what has been making those weird things happen. Our ghost stories make sense. Or maybe it is more like our ghosts have a sense of purpose. I have a theory about this. I think it is because Indians stay put and white people keep moving around. White people bury their dead in a graveyard full of people they don't know and then they move away themselves. Get a better job in a city on the West Coast or maybe retire to Florida. And those ghosts—even if they've stayed in the family home—they're surrounded by strangers. I think maybe those ghosts get to be like the homeless people you see wandering around the streets in the big cities these days. Talking to themselves, ignored unless they really get into your face, disconnected and forgotten.

8   But Indian people stay put—unless they're forced to move. Like the Cherokees being forced out of the south or the way the Abenakis were driven out of western Maine or the Stockbridge people or, to be honest, just about every Indian nation you can name at one time or another. There's still a lot of forcing Indian people to move going on today. I could tell you some stories about our own res. Last year they were planning to put in a big housing development that would have taken a lot of land up on Turkey Hill. That little mountain isn't officially ours anymore, but we hope to get it back one day. And that development would have polluted our water, cut down a lot of trees we care about. Maybe someday I will write a story about how that housing development got stalled and then this "recession-depression" came along and knocked the bottom out of the housing market. So that development went down the tubes. But some folks I know were involved in stopping

that development, and they might get in trouble if I told you what they did. And I am digressing, my writing instructor is probably writing in the margin of this story right now. Except he doesn't understand that is how we tell stories. In circles. Circling back to the fact that Indian people like to stay put. And because we stay put, close to the land where we were born (and even though my one-story house may not look like much, I'm the fifth generation of Painters to live in it and it stands on the same earth where a log cabin housed four generations before that and a bark lodge was there when the Puritans were trying to find a stone to stand on), we also stay close to the land where we're buried. Close to our dead. Close to our ghosts—which, I assume, do not feel as abandoned as white ghosts and so tend to be a lot less neurotic. We know them, they know us, and they also know what they can do. Which often is, pardon my French, to scare the shit out of us when we're doing the wrong things!

9   I've got a nephew named Tommy. Typical junior high. He's been staying with my wife and me the last six months. Him and some of the other kids his age decided to have some fun and so they went one night and hid in the graveyard near the road, behind some of the bigger stones there. They had a piece of white cloth tied onto a stick and a lantern. They waited till they saw people walking home past the graveyard and as soon as they were close they made spooky noises and waved that white cloth and flashed the light. Just about everybody took off! I guess they'd never seen some of those older folks move that fast before! The only one they didn't scare was Grama Big Eel. She just paid no attention to it at all and just kept on walking. She didn't even turn her head.

10   Next night Tommy was walking home by himself, right past the same graveyard. As soon as he hit that spot a light started flickering in the graveyard and he could see something white.

11   "Okay, you guys!" he said. "I know you're there. You're not scaring me!" He kept right on going, trying not to speed up too much. He knew it was them, but he also wondered how come the light was a different color tonight and how they were able to make it move so fast through that graveyard.

12   As soon as he got home, the phone rang. It was one of his friends who'd been with him in the graveyard the night before, scaring people.

13   "Thought you scared me, didn't you?" Tommy said.

14   "Huh?" his friend answered. "I don't know what you mean. The guys are all here. They've been here the last two hours playing Nintendo. We were just wondering if you wanted to go back down to the graveyard again tonight and spook people."

15   After that, you can bet that Tommy stopped goofing around in the graveyard.

16   There's a lot more stories like that one. The best stories we can tell, though, are always the stories where the jokes are on ourselves. Which brings me to the story I wanted to tell when I started writing this piece.

17   When I came back home, retired here, I came back alone. My wife and I had some problems and we split up. There were some things I did here that weren't too bad, but I was drinking too much. And when they say there's no fool like an old fool, I guess I ought to know who they was talking about. I'd always liked the young girls too. Especially those ones with the blond hair. Right now if there's any Indian women reading this I bet they are about ready to give up in disgust. They know the type. That was me. Oh honey, sweetie, wait up for Grampa Russell. Lemme buy you another beer, lemme just give you a little hug, honey, sweetie. People were getting pretty disgusted with me. Nobody said anything. That would have been interfering. But when they saw me sleeping it off next to the road with a bottle in my hand, they must have been shaking their heads. I've always been real tough and even now I like to sleep outside, even when it gets cold. I have got me a bed in the field behind our house. But I wasn't sleeping in no bed in those days. I was sleeping in the ditches. Tommy wasn't living with me then or he would have been really ashamed of his Uncle Russell.

18   One Saturday night, I was coming home real, real late. There's a little bridge that is down about a mile from my house on one of the little winding back roads that makes its way up to the

big highway that cuts through the res. I had been at one of those bars they built just a hundred yards past the line. I'd stayed out even later than the younger guys who had the car and so I was walking home. Staggering, more like. The moonlight was good and bright, though, so it was easy to make my way and I was singing something in Indian as I went. That little bridge was ahead of me and I saw her there on the bridge. It was a young woman with long pale hair. Her face was turned away from me. She was wearing a long dress and it showed off her figure real good. She looked like she was maybe in her twenties from her figure and the way she moved. I couldn't see her face. I knew there was some girls visiting from the Cherokees and figured maybe she was one of them. Some of those southern Indian girls have got that long blond hair and you can't tell they're Indian till you see it in their face or the way they carry themselves. And from the way she moved she was sure Indian. And she was out looking for something to do late at night.

19   "Hey, honey!" I yelled. "Hey, sweetie, wait for me. Wait up."

20   She paused there on the bridge and let me catch up to her. I came up real close.

21   "Hi, sweetie," I said. "Is it okay if I walk with you some?"

22   She didn't say anything, just kept her head turned away from me. I like that. I've always liked the shy ones... or at least the ones who pretend to be shy to keep you interested. I put my arm around her shoulders and she didn't take it off; she just kept walking and I walked with her. I kept talking, saying the kind of no sense things that an old fool says when he's trying to romance a young girl. We kept on walking and next thing I knew we were at the old quarry. That was okay by me. There was a place near the road where there's a kind of natural seat in the stones and that's right where she led me and we sat down together.

23   Oh, was that moon bright! It glistened on her hair and I kept my left arm tight around her. She felt awfully cold and I figured she wouldn't mind my helping her get warm. I still had the bottle in my right hand and I figured that would get her to turn her head and look at me. I still hadn't seen her face under that long pale hair of hers.

24   "Come on, honey, you want a drink, huh?" But it didn't work. She kept her face turned away. So I decided that a drink wasn't what she wanted at all. "Sweetie," I said, "why don't you turn around and give old Grampa Russell a little kiss?"

25   And she turned her head.

26   They say the first time she was seen on the reservation was about two hundred years ago. She was dressed then the way she was that night. Her hair loose and long, wearing an old-fashioned long dress and wearing those tall high-button shoes. I should have recognized those shoes. But no one ever does when they go to that

quarry with her. They never recognize who she is until she turns her face to look at them. That skull face of hers that is all bone. Pale and white as the moon.

27   I dropped the bottle and let go of her. I ran without looking back and I'm pretty sure that she didn't follow me. I ran and I ran and even in my sleep I was still running when I woke up the next morning on the floor inside the house. That day I went and talked to some people and they told me what I had to do if I didn't want the Bone Girl to come and visit me.

28   That was two years ago and I haven't had a drink since then and with Mary and me having gotten back together and with Tommy living with us, I don't think I'll ever go back to those ways again.

29   So that is about all I have to say in this story, about ghosts and all. About Indian ghosts in particular and why it is that I say that Indian ghosts aren't outsiders. They're what you might call familiar spirits.

●●

BONE GIRL

JOURNAL

1. **MLA Works Cited**   *Using this model, record this story here.*

Author's Last Name, First Name. "Title of the Story." *Title of the Book.* 3rd ed. Ed.

First Name Last Name. City: Publisher, year. Page number(s) of this story. Print.

2. **Main Character(s)**   *Describe each main character, and explain why you think each is a main character.*

3. **Supporting Characters**   *Describe each supporting character, and explain why you think each is a supporting character.*

4. **Setting and Props**   *Describe the setting(s) and all relevant prop(s).*

5. Sequence   *Outline the events of the story in order.*

6. Plot   *Tell the story in no more than two sentences.*

7. Conflicts   *Identify and explain all the conflicts involved here.*

8. Significant Quotations   *Explain the importance of each quotation completely. Record the page number in the parentheses.*

a. "But, even with that, I don't think that Indian ghosts *are* outsiders" ( ).

b. "I think it is because Indians stay put and white people keep moving around" ( ).

   c. "Huh?' his friend answered. 'I don't know what you mean. The guys are all here" (   ).

   d. "Come on, honey, you want a drink, huh?" (   ).

   e. "I dropped the bottle and let go of her" (   ).

9. **Literary Elements**   *Look at this chapter's title and explain why you think this story is placed in this chapter. Explain in which other chapter(s) you might place this story, as relevant to the literary element(s) of the chapter(s).*

10. **Foreshadowing, Irony, and/or Symbols**   *Explain examples of foreshadowing, irony, and/or symbols in this story.*

Follow-up Questions

10 Short Questions

What is the <u>best</u> answer for each?

____ 1. The narrator's heritage is
   a. white.
   b. Native American.
   c. other.

____ 2. The narrator is
   a. married.
   b. single.
   c. divorced.

____ 3. The narrator believes that Native spirits are
   a. all warlike or hurtful.
   b. scary.
   c. an extension of life.

____ 4. The narrator believes that Native spirits are
   a. similar to Western spirits.
   b. different from Western spirits.
   c. irrelevant to the living.

____ 5. The narrator's nephew
   a. tries to scare people.
   b. scares everyone.
   c. does not believe in spirits.

____ 6. The narrator's nephew seems to
   a. become a ghost.
   b. run into a ghost.
   c. be scared by his friends.

____ 7. The narrator is writing about this story
   a. to clear his conscience.
   b. to be a "cute Indian."
   c. for a writing course.

____ 8. The narrator has
   a. always been happily married.
   b. never been married.
   c. some marital problems.

____ 9. At first, the narrator does not think the Bone Girl is
   a. an available young girl.
   b. chilly from the weather.
   c. a spirit.

____ 10. After meeting with the Bone Girl, the narrator
   a. mends his life.
   b. continues his drinking and debauchery.
   c. dies.

5 Significant Quotations

What is the importance of each of these quotations?

1. "They're still with us and part of us. No farther away from us than the other side of a leaf that has fallen."

2. "I think it is because Indians stay put and white people keep moving around."

3. "He knew it was them, but he also wondered how come the light was a different color tonight and how they were able to make it move so fast through that graveyard."

4. "I still hadn't seen her face under that long pale hair of hers."

5. "That was two years ago […]."

2 COMPREHENSION ESSAY QUESTIONS

Use specific details and information from the story to answer these questions as completely as possible.

1. How is the narrator's idea of staying "put" significant to this story? Use specific details and information from the story to support your answer.

2. How is the title relevant to the story? Use specific details and information from the story to support your answer.

DISCUSSION QUESTIONS

Be prepared to discuss these questions in class.

1. Would you describe the Bone Girl as helpful or frightful?

2. What do you believe about spirits, and how does your thinking compare with the narrator's thinking?

WRITING

Use each of these ideas for writing an essay.

1. The narrator tells us, "I have a theory about this. I think it is because Indians stay put and white people keep moving around" (page 119). Thinking of your own family or community, write an essay that refutes or substantiates the narrator's thinking.

2. The encounter with the Bone Girl helps the narrator to straighten out his life. Many of us have had, or know of someone who has had, the experience of a supernatural intervention. Write about a supernatural intervention you know about and explain the effects this has had on the person involved.

Further Writing

1. The narrator refers to his excessive drinking. Research the effects alcohol has had on Native American communities.

2. The Bone Girl seems to be a rather benevolent spirit. Compare and contrast her with the spirit in Edgar Allan Poe's "The Masque of the Red Death" (available in a library).

STRONG TEMPTATIONS—STRATEGIC MOVEMENTS—THE INNOCENTS BEGUILED

Mark Twain

PRE-READING VOCABULARY
CONTEXT

Use context clues to define these words before reading. Use a dictionary as needed.

1. The children poured the water in a *bucket* in order to carry the water to the pool. *Bucket* means _____.

2. Don painted the house using a watery paint called *whitewash*. *Whitewash* means _____.

3. The *continents* of Asia, North America, and South America are all tremendous land masses. *Continent* means

   _____.

4. Little Leah and Kristin had a wonderful time playing on the beach and just generally *skylarking* together. *Skylarking* means

   _____.

5. Danny was not sure which suit to buy and *wavered* when he was at the counter, still unsure about which to buy. *Waver* means

   _____.

6. The sad woman looked so *melancholy* after she lost her dog. *Melancholy* means

   _____.

7. Robert went to *fetch* his mother at the train station. *Fetch* means

   _____.

8. During the cruise, Jane got off the ship to take many exciting *expeditions* ashore. *Expedition* means _____.

9. In an even trade, the boys *exchanged* one baseball glove for another. *Exchange* means _____.

10. Corey improved his *straightened means* when he took a job and finally had money to spend. *Straightened means* means

   _____.

11. The idea of painting the lawn's yellow spots green came as a great *inspiration* to Joe. *Inspiration* means

   _____.

12. During a lazy afternoon of floating around the pool, RoseAnn ran her fingers *tranquilly* and slowly through the water. *Tranquilly* means _____.

13. Helena is a good friend and never *ridicules* or makes fun of any of her friends. *Ridicule* means _____.

14. Pilar was so interested in the book that she became completely *absorbed* and did not notice anything around her. *Absorbed* means _____.

15. You could see the lazy boy's *reluctance* to help with all the work. *Reluctance* means _____.

16. Ali responded with *alacrity* to the wonderful invitation to see Springsteen for free. *Alacrity* means _____.

17. Little children, who are true *innocents,* are so pure and trusting that they believe everyone. *Innocent* means _____.

18. Don has always been able to earn a lot of money; he has never been *poverty-stricken. Poverty-stricken* means _____.

19. When Harold won all the money at the poker game, he *bankrupted* the other players. *Bankrupt* means _____.

20. After he took the job, Amar was *obliged* to show up on time. *Obliged* means _____.

PRE-READING VOCABULARY
STRUCTURAL ATTACK

Define these words by solving the parts. Use the Glossary or a dictionary as needed.

1. long-handled
2. topmost
3. steamboat
4. engine-bells
5. hurricane-deck
6. carelessly
7. poverty-stricken
8. passenger-coach

PRE-READING QUESTIONS

Try answering these questions as you read.

What are the "temptations"?

What are the "strategic movements"?

Who are "the innocents"?

What does Tom do?

What does Tom get everyone else to do?

STRONG TEMPTATIONS—STRATEGIC MOVEMENTS—THE INNOCENTS BEGUILED

MARK TWAIN

Mark Twain was born Samuel Langhorne Clemens in 1835. Growing up in Hannibal, Missouri, he enjoyed a childhood filled with the glamour of riverboats and the mysteries of the Mississippi. His father died when he was twelve, and Clemens became a printer's apprentice. For ten years he set type for newspapers from Iowa to New York. In 1857 he returned to the Mississippi and became a riverboat pilot. With the coming of the Civil War and decreased river traffic, he headed west and became a journalist. While working for a Nevada newspaper, he adopted the name "Mark Twain," a term riverboat crews used in measuring water depth. In 1869 he journeyed to Europe. In 1890 he married Olivia Langdon and they moved to her hometown of Elmira, New York, where they built a sizable estate that, arguably, contributed to his later financial problems. During the 1890s he suffered the loss of his wife and a daughter as well as financial problems. He died in 1910.

Twain developed a uniquely American style, unstifled by European dictates and reflecting the frontier he explored. His happiest works are set in his fictional St. Petersburg, Missouri, and include *Tom Sawyer* and *The Adventures of Huckleberry Finn*. The death of his wife and daughter led to what is generally agreed as darker and more obscure writing, but this story from *Tom Sawyer* is a classic tale recognized as part of American lore, a story of inspired American ingenuity.

Saturday morning was come, and all the summer world was bright and fresh, and brimming with life. There was a song in every heart; and if the heart was young the music issued at the lips. There was cheer in every face and a spring in every step. The locust trees were in bloom and the fragrance of the blossoms filled the air. Cardiff Hill, beyond the village and above it, was green with vegetation, and it lay just far enough away to seem a Delectable Land, dreamy, reposeful, and inviting.

2   Tom appeared on the sidewalk with a bucket of whitewash and a long-handled brush. He surveyed the fence, and all gladness left him and a deep melancholy settled down upon his spirit. Thirty yards of board fence nine feet high. Life to him seemed hollow, and existence but a burden. Sighing he dipped his brush and passed it along the topmost plank; repeated the operation; did it again; compared the insignificant whitewashed streak with the far-reaching continent of unwhitewashed fence, and sat down on a tree-box discouraged. Jim came skipping out at the gate with a tin pail, and singing "Buffalo Gals." Bringing water from the town pump had always been hateful work in Tom's eyes, before, but now it did not strike him so. He remembered that there was company at the pump. White, mulatto, and negro boys and girls were always there waiting their turns, resting, trading playthings, quarreling, fighting, skylarking. And he remembered that although the pump was only a hundred and fifty yards off, Jim never got back with a bucket of water under an hour—and even then somebody generally had to go after him. Tom said:

3   "Say, Jim, I'll fetch the water if you'll whitewash some."

4   Jim shook his head and said:

5   "Can't, Mars Tom. Ole missis, she tole me I got to go an' git dis water an' not stop foolin' roun' wid anybody. She say she spec' Mars Tom gwine to ax me to whitewash, an' so she tole me go 'long an' 'tend to my own business—she 'lowed *she'd* 'tend to de whitewashin'."

6   "Oh, never you mind what she said, Jim. That's the way she always talks. Gimme the bucket—I won't be gone only a minute. *She* won't ever know."

7   "Oh, I dasn't Mars Tom. Ole missis she'd take an' tar de head off'n me. 'Deed she would."

8   "*She!* She never licks anybody—whacks 'em over the head with her thimble—and who cares for that, I'd like to know. She talks awful, but talk don't hurt—anyways it don't if she don't cry. Jim, I'll give you a marvel. I'll give you a white alley!"

9   Jim began to waver.

10   "White alley, Jim! And it's a bully taw."

11   "My! Dat's a mighty gay marvel, *I* tell you! But Mars Tom I's powerful 'fraid ole missis—"

12   "And besides, if you will I'll show you my sore toe."

13   Jim was only human—this attraction was too much for him. He put down his pail, took the white alley, and bent over the toe with absorbing interest while the bandage was being unwound. In another moment he was flying down the street with his pail and a tingling rear, Tom was whitewashing with vigor, and Aunt Polly was retiring from the field with a slipper in her hand and triumph in her eye.

14   But Tom's energy did not last. He began to think of the fun he had planned for this day, and his sorrows multiplied. Soon the free boys would come tripping along on all sorts of delicious expeditions, and they would make a world of fun of him for having to work—the very thought of it burnt him like fire. He got out his worldly wealth and examined it—bits of toys, marbles, and trash; enough to buy an exchange of *work* maybe, but not half enough to buy so much as half an hour of pure freedom. So he returned his straightened means to his pocket, and gave up the idea of trying to buy the boys. At this dark and hopeless moment an inspiration burst upon him! Nothing less than a great, magnificent inspiration.

15   He took up his brush and went tranquilly to work. Ben Rogers hove in sight presently—the very boy, of all boys, whose ridicule he had been dreading. Ben's gait was the hop-skip-and-jump—proof enough that his heart was light and his anticipations high. He was eating an apple, and giving a long, melodious whoop, at intervals, followed by a deep-toned ding-dong-dong, ding-dong-dong, for he was personating a steamboat. As he drew near, he slackened speed, took the middle of the street, leaned far over to starboard and rounded to ponderously and with laborious pomp and circumstance—for he was personating the "Big Missouri," and considered himself to be drawing nine feet of water. He was boat, and captain, and engine-bells combined, so he had to imagine himself standing on his own hurricane-deck giving the orders and executing them:

16   "Stop her, sir! Ting-a-ling-ling!" The headway ran almost out and he drew up slowly toward the side-walk.

17   "Ship up to back! Ting-a-ling-ling!" His arms straightened and stiffened down his sides.

18   "Set her back on the stabboard! Ting-a-ling-ling! Chow! ch-chow-wow! Chow!" His right hand, meantime, describing stately circles—for it was representing a forty-foot wheel.

19   "Let her go back on the labboard! Ting-a-ling-ling! Chow-ch-chow-chow!" The left hand began to describe circles.

20   "Stop the stabboard! Ting-a-ling-ling! Stop the labboard! Come ahead on the stabboard! Stop her! Let your outside turn over slow! Ting-a-ling-ling! Chow-ow-ow! Get out that head-line! *Lively* now! Come—out with your spring-line—what're you about there!

Take a turn round that stump with the bight of it! Stand by that stage, now—let her go! Done with the engines, sir! Ting-a-ling-ling! *Sh't! sh't! sh't!*" (trying the gauge-cocks).

21   Tom went on whitewashing—paid no attention to the steamboat. Ben stared a moment and then said:

22   "Hi-*yi! You're* up a stump, ain't you!

23   No answer. Tom surveyed his last touch with the eye of an artist; then he gave his brush another gentle sweep and surveyed the result, as before. Ben ranged up alongside of him. Tom's mouth watered for the apple, but he stuck to his work. Ben said:

24   "Hello, old chap, you got to work, hey?"

25   Tom wheeled suddenly and said:

26   "Why it's you Ben! I warn't noticing."

27   "Say—*I'm* going in a swimming, *I* am. Don't you wish you could? But of course you'd druther *work*—wouldn't you? Course you would!"

28   Tom contemplated the boy a bit, and said:

29   "What do you call work?"

30   "Why ain't *that* work?"

31   Tom resumed his whitewashing, and answered carelessly:

32   "Well, maybe it is, and maybe it ain't. All I know, is, it suits Tom Sawyer."

33   "Oh come, now, you don't mean to let on that you *like* it?"

34   The brush continued to move.

35   "Like it? Well I don't see why I oughtn't to like it. Does a boy get a chance to whitewash a fence every day?"

36   That put the thing in a new light. Ben stopped nibbling his apple. Tom swept his brush daintily back and forth—stepped back to note the effect—added a touch here and there—criticised the effect again—Ben watching every move and getting more and more interested, more and more absorbed. Presently he said:

37   "Say, Tom, let *me* whitewash a little."

38   Tom considered, was about to consent; but he altered his mind:

39   "No—no—I reckon it wouldn't hardly do, Ben. You see, Aunt Polly's awful particular about this fence—right here on the street, you know—but if it was the back fence I wouldn't mind and *she* wouldn't. Yes, she's awful particular about this fence; it's got to be done very careful; I reckon there ain't one boy in a thousand, maybe two thousand, that can do it the way it's got to be done."

40   "No—is that so? Oh come, now—lemme just try. Only just a little—I'd let *you*, if you was me, Tom."

41   "Ben, I'd like to, honest injun; but Aunt Polly—well Jim wanted to do it, but she wouldn't let him; Sid wanted to do it, and she wouldn't let Sid. Now don't you see how I'm fixed? If you was to tackle this fence and anything was to happen to it—"

42   "Oh, shucks, I'll be just as careful. Now lemme try. Say—I'll, give you the core of my apple."

43   "Well, here—. No Ben, now don't. I'm afeard—"

44   "I'll give you *all* of it!"

45   Tom gave up the brush with reluctance in his face but alacrity in his heart. And while the late steamer "Big Missouri" worked and sweated in the sun, the retired artist sat on a barrel in the shade close by, dangled his legs, munched his apple, and planned the slaughter of more innocents. There was no lack of material; boys happened along every little while; they came to jeer, but remained to white-wash. By the time Ben was fagged out, Tom had traded the next chance to Billy Fisher for a kite, in good repair; and when *he* played out, Johnny Miller bought in for a dead rat and a string to swing it with—and so on, and so on, hour after hour. And when the middle of the afternoon came, from being a poor poverty-stricken boy in the morning, Tom was literally rolling in wealth. He had beside the things before mentioned, twelve marbles, part of a Jew's-harp, a piece of blue bottle-glass to look through, a spool cannon, a key that wouldn't unlock anything, a fragment of chalk, a stopper of a decanter, a tin soldier, a couple of tadpoles, six firecrackers, a kitten with only one eye, a brass door-knob, a dogcollar—but no dog—the handle of a knife, four pieces of orange peel, and a dilapidated old window-sash.

46   He had had a nice, good, idle time all the while—plenty of company—and the fence had three coats of whitewash on it! If he hadn't run out of whitewash, he would have bankrupted every boy in the village.

47   Tom said to himself that it was not such a hollow world, after all. He had discovered a great law of human action, without know-ing it—namely, that in order to make a man or a boy covet a thing, it is only necessary to make the thing difficult to attain. If he had been a great and wise philosopher, like the writer of this book, he would now have comprehended that Work consists of whatever a body is *obliged* to do, and that Play consists of whatever a body is not obliged to do. And this would help him to understand why constructing artificial flowers or performing on a treadmill is work, while rolling ten-pins or climbing Mont Blanc is only amusement. There are wealthy gentlemen in England who drive four-horse passenger-coaches twenty or thirty miles on a daily line, in the summer, because the privilege costs them considerable money; but if they were offered wages for the service, that would turn it into work and then they would resign.

48   The boy mused a while over the substantial change which had taken place in his worldly circumstances, and then wended toward headquarters to report.

● ●

STRONG TEMPTATIONS—STRATEGIC MOVEMENTS—THE INNOCENTS BEGUILED

JOURNAL

1. MLA Works Cited   *Using this model, record this story here.*

Author's Last Name, First Name. "Title of the Story." *Title of the Book.* 3rd ed. Ed.

First Name Last Name. City: Publisher, year. Page number(s) of this story. Print.

2. Main Character(s)   *Describe each main character, and explain why you think each is a main character.*

3. Supporting Characters   *Describe each supporting character, and explain why you think each is a supporting character.*

4. Setting and Props   *Describe the setting(s) and all relevant prop(s).*

5. Sequence   *Outline the events of the story in order.*

6. Plot   *Tell the story in no more than two sentences.*

7. Conflicts   *Identify and explain all the conflicts involved here.*

8. Significant Quotations   *Explain the importance of each quotation completely. Record the page number in the parentheses.*

a.   "He surveyed the fence, and all gladness left him [...]" (   ).

b.   "At this dark and hopeless moment an inspiration burst upon him! Nothing less than a great, magnificent inspiration" (   ).

c.   "Like it? Well I don't see why I oughtn't to like it. Does a boy get a chance to whitewash a fence every day?" (   ).

d. "Now don't you see how I'm fixed? If you was to tackle this fence and anything was to happen to it—"
"Oh, shucks, I'll be just as careful. Now lemme try. Say—I'll give you the core
of my apple [...]" ( ).

e. "And when the middle of the afternoon came, from being a poor poverty-
stricken boy in the morning, Tom was literally rolling in wealth" ( ).

9. **Literary Elements** *Look at this chapter's title and explain why you think this story
is placed in this chapter. Explain in which other chapter(s) you might place this story, as
relevant to the literary element(s) of the chapter(s).*

10. **Foreshadowing, Irony, and/or Symbols** *Explain examples of foreshadowing, irony,
and/or symbols in this story.*

FOLLOW-UP QUESTIONS

10 SHORT QUESTIONS

What is the <u>best</u> answer for each?

_____ 1. It is a
    a. sunny day.
    b. rainy day.
    c. cold day.

_____ 2. Tom
    a. does not paint the fence
       at all.
    b. wants to paint the fence.
    c. does not want to paint the
       fence.

_____ 3. Before, Tom had thought
    going to pump water
    was
    a. a chore.
    b. fun.
    c. a good escape.

_____ 4. Now, Tom would
    rather
    a. do chores.
    b. paint the fence.
    c. go to get water.

_____ 5. Ben seems to be
    a. a stranger to Tom.
    b. Tom's good
       friend.
    c. Tom's rival.

_____ 6. Ben is
    a. piloting a riverboat.
    b. pretending to pilot a
       riverboat.
    c. on a riverboat.

_____ 7. The boys consider riverboats
    to be
    a. fun and adventuresome.
    b. hard work.
    c. boring and dull.

_____ 8. Tom tells Ben Aunt Polly is
    "particular"
    a. to scare him away.
    b. to insult him.
    c. to lure him in.

_____ 9. Ben is
    a. the only painter.
    b. not the only painter.
    c. the only other boy.

_____ 10. Tom
    a. tricks the other boys into
       painting the fence.
    b. does not trick the other boys
       into painting the fence.
    c. cannot trick the other boys
       into painting the fence.

5 SIGNIFICANT QUOTATIONS

What is the importance of each of these quotations?

1. "Sighing he dipped his brush and passed it along the topmost plank; repeated the operation; did it again; compared the insignificant whitewashed streak with the far-reaching continent of unwhite washed fence, and sat down on a tree-box discouraged."

2. "Bringing water from the town pump had always been hateful work in Tom's eyes, before, but now it did not strike him so."

3. "Say, Tom, let *me* whitewash a little."

4. "Tom gave up the brush with reluctance in his face but alacrity in his heart."

5. "There are wealthy gentlemen in England who drive four-horse passenger-coaches twenty or thirty miles on a daily line, in the summer, because the privilege costs them considerable money; but if they were offered wages for the service, that would turn it into work and then they would resign."

2 Comprehension Essay Questions

Use specific details and information from the story to answer these questions as completely as possible.

1. The fence is central to this story. What is the significance of the fence? Use specific details and information from the story.

2. How does Tom trick the boys? Use specific details and information from the story to support your explanation.

Discussion Questions

Be prepared to discuss these questions in class.

1. Do you think what Tom does is fair, smart, or unfair? Use specific details from the story to support your thinking.

2. When have you tricked someone? Using specific details from the story, compare and contrast your trickery with the tricks Tom plays.

Writing

Use each of these ideas for writing an essay.

1. "Whitewashing" means to paint a surface with thin, white paint. "Whitewashing" has also come to mean cleaning up someone else's mess. Compare a time you used someone to clean up your mess or a time someone used you to clean up her or his mess to Tom's trickery.

2. "Whitewashing" also means to cover unpleasant facts with denials, lies, or half-truths. Tell the story of a time you or someone you know whitewashed facts.

Further Writing

1. Tom Sawyer in this story and Dee in "Everyday Use" by Alice Walker (available in a library) use ruses or pretenses to try to get what they want. Compare and contrast their manipulations and their goals.

2. Research the animal rights movement, and include a discussion of Twain's "A Dog's Tale" (available in a library), one of the most poignant and compelling pieces written that is germane to animal treatment.

THE RAIN CAME
GRACE OGOT

PRE-READING VOCABULARY
CONTEXT

Use context clues to define these words before reading. Use a dictionary as needed.

1. The tribe gathered together and joined in loyalty to the *chief* whom they chose to lead them. *Chief* means _____.

2. When Marna delivered her baby girl, the nurse handed Marna her *daughter* all wrapped up in a pink blanket. *Daughter* means

   _____.

3. Buzz wanted to know who was in his family hundreds of years ago and set out to research who his *ancestors* were. *Ancestor* means

   _____.

4. Heather went to a psychic to see if the psychic could give her a *prophecy* and predict her future. *Prophecy* means _____.

5. In order to *survive* the cold weather, Bob built a warm house and kept plenty of wood for the fireplace. *Survive* means _____.

6. *Household* may refer to a single home, or it may refer to a community of homes. *Household* means _____.

7. In order to keep his room clean, Robert had to *sacrifice* his messy habits. *Sacrifice* means _____.

8. When her husband died, Alicia was the *bereaved* one who cried more deeply than all others. *Bereaved* means _____.

9. Science fiction movies often feature horrible, man-eating *monsters* that threaten everyone. *Monster* means _____.

10. The rain came down in *torrents* so heavy that we could not see the cars in front of us. *Torrent* means _____.

11. When the head of the family died, all the family went into deep *mourning*, crying at the funeral and seeing no one for a year. *Mourning* means _____.

12. Nick prepared a fabulous Thanksgiving *feast* that included turkey, stuffing, potatoes, cranberries, and pumpkin pie. *Feast* means

    _____.

13. Debbie has naturally *maternal* feelings for her son and, as his mother, wants to protect him from harm. *Maternal* means

    _____.

14. When Amar thought he had lost his dog, he began to *sob* and the tears just flowed from his eyes. *Sob* means _____.

15. Deer, rabbits, and squirrels are all natural *denizens* of the northern woods. *Denizen* means _____.

16. When Kelli goes to church, she goes to watch a *sacred* and *holy* service that honors her God. *Sacred* and *holy* mean

    _____.

17. Even though he knew it would be difficult, Jack decided to make a *trek* across the desert to the next town. *Trek* means

    _____.

18. The people who give the services in church are called the clergy and the people who simply attend the service are called *laymen*. *Layman* means _____.

19. After mowing the lawn, washing the car, and painting the house, Patrick came in to take a nap because he was *exhausted*. *Exhausted* means _____.

20. No one dares to make Ken angry, because no one wants to face his boiling *wrath*. *Wrath* means

_____.

PRE-READING VOCABULARY
STRUCTURAL ATTACK

Define these words by solving the parts. Use the Glossary or a dictionary as needed.

1. breathlessly
2. anxiously
3. aimlessly
4. co-wife
5. hunger-stricken
6. glittering
7. bitterly
8. enthroned
9. forefather
10. enviable
11. rainmaker
12. disobeying
13. riverbank
14. lazily
15. midday
16. grandmother
17. neighboring
18. elder
19. fingered
20. barring
21. panicky
22. farewell
23. sorrowful
24. bewitching
25. beloved
26. barefooted
27. tongue-tied
28. unbelieving
29. painfully
30. wilderness
31. inhabited
32. sympathetically
33. frantically
34. unidentified
35. entangled

PRE-READING QUESTIONS

Try answering these questions as you read.

What is the prophecy?
What must Oganda do?
What does Osinda do?

THE RAIN CAME

GRACE OGOT

Grace Ogot was born in the Central Nyanga District of Kenya in 1930. With her father a teacher and surrounded by the wealth of oral stories around her, Ogot's writing reflects the integration of her formal learning with the rich traditions of her youth.

Continuing her formal education, Ogot went on to become a nurse and then a health administrator. During all this, she continued to write, later becoming involved in film and television and eventually becoming a United Nations' delegate. Her writing reflects her personal love for the stories of her culture and can be found in various collections.

The chief was still far from the gate when his daughter, Oganda, saw him. She ran to meet him. Breathlessly she asked her father, "What is the news, great Chief? Everyone in the village is anxiously waiting to hear when it will rain." Labong'o held out his hands for his daughter but he did not say a word. Puzzled by her father's cold attitude Oganda ran back to the village to warn the others that the chief was back.

2   The atmosphere in the village was tense and confused. Everyone moved aimlessly and fussed in the yard without

actually doing any work. A young woman whispered to her co-wife, "If they have not solved this rain business today, the chief will crack." They had watched him getting thinner and thinner as the people kept on pestering him. "Our cattle lie dying in the fields," they reported. "Soon it will be our children and then ourselves. Tell us what to do to save our lives, oh great Chief." So the chief had daily prayed with the Almighty through the ancestors to deliver them from their distress.

3   Instead of calling the family together and giving them the news immediately, Labong'o went to his own hut, a sign that he was not to be disturbed. Having replaced the shutter, he sat in the dimly lit hut to contemplate.

4   It was no longer a question of being the chief of hunger-stricken people that weighed Labong'o's heart. It was the life of his only daughter that was at stake. At the time when Oganda came to meet him, he saw the glittering chain shining around her waist. The prophecy was complete. "It is Oganda, Oganda, my only daughter, who must die so young." Labong'o burst into tears before finishing the sentence. The chief must not weep. Society had declared him the bravest of men. But Labong'o did not care anymore. He assumed the position of a simple father and wept bitterly. He loved his people, the Luo, but what were the Luo for him without Oganda? Her life had brought a new life in Labong'o's world and he ruled better than he could remember. How would the spirit of the village survive his beautiful daughter? "There are so many homes and so many parents who have daughters. Why choose this one? She is all I have." Labong'o spoke as if the ancestors were there in the hut and he could see them face to face. Perhaps they were there, warning him to remember his promise on the day he was enthroned when he said aloud, before the elders, "I will lay down life, if necessary, and the life of my household, to save this tribe from the hands of the enemy." "Deny! Deny!" he could hear the voice of his forefathers mocking him.

5   When Labong'o was consecrated chief he was only a young man. Unlike his father, he ruled for many years with only one wife. But people rebuked him because his only wife did not bear him a daughter. He married a second, a third, and a fourth wife. But they all gave birth to male children. When Labong'o married a fifth wife she bore him a daughter. They called her Oganda, meaning "beans," because her skin was very fair. Out of Labong'o's twenty children, Oganda was the only girl. Though she was the chief's favorite, her mother's co-wives swallowed their jealous feelings and showered her with love. After all, they said, Oganda was a female child whose days in the royal family were numbered. She would soon marry at a tender age and leave the enviable position to someone else.

6   Never in his life had he been faced with such an impossible decision. Refusing to yield to the rainmaker's request would mean sacrificing the whole tribe, putting the interests of the individual above those of the society. More than that. It would mean disobeying the ancestors, and most probably wiping the Luo people from the surface of the earth. On the other hand, to let Oganda die as a ransom for the people would permanently cripple Labong'o spiritually. He knew he would never be the same chief again.

7   The words of Ndithi, the medicine man, still echoed in his ears. "Podho, the ancestor of the Luo, appeared to me in a dream last night, and he asked me to speak to the chief and the people," Ndithi had said to the gathering of tribesmen. "A young woman who has not known a man must die so that the country may have rain. While Podho was still talking to me, I saw a young woman standing at the lakeside, her hands raised, above her head. Her skin was as fair as the skin of young deer in the wilderness. Her tall slender figure stood like a lonely reed at the riverbank. Her sleeply eyes wore a sad look like that of a bereaved mother. She wore a gold ring on her left ear, and a glittering brass chain around her waist. As I still marveled at the beauty of this young woman, Podho told me, 'Out of all the women in this land, we have chosen this one. Let her offer herself a sacrifice to the lake monster! And on that day, the rain will come down in torrents. Let everyone stay at home on that day, lest he be carried away by the floods.'"

8   Outside there was a strange stillness, except for the thirsty birds that sang lazily on the dying trees. The blinding midday heat had forced the people to retire to their huts. Not far away from the chief's hut, two guards were snoring away quietly. Labong'o removed his crown and the large eagle head that hung loosely on his shoulders. He left the hut, and instead of asking Nyabog'o the messenger to beat the drum, he went straight and beat it himself. In no time the whole household had assembled under the siala tree where he usually addressed them. He told Oganda to wait a while in her grandmother's hut.

9   When Labong'o stood to address his household, his voice was hoarse and the tears choked him. He started to speak, but words refused to leave his lips. His wives and sons knew there was great danger. Perhaps their enemies had declared war on them. Labong'o's eyes were red, and they could see he had been weeping. At last he told them. "One whom we love and treasure must be taken away from us. Oganda is to die." Labong'o's voice was so faint, that he could not hear it himself. But he continued. "The ancestors have chosen her to be offered as a sacrifice to the lake monster in order that we may have rain."

10   They were completely stunned. As a confused murmur broke out, Oganda's mother fainted and was carried off to her own hut. But the other people rejoiced. They danced around singing and chanting, "Oganda is the lucky one to die for the people. If it is to save the people, let Oganda go."

11   In her grandmother's hut Oganda wondered what the whole family were discussing about her that she could not hear. Her grandmother's hut was well away from the chief's court and, much as she strained her ears, she could not hear what was said. "It must be marriage," she concluded. It was an accepted custom for the family to discuss their daughter's future marriage behind her back. A faint smile played on Oganda's lips as she thought of the several young men who swallowed saliva at the mere mention of her name.

12   There was Kech, the son of a neighboring clan elder. Kech was very handsome. He had sweet, meek eyes and a roaring laughter. He would make a wonderful father, Oganda thought. But they would not be a good match. Kech was a bit too short to be her husband. It would humiliate her to have to look down at Kech each time she spoke to him. Then she thought of Dimo, the tall young man who had already distinguished himself as a brave warrior and an outstanding wrestler. Dimo adored Oganda, but Oganda thought he would make a cruel husband, always quarreling and ready to fight. No, she did not like him. Oganda fingered the glittering chain on her waist as she thought of Osinda. A long time ago when she was quite young Osinda had given her that chain, and instead of wearing it around her neck several times, she wore it round her waist where it could stay permanently. She heard her heart pounding so loudly as she thought of him. She whispered, "Let it be you they are discussing, Osinda, the lovely one. Come now and take me away…"

13   The lean figure in the doorway startled Oganda who was rapt in thought about the man she loved. "You have frightened me, Grandma," said Oganda laughing. "Tell me, is it my marriage you were discussing? You can take it from me that I won't marry any of them." A smile played on her lips again. She was coaxing the old lady to tell her quickly, to tell her they were pleased with Osinda.

14   In the open space outside the excited relatives were dancing and singing. They were coming to the hut now, each carrying a gift to put at Oganda's feet. As their singing got nearer Oganda was able to hear what they were saying: "If it is to save the people, if it is to give us rain, let Oganda go. Let Oganda die for her people, and for her ancestors." Was she mad to think that they were singing about her? How could she die? She found the lean figure of her grandmother barring the door. She could not get out. The

look on her grandmother's face warned her that there was danger around the corner. "Grandma, it is not marriage then?" Oganda asked urgently. She suddenly felt panicky like a mouse cornered by a hungry cat. Forgetting that there was only one door in the hut Oganda fought desperately to find another exit. She must fight for her life. But there was none.

15   She closed her eyes, leapt like a wild tiger through the door, knocking her grandmother flat to the ground. There outside in mourning garments Labong'o stood motionless, his hands folded at the back. He held his daughter's hand and led her away from the excited crowd to the little red-painted hut where her mother was resting. Here he broke the news officially to his daughter.

16   For a long time the three souls who loved one another dearly sat in darkness. It was no good speaking. And even if they tried, the words could not have come out. In the past they had been like three cooking stones, sharing their burdens. Taking Oganda away from them would leave two useless stones which would not hold a cooking pot.

17   News that the beautiful daughter of the chief was to be sacrificed to give the people rain spread across the country like wind. At sunset the chief's village was full of relatives and friends who had come to congratulate Oganda. Many more were on their way coming, carrying their gifts. They would dance till morning to keep her company. And in the morning they would prepare her a big farewell feast. All these relatives thought it a great honor to be selected by the spirits to die, in order that the society may live. "Oganda's name will always remain a living name among us," they boasted.

18   But was it maternal love that prevented Minya from rejoicing with the other women? Was it the memory of the agony and pain of childbirth that made her feel so sorrowful? Or was it the deep warmth and understanding that passes between a suckling babe and her mother that made Oganda part of her life, her flesh? Of course it was an honor, a great honor, for her daughter to be chosen to die for the country. But what could she gain once her only daughter was blown away by the wind? There were so many other women in the land, why choose her daughter, her only child! Had human life any meaning at all—other women had houses full of children while she, Minya, had to lose her only child!

19   In the cloudless sky the moon shone brightly, and the numerous stars glittered with a bewitching beauty. The dancers of all age groups assembled to dance before Oganda, who sat close to her mother, sobbing quietly. All these years she had been with her people she thought she understood them. But now she

discovered that she was a stranger among them. If they loved her as they had always professed why were they not making any attempt to save her? Did her people really understand what it felt like to die young? Unable to restrain her emotions any longer, she sobbed loudly as her age group got up to dance. They were young and beautiful and very soon they would marry and have their own children. They would have husbands to love and little huts for themselves. They would have reached maturity. Oganda touched the chain around her waist as she thought of Osinda. She wished Osinda was there too, among her friends. "Perhaps he is ill," she thought gravely. The chain comforted Oganda—she would die with it around her waist and wear it in the underground world.

20   In the morning a big feast was prepared for Oganda. The women prepared many different tasty dishes so that she could pick and choose. "People don't eat after death," they said. Delicious though the food looked, Oganda touched none of it. Let the happy people eat. She contented herself with sips of water from a little calabash [gourd].

21   The time for her departure was drawing near, and each minute was precious. It was a day's journey to the lake. She was to walk all night, passing through the great forest. But nothing could touch her, not even the denizens of the forest. She was already anointed with sacred oil. From the time Oganda received the sad news she had expected Osinda to appear any moment. But he was not there. A relative told her that Osinda was away on a private visit. Oganda realized that she would never see her beloved again.

22   In the late afternoon the whole village stood at the gate to say good-bye and to see her for the last time. Her mother wept on her neck for a long time. The great chief in a mourning skin came to the gate barefooted, and mingled with the people—a simple father in grief. He took off his wrist bracelet and put it on his daughter's wrist saying, "You will always live among us. The spirit of our forefathers is with you."

23   Tongue-tied and unbelieving Oganda stood there before the people. She had nothing to say. She looked at her home once more. She could hear her heart beating so painfully within her. All her childhood plans were coming to an end. She felt like a flower nipped in the bud never to enjoy the morning dew again. She looked at her weeping mother, and whispered, "Whenever you want to see me, always look at the sunset. I will be there."

24   Oganda turned southward to start her trek to the lake. Her parents, relatives, friends and admirers stood at the gate and watched her go.

25   Her beautiful slender figure grew smaller and smaller till she mingled with the thin dry trees in the forest. As Oganda walked the lonely path that wound its way in the wilderness, she sang a song, and her own voice kept her company.

26   *The ancestors have said Oganda must die*
         The daughter of the chief must be sacrificed,
         When the lake monster feeds on my flesh,
         The people will have rain.
         Yes, the rain will come down in torrents.
         And the floods will wash away the sandy beaches
         When the daughter of the chief dies in the lake.
         My age group has consented
         My parents have consented
         So have my friends and relatives.
         Let Oganda die to give us rain.
         My age group are young and ripe,
         Ripe for womanhood and motherhood
         But Oganda must die young,
         Oganda must sleep with the ancestors.
         Yes, rain will come down in torrents.

The red rays of the setting sun embraced Oganda, and she looked like a burning candle in the wilderness.

27   The people who came to hear her sad song were touched by her beauty. But they all said the same thing. "If it is to save the people, if it is to give us rain, then be not afraid. Your name will forever live among us."

28   At midnight Oganda was tired and weary. She could walk no more. She sat under a big tree, and having sipped water from her calabash, she rested her head on the tree trunk and slept.

29   When Oganda woke up in the morning the sun was high in the sky. After walking for many hours, she reached the *tong'*, a strip of land that separated the inhabited part of the country from the sacred place *(kar lamo)*. No layman could enter this place and come out alive—only those who had direct contact with the spirits and the Almighty were allowed to enter this holy of holies. But Oganda had to pass through this sacred land on her way to the lake, which she had to reach at sunset.

30   A large crowd gathered to see her for the last time. Her voice was now hoarse and painful, but there was no need to worry anymore. Soon she would not have to sing. The crowd looked at Oganda sympathetically, mumbling words she could not hear. But none of them pleaded for life. As Oganda opened the gate, a child, a young child, broke loose from the crowd, and ran toward her. The child took a small earring from her sweaty hands and gave it to Oganda saying, "When you reach the world of the dead, give

this earring to my sister. She died last week. She forgot this ring." Oganda, taken aback by the strange request, took the little ring, and handed her precious water and food to the child. She did not need them now. Oganda did not know whether to laugh or cry. She had heard mourners sending their love to their sweethearts, long dead, but this idea of sending gifts was new to her.

31   Oganda held her breath as she crossed the barrier to enter the sacred land. She looked appealingly at the crowd, but there was no response. Their minds were too preoccupied with their own survival. Rain was the precious medicine they were longing for, and the sooner Oganda could get to her destination the better.

32   A strange feeling possessed Oganda as she picked her way in the sacred land. There were strange noises that often startled her, and her first reaction was to take to her heels. But she remembered that she had to fulfill the wish of her people. She was exhausted, but the path was still winding. Then suddenly the path ended on sandy land. The water had retreated miles away from the shore leaving a wide stretch of sand. Beyond this was the vast expanse of water.

33   Oganda felt afraid. She wanted to picture the size and shape of the monster, but fear would not let her. The society did not talk about it, nor did the crying children who were silenced by the mention of its name. The sun was still up, but it was no longer hot. For a long time Oganda walked ankledeep in the sand. She was exhausted and longed desperately for her calabash of water. As she moved on, she had a strange feeling that something was following her. Was it the monster? Her hair stood erect, and a cold paralyzing feeling ran along her spine. She looked behind, sideways and in front, but there was nothing, except a cloud of dust.

34   Oganda pulled up and hurried but the feeling did not leave her, and her whole body became saturated with perspiration.

35   The sun was going down fast and the lake shore seemed to move along with it.

36   Oganda started to run. She must be at the lake before sunset. As she ran she heard a noise coming from behind. She looked back sharply, and something resembling a moving bush was frantically running after her. It was about to catch up with her.

37   Oganda ran with all her strength. She was now determined to throw herself into the water even before sunset. She did not look back, but the creature was upon her. She made an effort to cry out, as in a nightmare, but she could not hear her own voice. The creature caught up with Oganda. In the utter confusion, as Oganda came face-to-face with the unidentified creature, a strong hand grabbed her. But she fell flat on the sand and fainted.

38   When the lake breeze brought her back to consciousness, a man was bending over her. "......!!" Oganda opened her mouth

to speak, but she had lost her voice. She swallowed a mouthful of water poured into her mouth by the stranger.

39   "Osinda, Osinda! Please let me die. Let me run, the sun is going down. Let me die, let them have rain." Osinda fondled the glittering chain around Oganda's waist and wiped the tears from her face.

40   "We must escape quickly to the unknown land," Osinda said urgently. "We must run away from the wrath of the ancestors and the retaliation of the monster."

41   "But the curse is upon me, Osinda, I am no good to you anymore. And moreover the eyes of the ancestors will follow us everywhere and bad luck will befall us. Nor can we escape from the monster."

42   Oganda broke loose, afraid to escape, but Osinda grabbed her hands again.

43   "Listen to me, Oganda! Listen! Here are two coats!" He then covered the whole of Oganda's body, except her eyes, with a leafy attire made from the twigs of *Bwombwe*. "These will protect us from the eyes of the ancestors and the wrath of the monster. Now let us run out of here." He held Oganda's hand and they ran from the sacred land, avoiding the path that Oganda had followed.

44   The bush was thick, and the long grass entangled their feet as they ran. Halfway through the sacred land they stopped and looked back. The sun was almost touching the surface of the water. They were frightened. They continued to run, now faster, to avoid the sinking sun.

45   "Have faith, Oganda—that thing will not reach us."

46   When they reached the barrier and looked behind them trembling, only a tip of the sun could be seen above the water's surface.

47   "It is gone! It is gone!" Oganda wept, hiding her face in her hands.

48   "Weep not, daughter of the chief. Let us run, let us escape."

49   There was a bright lightning. They looked up, frightened. Above them black furious clouds started to gather. They began to run. Then the thunder roared, and the rain came down in torrents.

THE RAIN CAME

JOURNAL

1. MLA Works Cited   *Using this model, record this story here.*

Author's Last Name, First Name. "Title of the Story." *Title of the Book.* 3rd ed. Ed.

First Name Last Name. City: Publisher, year. Page number(s) of this story. Print.

2. Main Character(s)   *Describe each main character, and explain why you think each is a main character.*

3. Supporting Characters   *Describe each supporting character, and explain why you think each is a supporting character.*

4. Setting and Props   *Describe the setting(s) and all relevant prop(s).*

5. Sequence   *Outline the events of the story in order.*

6. Plot   *Tell the story in no more than three sentences.*

7. Conflicts   *Identify and explain all of the conflicts involved.*

8. Significant Quotations   *Explain the importance of each quotation completely. Record the page number in the parentheses.*

a. "The prophecy was complete. 'It is Oganda, my only daughter, who must die so young'" (   ).

b. "A long time ago when she was quite young Osinda had given her that chain […]. She heard her heart pounding so loudly as she thought of him" (   ).

c. "Unable to restrain her emotions any longer, she sobbed loudly as her age group got up to dance" ( ).

d. "As she moved on, she had a strange feeling that something was following her. Was it the monster?" ( ).

e. "Listen to me, Oganda! Listen! Here are two coats!" ( ).

9. **Literary Elements**   *Look at this chapter's title and explain why you think this story is placed in this chapter. Explain in which other chapter(s) you might place this story, as relevant to the literary element(s) of the chapter(s).*

10. **Foreshadowing, Irony, and/or Symbols**   *Explain examples of foreshadowing, irony, and/or symbols in this story.*

FOLLOW-UP QUESTIONS

10 SHORT QUESTIONS

What is the <u>best</u> answer for each?

____ 1. The chief
   a. is distressed.
   b. is happy.
   c. does not care.

____ 2. Oganda is
   a. distressed.
   b. proud.
   c. happy.

____ 3. Oganda is
   a. happy about the prophecy.
   b. described in the prophecy.
   c. not described in the prophecy.

____ 4. Oganda's mother is
   a. distressed.
   b. proud.
   c. happy.

____ 5. The tribe's people
   a. are distressed.
   b. do not care.
   c. are happy.

____ 6. The tribe's people
   a. celebrate.
   b. mourn.
   c. do nothing.

____ 7. Oganda feels that
   a. the people understand her.
   b. the people do not understand her.
   c. the people are her saviors.

____ 8. Oganda is
   a. happy to be sacrificed.
   b. proud to be sacrificed.
   c. not happy to be sacrificed.

____ 9. Oganda enters the sacred place
   a. with fear.
   b. without fear.
   c. with many other people.

____ 10. In the end, Oganda
   a. is killed by the lake monster.
   b. dies quietly.
   c. is saved from the lake monster.

5 SIGNIFICANT QUOTATIONS

What is the importance of each of these quotations?

1. "On the other hand, to let Oganda die as a ransom for the people would permanently cripple Labong'o spiritually."

2. "At sunset the chief's village was full of relatives and friends who had come to congratulate Oganda."

3. "She wanted to picture the size and shape of the monster, but fear would not let her."

4. "These will protect us from the eyes of the ancestors and the wrath of the monster."

5. "Then the thunder roared, and the rain came down in torrents."

2 Comprehension Essay Questions

Use specific details and information from the story to answer these questions as completely as possible.

1. What are the conflicting emotions in this story? Use specific details and information from the story to support your answer.

2. What is Osinda's role in this story? Use specific details and information from the story to support your answer.

Discussion Questions

Be prepared to discuss these questions in class.

1. Tribal law exists for the good of the tribe as a whole, and not necessarily for the good of any one member. What is the role of tribal law in this story?

2. Why do you think the rain came? Use details from the story to support your answer.

Writing

Use each of these ideas for writing an essay.

1. We all have obligations that we have to fulfill. Think of a specific obligation you have and write about a specific occasion when this obligation has been either good or bad for you.

2. Sometimes the only way to resolve a situation is to escape it. Describe a time when you or someone you know has solved a situation by escaping the situation.

Further Writing

1. Compare and contrast Oganda with Bindeh in R. Sarif Easmon's "Bindeh's Gift" (available in a library).

2. Tribal law has been mentioned before. Research tribal law and explain "The Rain Came" as an example of tribal law.

WHAT'S IN A NAME?

JIALIN PENG

PRE-READING VOCABULARY
CONTEXT

Use context clues to define these words before reading. Use a dictionary as needed.

1. The children obeyed their parents' rules out of a sense of *filial obedience. Filial obedience* means _____.

2. By making tiny little observations, Sherlock Holmes is able to *deduce* many facts about people that he meets. *Deduce* means

   _____.

3. Although the *literal* meaning for the word "cat" is "four-legged feline," many people add feelings of softness or fear to the word. *Literal* means _____.

4. When the *Great Cultural Revolution* came to China, the old system of emperors fell to the new system of communism. *Great Cultural Revolution* means _____.

5. Rich owns several businesses and is a true *capitalist*, trying to make money by his own efforts. *Capitalist* means

   _____.

6. Theo has many *virtues*, which include his honesty, kindness, thoughtfulness, loyalty, and willingness to work. *Virtue* means

   _____.

7. Karl Marx described the poor class of workers, farmers, and generally anyone who was underpaid as the *proletariat. Proletariat* means _____.

8. Su Lin was very loyal to his family and always shared a sense of *kinship* with family members at family gatherings. *Kinship* means

_____.

9. Revisionists are often *reactionaries* who would like things to be the way they were in the past. *Reactionary* means _____.

10. Revolutionaries cause great change while *counter-revolutionaries* work against the revolution or change. *Counter-revolutionary* means

_____.

11. During the revolution in China, bands of young men joined the feared *Red Guard* to enforce the revolution. *Red Guard* means

_____.

12. When Pilar sought to criticize and hurt her sister, she suffered the *consequence* of her sister not talking to her. *Consequence* means

_____.

13. In Western culture, one's *surname* is one's family name or last name, such as Smith, Brown, or Kennedy. *Surname* means

_____.

14. The poor *peasants* worked the farmland from morning until night and received barely enough to eat. *Peasant* means

_____.

15. The *timid* rabbit hid under the bushes and only came out when it was sure no one would hurt it. *Timid* means _____.

16. When Laura and Dave became engaged, they announced their *betrothal* at a dinner party. *Betrothal* means

_____.

17. For the wedding, the parents planned a fabulous *feast* of shrimp and lobster and filet mignon. *Feast* means _____.

18. Whenever our *clan* gets together, all the grandparents and parents and aunts and uncles and cousins are there. *Clan* means

_____.

19. Francis saved his *veto* vote for an important time, because he knew he could only vote "no" once. *Veto* means

_____.

20. Jack was a *bachelor* until he proposed and then married Tricia.

Bachelor means _____.

PRE-READING VOCABULARY
STRUCTURAL ATTACK

Define these words by solving the parts. Use the Glossary or a dictionary as needed.

1. mishap
2. expectation
3. revolutionary
4. inconvenient
5. schoolmate
6. standard-bearer
7. thoroughly
8. immediately
9. handwritten
10. bewilderment
11. boundless
12. landlord
13. honorable
14. maternal
15. shameful
16. painful
17. discarding
18. imprisonment
19. rehabilitated
20. unskilled
21. bad-mouth
22. shrewish
23. unbearable
24. go-between
25. half-paralyzed
26. departed
27. humbling
28. prohibition

PRE-READING QUESTIONS

Try answering these questions as you read.

What is the narrator's first choice? Next? Next?
What effects do the changes have on his life?

WHAT'S IN A NAME?

JIALIN PENG

Jialin Peng was born in China in 1948. This story reflects some of the lighter tension felt by Jialin Peng as a result of the Cultural Revolution in China. After millennia of relatively stable rule under the dynastic system, China then experienced the continuing communist revolution. As in most revolutions, the heat of revolution produced victims, and those who did not support the revolution were often sent to prison or worse. Although today we may see the more stable, thermidor stage of the revolution, Jialin Peng's story offers insight into some social and political complications of the revolution while also offering insight into the Chinese name selection process. Other stories may be found in *Wild Cat: Stories of the Cultural Revolution.*

W*hat's in a name? That which we call a rose*
By any other name would smell as sweet.
W. SHAKESPEARE

2   I adore Shakespeare, but in China a rose smells different when you give it another name. My names—family name, given name and adopted name—caused me no end of trouble.

3   My name was Chou Dexiao. Chou was my family name; Dexiao, the name given me by my father. *De* means "virtue" and *xiao* means "filial obedience." From the name you may deduce my father's high expectations. With this name I lived eighteen years

without mishap. When people used my name, they were not conscious of its literal meaning. A rose is a rose.

4   But a rose can decay. The Great Cultural Revolution began, and suddenly we found everything had the smell of social class: the girls' long braids stank of the capitalist class, so they had them cut short. My name reeked of the ruling class of feudalist times. Virtue and filial obedience—the Revolutionary Proletariat did not like them. Therefore, I had to change my name to a revolutionary one. But that was more easily said than done, because for each revolutionary name, there might be thousands of people who wanted to use it. And it was inconvenient to share the same name with so many people, especially with your schoolmates.

5   In our class alone, there had already been two Zaofans (rebel), two Gemings (revolution), two Weibiaos (defenders of Lin Biao) and three Weidongs (defenders of Mao Zedong). I didn't want to share any of these names with my classmates. So I thought and thought, then I had an idea: why not call myself Weiqing (the defender of Jiang Qing)? Comrade Jiang Qing was the wife of our "great leader, great teacher, great commander and great helmsman" Chairman Mao Zedong. And she herself was the "standard-bearer of the Great Proletarian Cultural Revolution."

6   I was thrilled to have found a name so thoroughly revolutionary. I immediately started going through the name-changing procedures. All I had to do was to write a *dazibao* and put it on a wall at school. *Dazibao* literally meant a public poster handwritten in big fat characters. In the first days of the Cultural Revolution, millions upon millions of *dazibaos* appeared all over China, stuck to walls, pasted on doors and windows and hanging from wires. They denounced the enemies of the Revolution, criticized the corruption of Capitalism, Revisionism and Feudalism, and even made proclamations such as: A REVOLUTIONARY CROSSES THE STREET ON A RED LIGHT! and CAPITALIST SONS OF BITCHES ARE NOT SERVED IN THIS RESTAURANT!

7   I had hardly finished writing my new name for the first time when a voice thundered over my shoulder, "Do you want to be a counter-revolutionary?" I was astounded, and gazed in bewilderment at the speaker, Wang Zaofan, the head of a major Red Guard organization in our school. The name Zaofan meant "rebel" but his original name was Wenbin, meaning "gentle."

8   "Look," he said. "Your family name is Chou; it means 'hate.' What does 'Chou Weiqing' mean?"

9   I was so scared that I broke out in a cold sweat. My new name could imply that I hated Chairman Mao's wife! My God! If I had not shared the same desk all through school with Zaofan and if I had not let him copy from my papers in examinations, the consequences would have been too ghastly to contemplate!

10   Obviously, if I wanted to give myself a revolutionary name, I'd have to change my family name as well. I had read a report in a newspaper about a boy who, in order to express his boundless respect for the great leader Chairman Mao, had changed his own family name Mu to Mao. I was going to use him as my example. But this time I first consulted Wang Zaofan.

11   "You want to name yourself *Mao* too? Hah! Pee on the ground and look at your image to see if you're worthy of the name Mao. What kind of person was your father?" he snarled with curled lips. Zaofan was seven inches shorter than I, so for greater emphasis he jumped up on a chair and continued, "What kind of person was your grandfather?"

12   I knew what he was getting at. Before their deaths, my father had been a rightist and my grandfather a landlord. I was not worthy of so great and honorable a family name as Mao; absolutely not.

13   Finally, I adopted my mother's family name, Qin, as my own. Before the decision was made, I carried out as thorough a research as possible. I consulted three different dictionaries. They all defined the character *Qin* as follows: the Qin Dynasty (221–207 B.C.); another name for Shaanxi Province; a surname.

14   None of the definitions looked like a potential trouble-maker. I also investigated my maternal history. My mother's parents were poor peasants, her father's father was a poor peasant, and so was her father's father's father. Therefore, I concluded with relief, Qin should be a safe surname for me.

15   To be honest, I was glad to change my old family name. My father had divorced my mother after he became a rightist in 1957. Then he'd died somewhere. I'd been raised by my mother, who earned her living as a primary school teacher. I could hardly remember what my father looked like. It was shameful and painful to be a rightist's son! So it was not simply that I had no affection for my father, I positively hated him. By discarding his name, I intended to make a clean break from him, and wash his reactionary taint off myself.

16   With this thoroughly new name, Qin Weiqing, I lived another ten years. Before long I found the name was far from being as good as I had thought. People began to hate Jiang Qing. Scandalous rumours about her spread from mouth to mouth throughout the country. Even the threat of imprisonment did not stop people from whispering. Could you expect them to be nice to a fellow who'd named himself Jiang Qing's defender? And in fact, I myself had also come to hate this woman. So after the downfall of the Gang of Four, headed by Jiang Qing, the first thing I did was to apply to resume my old given name, Dexiao. I continued to use the surname Qin, for it showed my love for my mother.

17   The year I turned thirty-two, the government removed the label "rightist" from just about everyone. My father was among the rehabilitated. So I was finally free of his reactionary mark.

18   I was now a skilled turner in a factory. Some people said I was quite handsome. However, with a wage of only 36 yuan per month and without powerful and rich parents, I found it very hard to find a wife. My mother was so anxious about me that her hair turned white. An old Chinese woman suffers untold anxiety until she sees her son married. She asked all her acquaintances to look for a girl for me. Thanks to an introduction by an aunt of one of my mother's former pupils, I was finally brought together with a potential marriage partner. Her name was Yue Meihua. Though *Meihua* meant "beautiful flower," she wasn't beautiful at all. The girl, an unskilled laborer in a cotton mill, was twenty-eight. Her parents were peasants who lived in a village far from our city. All of which meant that she was not a girl with a high "selling price."

19   All the same, I liked her very much. Perhaps it was because she was so gentle, even shy. She would always blush before she started to speak to a strange man, and one never heard her speak or laugh loudly. I didn't agree with the aesthetic standard of ancient China which required a woman not to show her teeth while smiling; still I preferred a gentle, timid girl, for I'd been frightened by a few neighbors' wives. They enjoyed quarrelling too much, and for them the greatest pleasure in life was to bad-mouth their husbands. I could often hear them, in the small hours of the morning, cursing their husbands instead of making love to them. But my Meihua was quieter than a sleeping flower.

20   Besides, for my sake, my mother had suffered too much already and I didn't want to hurt her by marrying a shrewish girl. As some of my married friends had told me, the most unbearable business, for a man, was to be a buffer in clashes between his mother and his wife.

21   Evidently, Yue Meihua liked me too. So I wrote a letter and proposed to her. A few days later, the go-between—the aunt of my mother's former pupil—told me that the girl liked me but could not accept until she got her parents' approval, and it was very likely that her mother would come and have a look at me.

22   Of course, the news gave my mother hope. But it added to her worries because it was said of people in the country that they didn't marry off their daughters, but sold them at high prices. It happened that a couple of days earlier, my mother had read a tragic story reported in the newspaper. A bride refused to go into the bridal chamber because the bridegroom was unable to satisfy her parents' additional economic demands. The poor bridegroom, who was up to his ears in debt already, killed the bride and then himself. If Meihua's parents asked for extravagant betrothal gifts, what would we do?

23   When her mother arrived, Meihua took me to see her. All I remember about the meeting was that the top button of my new shirt seemed determined to strangle me. The day was sweltering and I was terribly thirsty. But I do recall what happened at the end of the interview. Her mother filled the pockets of my new jacket with peanuts which she had grown herself. I was half-paralyzed and murmured some words no one could understand. Meihua blushed and said softly, "Say thank you to Mama, you foolish man." I came to my senses at once. Wonderful! The old lady was fond of me!

24   Then her mother and my mother met. Exceeding our hopes, the negotiations went off without a hitch. Although Meihua's mother was unable to read or write, she had an enlightened mind. She did not ask for betrothal gifts.

25   Now what we needed was her father's approval. That would be no problem, Meihua assured me. Her father had never questioned any decision made by her mother. Therefore, no sooner had her mother departed than we began to prepare for the wedding. My close friends and relatives went into action. Three friends asked for a few days sick leave to make a bed and a wardrobe for us. A cousin who was a truck-driver made plans to go to some out-of-the-way town to fetch food for the wedding feast. My mother withdrew all her savings from the bank and went on a shopping spree. How happy and excited she was!

26   Then came the blow. Meihua's parents suddenly refused to let me marry her. The wedding was off. It was not her mother nor her father but some elders of the clan who had exercised their veto. They made a declaration: if Meihua marries the man named Qin, we will expel her from the clan. And after the marriage, if she appears in our village, we will break her legs.

27   Why? All they knew about me was my name. But it was nothing else than my name that killed the wedding!

28   To understand, one must go back more than 800 years, to the year 1142. That year, an evil Prime Minister, Qin Hui, concocted a charge against a great national hero, Marshal Yue Fei, and had him put to death. But people loved Yue Fei very much. Soon he was rehabilitated, and from then on, Yue Fei's tomb has become a scenic spot in Huangzhou City. Out of indignation, people cast two iron effigies in a kneeling position, to represent Qin Hui and his conspiratorial wife. Since then the two have been humbling themselves in front of the tomb for hundreds of years. And since Yue Fei's execution, people named Yue have adopted an unwritten prohibition against marrying people named Qin.

29   So, I remain a bachelor. What's in a name? That which we call a rose by any other name may smell of stinkweed.

• •

WHAT'S IN A NAME?

JOURNAL

1. **MLA Works Cited** *Using this model, record this story here.*

   Author's First Name, Last Name. "Title of the Story." *Title of the Book.* 3rd ed. Ed.

   First Name Last Name. City: Publisher, year. Page number(s) of this story. Print.

   (Note: Chinese names are not inverted.)

2. **Main Character(s)** *Describe each main character, and explain why you think each is a main character.*

3. **Supporting Characters** *Describe each supporting character, and explain why you think each is a supporting character.*

4. **Setting and Props** *Describe the setting(s) and all relevant prop(s).*

5. Sequence   *Outline the events of the story in order.*

6. Plot   *Tell the story in no more than two sentences.*

7. Conflicts   *Identify and explain all the conflicts involved here.*

8. Significant Quotations   *Explain the importance of each quotation completely. Record the page number in the parentheses.*

a. "My name reeked of the ruling class of feudalist times. Virtue and filial obedience—the Revolutionary Proletariat did not like them" ( ).

b. "Obviously, if I wanted to give myself a revolutionary name, I'd have to change my family name as well" ( ).

c. "My mother's parents were poor peasants, her father's father was a poor peasant, and so was her father's father's father. I concluded with relief, Qin should be a safe surname for me" ( ).

d. "My mother withdrew all her savings from the bank and went on a shopping spree. How happy and excited she was!" ( ).

e. "But it was nothing else than my name that killed the wedding!" ( ).

9. **Literary Elements**   *Look at this chapter's title and explain why you think this story is placed in this chapter. Explain in which other chapter(s) you might place this story, as relevant to the literary element(s) of the chapter(s).*

10. **Foreshadowing, Irony, and/or Symbols**   *Explain examples of foreshadowing, irony, and/or symbols in this story.*

FOLLOW-UP QUESTIONS

10 SHORT QUESTIONS

What is the <u>best</u> answer for each?

____ 1. "Chou" means
    a. love.
    b. hate.
    c. nothing.

____ 2. "De" means
    a. goodness.
    b. hate.
    c. nothing.

____ 3. "Xiao" means
    a. dedication.
    b. hate.
    c. nothing.

____ 4. This story takes place during
    a. the communist era.
    b. the rightist era.
    c. the capitalist era.

____ 5. The narrator is sympathetic to
    a. the rightist movement.
    b. the communist movement.
    c. the reactionary movement.

____ 6. For a new name, the narrator selects
    a. Mao's name.
    b. Mao's wife's name.
    c. Mao's prior name.

____ 7. His choice is not good because it suggests
    a. he respects Mao.
    b. he respects Mao's wife.
    c. he hates Mao's wife.

____ 8. His next new name
    a. comes from his father.
    b. comes from his mother.
    c. reflects his politics.

____ 9. His intended mother- and father-in-law
    a. accept him.
    b. do not accept him.
    c. want more money from him.

____ 10. Ultimately, he cannot marry his intended
    a. because his new name offends his fiancée's family.
    b. because his new name is reminiscent of a fallen hero.
    c. both a and b.

5 SIGNIFICANT QUOTATIONS

What is the importance of each of these quotations?

1. "I was thrilled to have found a name so thoroughly revolutionary."

2. "My new name could imply that I hated Chairman Mao's wife!"

3. "Finally, I adopted my mother's family name, Qin, as my own. Before the decision was made, I carried out as thorough a research as possible."

4. "Therefore, no sooner had her mother departed than we began to prepare for the wedding."

5. "And since Yue Fei's execution, people named Yue have adopted an unwritten prohibition against marrying people named Qin."

2 COMPREHENSION ESSAY QUESTIONS

Use specific details and information from the story to answer these questions as completely as possible.

1. What are the narrator's problems in selecting a name? Use specific details and information from the story to support your explanation.

2. What are the consequences of the names on the narrator's life? Use specific details and information from the story to support your explanation.

DISCUSSION QUESTIONS

Be prepared to discuss these questions in class.

1. How are the narrator's experiences with his names different from yours?

2. Find out what your name means. How is your family's name selection process different from the narrator's?

WRITING

Use each of these ideas for writing an essay.

1. Our names are often a very central part of our self-identity. Tell what effects your name has had on your life.

2. Choose another name for yourself. Write an essay describing your selection process and then explain how this new name might change your life.

Further Writing

1. Research your own first and last names.

2. Consult with family members and develop your own family tree. Note any significant patterns, consistencies, inconsistencies, etc.

   Anthropological graphing usually uses this format, using △ for male, ○ for female, = for marriage, and | for child of.

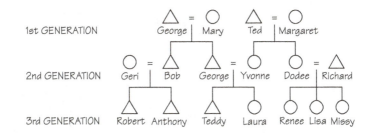

1st GENERATION	△ = ○ George | Mary	△ = ○ Ted | Margaret
2nd GENERATION	○ = △ Geri | Bob	△ = ○ George | Yvonne	○ = △ Dodee | Richard
3rd GENERATION	△ △ Robert Anthony	△ ○ Teddy Laura	○ ○ ○ Renee Lisa Missy

For instance, you would read this thus:

George marries Mary and Ted marries Margaret. George and Mary have two sons (Bob and George). Ted and Margaret have two daughters (Yvonne and Dodee). Bob marries Geri and they have two sons (Robert and Anthony). George marries Yvonne and they have two children (Teddy and Laura). Dodee marries Richard and they have three children (Renee, Lisa, and Missy). Thus, here the third generation are respective cousins.

You will find this to be a very informative and challenging assignment. Now try diagramming your own family. Noting birth places, residence places, occupations, or any other concern, you may find interesting patterns—or lack of patterns—in your family. Record your family here:

1st generation

2nd generation

3rd generation

NOTES

Plot and Foreshadowing

A story is based around a simple skeleton of events called a **plot.** Around this basic plot, a logical order of events, or **sequence,** occurs that builds tension or, in mysteries, suspense. In stories we call the events in the sequence a **story line.**

Have you ever gone to the movies and watched the end credits roll while you were still waiting for the movie to get going? You looked at the person sitting next to you, felt cheated, and said, "What happened?" What happened is that somewhere along the line, the storyteller failed.

In a well-written story, one event logically leads to another event, and then to another, and so on, so that each word and action counts and builds tension that carries your interest. The tension peaks at the **climax** and then resolves in the **dénouement.** When any of these pieces are missing, poorly developed, or unbelievable, we are disappointed. (Movie sequels, in fact, purposely stop at the climax and before the dénouement so that we will return for the next episode.)

Each story in this chapter depends on the flow of events in the story. First, outside forces overwhelm Songsam and Tokjae in "Cranes." Next, Raju in "Trail of the Green Blazer" and then the narrator in "Yoruba" are each caught in spinning events. More events churn the characters in "The Madman," and then Delia finally seems to take control of events in "Sweat."

Foreshadowing is a technique some authors use to help explain or predict events to come. The author may sprinkle information or hints throughout the story to help predict actions that are yet to happen. All these stories contain information on events to come. In "Cranes" and "Yoruba," the authors present a story-in-a-story that helps explain events to come. In "Trail of the Green Blazer," "The Madman," and "Sweat," each character's situation offers information on the actions to come. If you do not pick up the hints along the way, look back and notice the hints that might have helped you to predict the often surprising endings.

CRANES

Hwang Sunwon

PRE-READING VOCABULARY
CONTEXT

Use context clues to define these words before reading. Use a dictionary as needed.

1. George watched the beautiful white *crane* as it flew into the water
   and pulled in its wings to stand stately and search for food.
   Crane means _____.

2. After World War II, Korea was divided into two separate countries,
   marked at the *38th parallel* or line of latitude. *38th parallel* means

   _____.

3. Alex loves *autumn* when the leaves turn a range of colors and the
   weather turns cool, waiting for winter. *Autumn* means

   _____.

4. War is often a major *conflict* over which country should own what
   property. *Conflict* means _____.

5. Ti Lu had a round and bulging *wen* on the side of his neck and his
   doctor decided to remove it by surgery. *Wen* means

   _____.

6. When Teddy had to make a trip to Switzerland, Laura missed him in
   his *absence* from home. *Absence* means

   _____.

7. Missy had to remove the thorny *burrs* from the dog's fur after the dog
   romped in the weeds. *Burr* means _____.

8. The guards tied the criminal's hands behind his back and *bound* them
   with nylon cords. *Bound* means _____.

9. Karl was taken *prisoner* and locked up in the jail after he robbed the bank and got caught. *Prisoner* means _____.

10. Police walked on either side of the prisoner and *escorted* him into the courtroom. *Escorted* means _____.

11. While *bastard* literally means "one born to unwed parents," the word is often used to insult someone. *Bastard* means

   _____.

12. Dave *glared* unbelievingly at the television as he watched his favorite team lose the game in the last seconds. *Glared* means

   _____.

13. Renee was on a *mission* as she searched store after store to find the perfect gift for her sister. *Mission* means _____.

14. Ted enjoys collecting guns and is especially proud of the Navy *pistol* he carried while flying during World War II. *Pistol* means

   _____.

15. In order to plant the seeds evenly, the farmer was *tilling* the soil to make rows for planting. *Tilling* means _____.

16. Michelle had a *suspicion* that everyone was planning a surprise party when she came across a closet filled with balloons. *Suspicion* means

   _____.

17. When the countries went to war, many people tried to leave before the *invasion* of one country into another. *Invasion* means

   _____.

18. The robber tried to *flee* the police by running down an alley and jumping over a fence. *Flee* means _____.

19. The hunters placed a carefully designed *snare* so that they could trap the wild lion. *Snare* means _____.

20. Vernie watched the eagles *soar* high above the treetops as they flew off into the blue sky. *Soar* means _____.

PRE-READING VOCABULARY
STRUCTURAL ATTACK

Define these words by solving the parts. Use the Glossary or a dictionary as needed.

1. driftwood
2. temporarily
3. vice-chairman
4. backside
5. fistful
6. widower
7. armload
8. demilitarized
9. governor-general
10. disappeared
11. loosened

PRE-READING QUESTIONS

Try answering these questions as you read.

What does Songsam do?

What does he feel?

What does Tokjae do?

What does he feel?

CRANES

Hwang Sunwon

Hwang Sunwon was born in northern Korea in 1915. The confusion of war and the love of literature are themes that entwine in Hwang Sunwon's life. When he was born, the Japanese occupied Korea, and his father was imprisoned as a resister. After World War II, Korea was divided at the 38th parallel into the Soviet-influenced North and the American-influenced South. With the coming of the Korean War, Hwang Sunwon left the North and moved to the South. During his youth and between open war, Hwang Sunwon was educated in Japanese and later attended the Waseda University in Tokyo, where he majored in English literature. He became an esteemed writer and a professor, and his writing reflects the isolation and disruption of war. His writings can be found in novels and short story collections.

The village just north of the thirty-eighth parallel was quiet beneath the clear, lofty autumn sky.

2 A white gourd lay where it had tumbled, leaning against another on the dirt-floored space between the rooms of an abandoned house.

3 An old man Songsam happened to meet put his long tobacco pipe behind his back. The children, as children would, had already fled from the street to keep their distance. Everyone's face was masked with fear.

4 Overall, the village showed few signs of the conflict that had just ended. Still, it did not seem to Songsam to be the same village where he had grown up.

5 He stopped walking at a grove of chestnut trees on the hill behind the village. He climbed one of the trees. In his mind, from far away, he could hear the shouts of the old man with a wen. Are you kids climbing my chestnut tree again?

6   Had that old man died during Songsam's absence? He had not seen him among the men he had met so far in the village. Hanging onto the tree, Songsam looked up at the clear autumn sky. Though he did not shake the branch, some of the remaining chestnut burrs burst open, and the nuts fell to the ground.

7   When he reached the house that was being used temporarily as the Public Peace Office, he found someone there bound tightly with rope. This was the first young man he had seen in the village. As Songsam drew closer and examined his face, he was taken aback. It was none other than his boyhood friend Tokjae.

8   Songsam asked one of the security guards from his detachment who had accompanied him from Ch'ont'ae what the situation was. The guard answered that the prisoner had been vice-chairman of the Communist Farmers' Alliance and that he had just been captured while hiding in his own house here in the village.

9   Songsam squatted by the house and lit a cigarette. Tokjae was to be escorted to Ch'ongdan by one of the young security guards.

10   After a while Songsam lit a cigarette from the one he had been smoking, then stood up.

11   "I'll take the guy myself."

12   Tokjae kept his face turned away; he did not even glance at Songsam.

13   They left the village.

14   Songsam kept smoking, but he could not taste the tobacco. He just sucked and puffed. He suddenly realized that Tokjae might like a smoke. He recalled when they were boys how they had shared a smoke of dried pumpkin leaves, hiding from the adults in the corner of the wall around the house. But how could he offer a guy like this a cigarette?

15   Once, when they were boys, he had gone with Tokjae to steal chestnuts from the old man with the wen. Songsam was taking his turn climbing the tree when suddenly they heard the old man shouting. Songsam slid down the tree and got chestnut burrs stuck in his rear end. Yet he dashed off without doing anything about them. Once they had run far enough that the old man could not catch them, he turned his backside toward Tokjae. It hurt even more to have the prickly chestnut spines pulled out. Tears ran freely down Songsam's face. Tokjae held out a fistful of his own chestnuts, then thrust them into Songsam's pocket.

16   Songsam had just lit a cigarette from the last one he had smoked, but he tossed it away. He made up his mind not to smoke anymore while he was escorting this bastard Tokjae.

17   They reached the mountain ridge road. He had often come to the ridge with Tokjae to cut fodder before Songsam moved to

the area around Ch'ont'ae, south of the thirty-eighth parallel, two years before the Liberation in 1945.

18 Songsam felt an inexplicable urge. He burst out shouting. "You bastard, how many people have you killed?"

19 Tokjae glanced toward Songsam, then looked away again.

20 "How many people have you killed?"

21 Tokjae turned his face toward Songsam and glared. The light in his eyes grew fierce and his mouth, which was surrounded by a stubble beard, twitched.

22 "So, is that what you've been doing? Killing people?"

23 That bastard! Still, Songsam felt a clearing in the center of his chest, as if something caught there had been released. But then he said, "Why wouldn't someone like the vice-chairman of the Farmers' Alliance try to escape? You must have been hiding out because you had been given some assignment."

24 Tokjae did not respond.

25 "Well? Answer me. What kind of mission were you hiding out to do?"

26 Silent, Tokjae just kept walking. The guy certainly seemed cowed. At a time like this, it would be good to get a look at his face. But Tokjae did not turn toward Songsam again.

27 Songsam took hold of the pistol in his belt.

28 "It's no use trying to explain your way out of it. You'll have to be shot anyway, so go ahead and tell the truth."

29 Tokjae began to speak. "I'm not trying to get out of anything. First and last, I'm the son of a dirt farmer. I was made vice-chairman of the Farmers' Alliance because they said I was a hard worker. If that's a crime worthy of death, there is nothing I can do. The only skill I've got is tilling the ground." After a moment he continued. "My father is sick in bed at home. It's been six months now."

30 Tokjae's father was a widower, a poor farmer who had grown old with only his son by his side. Seven years ago his back had already been bent, and his face had dark age spots.

31 "Are you married?"

32 "Yes," Tokjae answered after a moment.

33 "Who to?"

34 "To Shorty."

35 Not Shorty! Now that's interesting. Shorty, a fat little girl who knew the breadth of the earth but not the height of the sky. Always such a prig. Songsam and Tokjae had hated that about her. They were always teasing and laughing at her. So that's who Tokjae had married.

36 "And how many kids do you have?"

37 "Our first is due this fall."

38 Songsam tried to stifle a smile that rose to his lips in spite of himself. Asking how many children Tokjae had and having him

answer that the first was due in autumn was so funny he could not stand it. Shorty—holding up her armload of a belly on that little body. But Songsam realized that this was not the place to laugh or joke about such things.

39 "Anyway, don't you think it looks suspicious that you stayed behind and didn't flee?"

40 "I tried to go. They said if there was an invasion from the south, every last man who was a man would be captured and killed, so all the men between seventeen and forty were forced to head north. I really didn't have any choice. I thought I would carry my father on my back and go. But he wouldn't stand for it. He said if a farmer leaves the fields he has already tilled and planted, where can he go? My father has always depended on me alone. He's grown old farming all these years, and I have to be the one to close his eyes when the end comes. The truth is, people like us who just till the ground wouldn't be any better off even if we *did* flee..."

41 Songsam himself had fled the past June. One night he secretly spoke to his father about escaping, but his father had said the same thing as Tokjae's. How could a farmer flee and leave his work behind? Songsam fled alone. As he wandered along the strange roads through strange towns in the south, he never stopped thinking of the farm work he had left to his old parents and his wife and children. Fortunately, then as now, his family was healthy.

42 They crossed the ridge. Now, somehow, Songsam was the one who kept his eyes averted. The autumn sun was hot on his forehead. What a perfect day this would be for harvesting, he thought.

43 After they had gone down the far side of the ridge, Songsam hesitated.

44 It looked like a group of people wearing white clothes were stooped over working in the middle of the field. It was actually a flock of cranes, here in the so-called Demilitarized Zone at the thirty-eighth parallel. Even though people were no longer living here, the cranes remained as before.

45 Once when Songsam and Tokjae were about twelve years old, they had secretly set a snare and caught a crane. They even bound its wings with a straw rope. The two boys came out to the place they kept the crane almost every day; they would hold the crane around the neck and raise a ruckus trying to ride on its back. Then one day they heard the adults in the village talking in whispers. Some people had come from Seoul to hunt cranes. They had special permission from the Japanese governor-general to collect

specimens of some kind. When they heard this, the two boys raced off to the field. They were not worried about being caught by the adults and scolded. Now they had only one thought: their crane must not die. Without stopping to catch their breath, they scrambled through the weeds. They took the snare off the crane's leg and loosened the straw rope from its wings. But the crane could hardly walk, probably because it had been tied up for so long. The boys held the crane up between them and tossed it into the air. They heard a gunshot. The bird flapped its wings two, three, four times, but fell back to the ground. It was hit! But in the next instant, another crane in the grass nearby spread its wings. Their own crane, which had been lying on the ground, stretched out its long neck, gave a cry, and rose into the sky, too. They circled over the boys' heads, then flew off into the distance. The boys could not take their eyes off the spot in the blue sky where the cranes had disappeared.

46   "Let's go catch a crane." Songsam said abruptly.

47   Tokjae was bewildered. He did not know what was going on.

48   "I'll make a snare out of this, and you drive the cranes this way." Songsam untied Tokjae's bonds and took the cord. Before Tokjae knew it, Songsam was crawling through the grass.

49   At once. Tokjae's face went white. The words "you'll have to be shot" flashed through his mind. At any moment a bullet would come from wherever Songsam had crawled.

50   Some distance away, Songsam rose and turned toward Tokjae. "What do you mean standing there like an idiot! Go drive some cranes this way!"

51   Only then did Tokjae realize what was happening. He started crawling through the weeds.

52   Above, two cranes were soaring, their vast wings spread against the high, blue autumn sky.

• •

CRANES

Journal

1. MLA Works Cited   *Using this model, record this story here.*

Author's First Name Last Name. "Title of the Story." *Title of the Book.* 3rd ed. Ed.

First Name Last Name. City: Publisher, year. Page number(s) of this story.

(Note: Korean names are not inverted.)

2. Main Character(s)   *Describe each main character, and explain why you think each is a main character.*

3. Supporting Characters   *Describe each supporting character, and explain why you think each is a supporting character.*

4. Setting and Props   *Describe the setting(s) and all relevant prop(s).*

5. Sequence   *Outline the events of the story in order.*

6. Plot   *Tell the story in no more than two sentences.*

7. Conflicts   *Identify and explain all the conflicts involved here.*

8. Significant Quotations   *Explain the importance of each quotation completely. Record the page number in the parentheses.*

   a. "In his mind, far away, he could hear the shouts of the old man with a wen. Are you kids climbing my chestnut tree again?" ( ).

   b. "The guard announced that the prisoner had been vice-chairman of the Communist Farmers' Alliance and that he had just been captured while hiding in his own house here in the village" ( ).

c. "Songsam tried to stifle a smile that rose to his lips in spite of himself. [...] But Songsam realized that this was not the place to laugh or joke about such things" ( ).

d. "Once when Songsam and Tokjae were about twelve years old, they had secretly set a snare and caught a crane" ( ).

e. "What do you mean standing there like an idiot! Go drive some cranes this way!" ( ).

9. **Literary Elements**   *Look at this chapter's title and explain why you think this story is placed in this chapter. Explain in which other chapter(s) you might place this story, as relevant to the literary element(s) of the chapter(s).*

10. **Foreshadowing, Irony, and/or Symbols**   *Explain examples of foreshadowing, irony, and/or symbols in this story.*

FOLLOW-UP QUESTIONS

10 SHORT QUESTIONS

What is the <u>best</u> answer for each?

____ 1. In the beginning of this story, Songsam looks on Tokjae as
   a. a friend.
   b. the enemy.
   c. a stranger.

____ 2. In the beginning of the story, Songsam thinks Tokjae is
   a. a murderer.
   b. a poor farmer.
   c. an old man.

____ 3. Songsam assumes the worst about Tokjae because Tokjae is
   a. a poor farmer.
   b. an old man.
   c. a government official.

____ 4. In truth, Tokjae is
   a. a poor farmer.
   b. an old man.
   c. a stranger.

____ 5. In fact, Songsam and Tokjae
   a. are strangers.
   b. are sons of the old man.
   c. grew up together.

____ 6. All that seems to separate Songsam and Tokjae is
   a. a long-standing hatred.
   b. a family feud.
   c. a separation by the governments.

____ 7. As children, Songsam and Tokjae
   a. never talked to each other.
   b. were best friends.
   c. hated each other.

____ 8. As children, Songsam and Tokjae
   a. killed a crane.
   b. kept a crane.
   c. shot a crane.

____ 9. As children, Songsam and Tokjae
   a. gave a crane freedom.
   b. killed a crane.
   c. shot a crane.

____ 10. The two cranes at the end probably symbolize
   a. freedom.
   b. capture.
   c. death.

5 SIGNIFICANT QUOTATIONS

What is the importance of each of these quotations?

1. "Overall, the village showed few signs of the conflict that had just ended. Still, it did not seem to Songsam to be the same village where he had grown up."

2. "Songsam felt an inexplicable urge. He burst out shouting, 'You bastard, how many people have you killed?'"

3. "First and last, I'm the son of a dirt farmer. I was made vice-chairman of the Farmers' Alliance because they said I was a hard worker."

4. "Their own crane, which had been lying on the ground, stretched out its long neck, gave a cry, and rose into the sky, too."

5. "Above, two cranes were soaring, their vast wings spread against the high, blue autumn sky."

2 Comprehension Essay Questions

Use specific details and information from the story to answer these questions as completely as possible.

1. What is the relationship between Songsam and Tokjae? Use specific details and information from the story to support your answer.

2. How does the title relate to the story? Explain the significance of the title using specific details and information from the story.

Discussion Questions

Be prepared to discuss these questions in class.

1. How does Songam feel at first? In the end?

2. What do you think becomes of Tokjae? Use details from the story to support your prediction.

Writing

Use each of these ideas for writing an essay.

1. We all have tender childhood memories. Focus on a specific memory— one specific occasion, one specific day or moment—and describe that memory so that the reader can taste, hear, smell, see, and/or feel it.

2. Things change as we grow older. Tell about something in your life that has changed and contrast what was before with what is today.

Further Writing

1. Contrast the central characters in this story with the central characters in Leo Tolstoy's "God Sees the Truth, but Waits" (page 337).

2. Contrast the spy in the movie *The Patriot* with the central characters in this story.

TRAIL OF THE GREEN BLAZER
R. K. NARAYAN

PRE-READING VOCABULARY
CONTEXT

Use context clues to define these words before reading. Use a dictionary as needed.

1. Anthony decided to buy a navy *blazer* with gold buttons in place of a sport coat. *Blazer* means _____.

2. Raja wore a beautiful silk *sari* that was trimmed in delicate flowers and that flowed in the breeze. *Sari* means _____.

3. In order to sell his baseball cards, Matt rented a *stall* at the flea market and hung a big banner out in front. *Stall* means

   _____.

4. Rudy thought the vase was too expensive, so he *haggled* with the salesperson to lower the price. *Haggle* means _____.

5. The open drawer with all the money in it was an open *invitation* to the thief to steal the money. *Invitation* means

   _____.

6. After tilling the soil and planting the seeds, the poor *peasant* waited for food to grow so he could eat. *Peasant* means

   _____.

7. The boy was a true *idler* and chose to do nothing all day rather than get a job. *Idler* means _____.

8. Americans use dollars and cents to pay for things while some Asians use *annas* and *rupees*. *Anna* and *rupee* mean _____.

9. Thomas was able to connect tiny wires back and forth between his fingers and everyone was amazed at his *deftness*. *Deftness* means

   _____.

10. Everyone thought the thief was *reformed* and on his way to becoming an honest man when he stopped stealing. *Reformed* means

_____.

11. When Theo sold shoes, he was paid an extra *commission* on each pair he sold. *Commission* means _____.

12. Even though she knew her brother's toothache hurt him, Christina had to *suppress* a laugh because he looked so funny. *Suppress* means

_____.

13. The little boy cried when he lost the string and his big round red *balloon* sailed off into the sky. *Balloon* means _____.

14. When Patrick wants to get away from it all, he tries to find a quiet and *secluded* place where no one can find him. *Secluded* means

_____.

15. Eliot dug a small *well* to find water and put a wooden fence around the hole so no one would fall in. *Well* means _____.

16. Artie was greatly *disappointed* when the wonderful surprise he ordered for Carol arrived late and damaged. *Disappointed* means

_____.

17. Ethan felt such *pity* for the little puppy stuck at the dog pound that he decided to adopt the puppy and take it home. *Pity* means

_____.

18. The snake moved slowly and no one saw it *sidle* up next to the house to wait for darkness and silence. *Sidle* means _____.

19. The dog dropped his head and *cowered* in the corner when he was yelled at for doing something wrong. *Cower* means _____.

20. After years of law school and a successful career, Shirley was

appointed the head *magistrate* for legal affairs. *Magistrate* means

_____.

Use context clues from the text to solve this word.

"It had to be finely balanced and calculated—the same sort of calculations as carry a *shikari* through his tracking of game and see him safely home again" (193–194)

Shikari means _____.

PRE-READING VOCABULARY
STRUCTURAL ATTACK

Define these words by solving the parts. Use the Glossary or a dictionary as needed.

1. villagers
2. twosome
3. marketplace
4. loincloth
5. overshadowed
6. involuntarily
7. fondness
8. shopman
9. motherless
10. carelessness
11. unworthy
12. semicircle

PRE-READING QUESTIONS

Try answering these questions as you read.

Who is the Green Blazer?

Who is Raju?

What is Raju doing?

What does Raju then decide to do?

TRAIL OF THE GREEN BLAZER

R. K. NARAYAN

Rasipuram Krishnaswamy (R. K.) Narayan was born in the Indian city of Madras in 1906. Perhaps because his father was an English teacher, Narayan has chosen to write in non-native English. He has become a prolific writer, often focusing on the combination of, and even open confrontation between, people from different walks of life. He is generally sympathetic to the lower classes and social commentary often emerges through his characters and their plights. His writings can be found in numerous novels and short story collections.

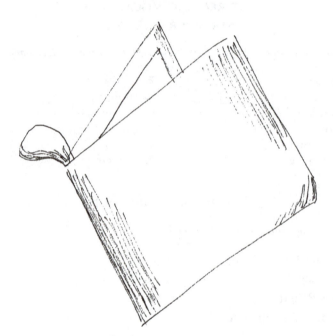

The Green Blazer stood out prominently under the bright sun and blue sky. In all that jostling crowd one could not help noticing it. Villagers in shirts and turbans, townsmen in coats and caps, beggars bare-bodied and women in multicolored saris were thronging the narrow passage between the stalls and moving in great confused masses, but still the Green Blazer could not be missed. The jabber and babble of the marketplace was there, as people harangued, disputed prices, haggled or greeted each other; over it all boomed the voice of a Bible-preacher, and when he paused for breath, from another corner the loudspeaker of a health van amplified on malaria and tuberculosis. Over and above it all the Green Blazer seemed to cry out an invitation. Raju could not ignore it. It was not in his nature to ignore such a persistent invitation. He kept himself half-aloof from the crowd; he could not afford to remain completely aloof or keep himself in it too conspicuously. Wherever he might be, he was harrowed by the fear of being spotted by a policeman; today he wore a loincloth and was bare-bodied, and had wound an enormous turban over his head, which overshadowed his face completely, and he hoped that he would be taken for a peasant from a village.

2   He sat on a stack of cast-off banana stalks beside a shop awning and watched the crowd. When he watched a crowd he did it with concentration. It was his professional occupation. Constitutionally he was an idler and had just the amount of energy to watch in a crowd and put his hand into another person's pocket. It was a gamble, of course. Sometimes he got nothing out of a venture, counting himself lucky if he came out with his fingers intact. Sometimes he picked up a fountain pen, and the "receiver" behind the Municipal Office would not offer even four annas for it, and there was always the danger of being traced through it. Raju promised himself that someday he would leave fountain pens alone; he wouldn't touch one even if it were presented to him on a plate; they were too much bother—inky, leaky and next to worthless if one could believe what the receiver said about them. Watches were in the same category, too.

3   What Raju loved most was a nice, bulging purse. If he saw one he picked it up with the greatest deftness. He took the cash in it, flung it far away and went home with the satisfaction that he had done his day's job well. He splashed a little water over his face and hair and tidied himself up before walking down the street again as a normal citizen. He bought sweets, books and slates for his children, and occasionally a jacket-piece for his wife, too. He was not always easy in mind about his wife. When he went home with too much cash, he had always to take care to hide it in an envelope and shove it under a roof tile. Otherwise she asked too many questions and made herself miserable. She liked to believe that he was reformed and earned the cash he showed her as commission; she never bothered to ask what the commissions were for; a commission seemed to her something absolute.

4   Raju jumped down from the banana stack and followed the Green Blazer, always keeping himself three steps behind. It was a nicely calculated distance, acquired by intuition and practise. The distance must not be so much as to obscure the movement of the other's hand to and from his purse, nor so close as to become a nuisance and create suspicion. It had to be finely balanced and calculated—the same sort of calculations as carry a *shikari* through

his tracking of game and see him safely home again. Only this hunter's task was more complicated. The hunter in the forest could count his day a success if he laid his quarry flat; but here one had to extract the heart out of the quarry without injuring it.

5   Raju waited patiently, pretending to be examining some rolls of rush mat, while the Green Blazer spent a considerable length of time drinking a coconut at a nearby booth. It looked as though he would not move again at all. After sucking all the milk in the coconut, he seemed to wait interminably for the nut to be split and the soft white kernel scooped out with a knife. The sight of the white kernel scooped and disappearing into the other's mouth made Raju, too, crave for it. But he suppressed the thought; it would be inept to be spending one's time drinking and eating while one was professionally occupied; the other might slip away and be lost forever.... Raju saw the other take out his black purse and start a debate with the coconut-seller over the price of coconuts. He had a thick, sawing voice which disconcerted Raju. It sounded like the growl of a tiger, but what jungle-hardened hunter ever took a step back because a tiger's growl sent his heart racing involuntarily! The way the other haggled didn't appeal to Raju either; it showed a mean and petty temperament...too much fondness for money. Those were the narrow-minded troublemakers who made endless fuss when a purse was lost....The Green Blazer moved after all. He stopped before a stall flying colored balloons. He bought a balloon after an endless argument with the shopman—a further demonstration of his meanness. He said, "This is for a motherless boy. I have promised it to him. If it bursts or gets lost before I go home, he will cry all night, and I wouldn't like it at all."

6   Raju got his chance when the other passed through a narrow stile, where people were passing four-thick in order to see a wax model of Mahatma Gandhi reading a newspaper.

7   Fifteen minutes later Raju was examining the contents of the purse. He went away to a secluded spot, behind a disused well. Its crumbling parapet seemed to offer an ideal screen for his activities. The purse contained ten rupees in coins and twenty in currency notes and a few annas in nickel. Raju tucked the annas at his waist in his loincloth. "Must give them to some beggars," he reflected generously. There was a blind fellow yelling his life out at the entrance to the fair and nobody seemed to care. People seemed to have lost all sense of sympathy these days. The thirty rupees he bundled into a knot at the end of his turban and wrapped this again round his head. It would see him through the rest of the month. He could lead a clean life for at least a fortnight and take his wife and children to a picture.

8   Now the purse lay limp within the hollow of his hand. It was only left for him to fling it into the well and dust off his hand

and then he might walk among princes with equal pride at heart. He peeped into the well. It had a little shallow water at the bottom. The purse might float, and a floating purse could cause the worst troubles on earth. He opened the flap of the purse in order to fill it up with pebbles before drowning it. Now, through the slit at its side, he saw a balloon folded and tucked away. "Oh, this he bought...." He remembered the other's talk about the motherless child. "What a fool to keep this in the purse," Raju reflected. "It is the carelessness of parents that makes young ones suffer," he ruminated angrily. For a moment he paused over a picture of the growling father returning home and the motherless one waiting at the door for the promised balloon, and this growling man feeling for his purse...and, oh! it was too painful!

9   Raju almost sobbed at the thought of the disappointed child—the motherless boy. There was no one to comfort him. Perhaps this ruffian would beat him if he cried too long. The Green Blazer did not look like one who knew the language of children. Raju was filled with pity at the thought of the young child—perhaps of the same age as his second son. Suppose his wife were dead...(personally it might make things easier for him, he need not conceal his cash under the roof); he overcame this thought as an unworthy side issue. If his wife should die it would make him very sad indeed and tax all his ingenuity to keep his young ones quiet....That motherless boy must have his balloon at any cost, Raju decided. But how? He peeped over the parapet across the intervening space at the far-off crowd. The balloon could not be handed back. The thing to do would be to put it back into the empty purse and slip it into the other's pocket.

10   The Green Blazer was watching the heckling that was going on as the Bible-preacher warmed up to his subject. A semicircle was asking, "Where is your God?" There was a hubbub. Raju sidled up to the Green Blazer. The purse with the balloon (only) tucked into it was in his palm. He'd slip it back into the other's pocket.

11   Raju realized his mistake in a moment. The Green Blazer caught hold of his arm and cried, "Pickpocket!" The hecklers lost interest in the Bible and turned their attention to Raju, who tried to look appropriately outraged. He cried, "Let me go." The other, without giving a clue to what he proposed, shot out his arm and hit him on the cheek. It almost blinded him. For a fraction of a second Raju lost his awareness of where and even who he was. When the dark mist lifted and he was able to regain his vision, the first figure he noticed in the foreground was the Green Blazer, looming, as it seemed, over the whole landscape. His arms were raised ready to strike again. Raju cowered at the sight. He said, "I...I was trying to put back your purse." The other gritted his

teeth in fiendish merriment and crushed the bones of his arm. The crowd roared with laughter and badgered him. Somebody hit him again on the head.

12   Even before the Magistrate Raju kept saying, "I was only trying to put back the purse." And everyone laughed. It became a stock joke in the police world. Raju's wife came to see him in jail and said, "You have brought shame on us," and wept.

13   Raju replied indignantly, "Why? I was only trying to put it back."

14   He served his term of eighteen months and came back into the world—not quite decided what he should do with himself. He told himself, "If ever I pick up something again, I shall make sure I don't have to put it back." For now he believed God had gifted the likes of him with only one-way deftness. Those fingers were not meant to put anything back.

TRAIL OF THE GREEN BLAZER

Journal

1. MLA Works Cited   *Using this model, record this story here.*

Author's Last Name, First Name. "Title of the Story." *Title of the Book.* 3rd ed. Ed.

First Name Last Name. City: Publisher, year. Page number(s) of this story. Print.

2. Main Character(s)   *Describe each main character, and explain why you think each is a main character.*

3. Supporting Characters   *Describe each supporting character, and explain why you think each is a supporting character.*

4. Setting and Props   *Describe the setting(s) and all relevant prop(s).*

5. Sequence   *Outline the events of the story in order.*

6. Plot   *Tell the story in no more than two sentences.*

7. Conflicts   *Identify and explain all the conflicts involved here.*

8. Significant Quotations   *Explain the importance of each quotation completely. Record the page number in the parentheses.*

a. "The Green Blazer stood out prominently under the bright sun and blue sky" (   ).

b. "When he went home with too much cash, he had always to take care to hide it in an envelope and shove it under a roof tile" (   ).

c. "He said, 'This is for a motherless boy' " ( ).

d. "Now, through the slit at its side, he saw a balloon folded and tucked away" ( ).

e. "Those fingers were not meant to put anything back" ( ).

9. **Literary Elements**   *Look at this chapter's title and explain why you think this story is placed in this chapter. Explain in which other chapter(s) you might place this story, as relevant to the literary element(s) of the chapter(s).*

10. **Foreshadowing, Irony, and/or Symbols**   *Explain examples of foreshadowing, irony, and/or symbols in this story.*

Follow-up Questions

10 Short Questions

What is the <u>best</u> answer for each?

_____ 1. Raju is
   a. a pickpocket.
   b. an honest family man.
   c. an honest citizen.

_____ 2. The Green Blazer is probably
   a. a native to the bazaar.
   b. a visitor to the bazaar.
   c. a worker's jacket.

_____ 3. The green blazer implies
   a. the person wearing it has money.
   b. the person wearing it is different from the others.
   c. both a. and b.

_____ 4. Raju prefers to find
   a. fountain pens.
   b. watches.
   c. money.

_____ 5. Raju has
   a. just learned how to pick pockets.
   b. picked pockets before.
   c. never picked pockets before.

_____ 6. Raju's wife thinks
   a. Raju has an honest job.
   b. Raju is not reformed.
   c. Raju is still a thief.

_____ 7. At first, the money makes Raju feel
   a. satisfied.
   b. disappointed.
   c. guilty.

_____ 8. Then, the balloon makes Raju feel
   a. satisfied.
   b. disappointed.
   c. guilty.

_____ 9. Raju decides to
   a. throw the purse away.
   b. return the purse and the balloon.
   c. keep the purse and the balloon.

_____ 10. Raju gets in trouble because
   a. he keeps the purse and the balloon.
   b. he throws away the purse and the balloon.
   c. he tries to return the purse and the balloon.

5 Significant Quotations

What is the importance of each of these quotations?

1. "Over and above it all the Green Blazer seemed to cry out an invitation."

2. "She liked to believe that he was reformed and earned the cash he showed her as commission […]."

3. "Fifteen minutes later Raju was examining the contents of the purse."

4. "Raju almost sobbed at the thought of the disappointed child—the motherless boy."

5. "Raju realized his mistake in a moment."

2 Comprehension Essay Questions

Use specific details and information from the story to answer these questions as completely as possible.

1. How is the title relevant to the story? Use specific details and information from the story to support your answer.

2. What is the role of the balloon in this story? Use specific details and information from the story to support your answer.

Discussion Questions

Be prepared to discuss these questions in class.

1. What is Raju's profession and do you think he is good at it?

2. What is the irony in this story?

Writing

Use each of these ideas for writing an essay.

1. At one time or another, we have all done something wrong and gotten caught. Write about a time that you or someone you know has gotten caught and what the consequences have been.

2. We all have things that we need to change or reform. Tell about one specific thing that you or someone you know has changed, and contrast the old behavior with the new.

Further Writing

1. Compare and contrast Raju with the two desperados in O. Henry's "The Ransom of Red Chief" (page 288).

2. In some cultures, thieves are very nearly considered an actual social class. Research social class structures in Middle Eastern and/or Asian cultures.

YORUBA

Migene Gonzalez-Wippler

Pre-reading Vocabulary
Context

Use context clues to define these words before reading. Use a dictionary as needed.

1. When Ben's mother went to work, his *nanny* saw to it that he was
   dressed and fed and ready for school each day. *Nanny* means

   _____.

2. The rainstorm was *mammoth*, covering over half the country with
   clouds and rain. *Mammoth* means _____.

3. Services, or *masses*, are usually celebrated daily at the Catholic
   church in town. *Mass* means _____.

4. Maureen put all her clothes in her closet, picked up all her belongings,
   and generally kept her room *immaculate*. *Immaculate* means

   _____.

5. To keep from getting a sunburn, Jennifer walked through town with
   a large pink *parasol* that looked like an umbrella. *Parasol* means

   _____.

6. Since it was the weekend, Lisa broke from her usual weekday *routine*
   and went to the mall instead of going to work. *Routine* means

   _____.

7. Margaret loved the beautiful beads on the *rosary* chain she used
   to count her prayers as she said them. *Rosary* means

   _____.

8. Since they had never met before, Allison *introduced* her brother Jacob
   to her friend Zachary. *Introduce* means _____.

9. Plowing the field and then later harvesting the crops was hard work
for the poor *peasant. Peasant* means _____.

10. Ashley and Caitlin love going to the *beach* where they make
sandcastles and swim in the ocean. *Beach* means

_____.

11. Hatem planned to take Rte. 1, but Rte. 1 was blocked and the *detour*
took him way out of his way. *Detour* means _____.

12. Reid decided to *initiate* his own baseball team and started it by
sending out flyers to his friends to encourage them to join. *Initiate*
means _____.

13. The priest *anointed* the baby's head with holy water when he blessed
the baby. *Anointed* means _____.

14. To keep her gown from getting wet in the rain, Missy put on a large
mantle that flowed from her shoulders over her gown. *Mantle*
means _____.

15. My *mammy* gave birth to me and has taken care of me ever since
I was born. *Mammy* means _____.

16. The pastor of our church offered a *blessing* to all the new babies by
saying a prayer for them. *Blessing* means _____.

17. A human baby grows for nine months within her or his mother's
womb. Womb means _____.

18. With more rain than usual and mild weather, the farm produced
a huge *bounty* of more food than ever. *Bounty* means

_____.

19. Karen *exchanged* the red shoes for the white ones when she knew she would not wear the red. *Exchanged* means _____.

20. Mary Beth *adores* the beautiful new dollhouse Donald built especially for her. *Adore* means

_____.

PRE-READING VOCABULARY
STRUCTURAL ATTACK

Define these words by solving the parts. Use the Glossary or a dictionary as needed.

1. marketplace
2. shantytown
3. sundress
4. sunbonnet
5. majestically
6. fiery
7. unusually
8. compilation
9. obediently
10. throaty
11. luxurious
12. voluminous
13. undercurrent
14. fruitless
15. impassioned
16. encrusted

PRE-READING QUESTIONS

Try answering these questions as you read.

Who is María?
Who is Yemayá?
What is Yoruba?

YORUBA

Migene Gonzalez-Wippler

Migene Gonzalez-Wippler is a resident of Puerto Rico. She is a recognized authority on the Santeria religion. This story is taken from her book *The Santeria Experience*. More of her writing can be found in *Santeria: African Magic in Latin America*.

Arecibo, tucked in a fold of Puerto Rico's northeastern coast, is one of the oldest towns in the western hemisphere. Originally an Indian village ruled by a Taíno chieftain called Aracibo, it was founded by the Conquistadores in 1616.

2   In the late nineteen forties, when I was three years old, my mother hired María, a black woman of mammoth proportions, to be my nanny. María's skin was like shiny mahogany with almost iridescent tones, and her smile was radiant. I never saw María angry or sad, and if she was ever prey to these dismal human moods, she was quite adept at hiding them from me. I thought her very beautiful, and soon I would take my meals only if María ate with me and would not fall asleep unless María sat by my side.

3   María took me everywhere she went. To the marketplace where she did our daily shopping and to the shantytown where her numerous family lived. To daily mass, for she was a devout Catholic, and to the neighborhood store where she placed her occasional bets with the numbers. My mother took a dim view of these escapades, but I was so healthy and so happy in María's care that my mother eventually relented and let her take full charge of me.

4   Each morning María would put me in a frothy sundress with a matching sunbonnet, white sandals, and socks which she bleached daily to ensure their whiteness. Underneath the bonnet, my long black hair would be meticulously braided and tied with silk ribbons matching the color of my dress. María was partial to the scent of Parma violets, and all my clothes exuded a faint violet fragrance.

5   Once my morning toilet was finished, María would march me proudly into our dining room, where my parents and grandparents would make proper sounds of praise and admiration at my dazzling pulchritude. Then, under María's watchful eyes, I would sit to breakfast without wrinkling my skirts or soiling my ruffles. After a substantial breakfast, María sailed majestically out of the house with me in tow, her long, immaculate skirts crackling with starch. On her shoulder was a huge parasol to protect us from the fiery Caribbean sun, while from her wrist dangled a fan to bring us relief from the stifling heat. Since air conditioning had barely made its appearance on the island, the fan was more than an ornament. But female vanity had long turned a necessary instrument into a thing of beauty, and fans had become the objects of both pride and delight, some of them made of fine sandalwood and hand-painted with exquisite landscapes by renowned artists. Others were of peacock or ostrich feathers, or of Chantilly lace embroidered with seed pearls. María had purchased her fan from a merchant marine sailor who had brought if from Spain. Its unusually wide span was of ebony, carved with intricate flowery designs and highlighted with delicate touches of color that made the flower patterns dance with light.

6   It was María who first taught me that with a flick of the wrist and the opening and closing of a fan, a woman can tell an admirer that she is angry or jealous, that she welcomes his advances or finds him a crashing bore. María taught me all this and more during the twelve years I remained in her care.

7   I was thrilled at the idea of going to school, which opened the day after I turned five, and talked about it incessantly with María. My mother had promised me an especially nice party to celebrate my birthday, and my grandfather had a famous designer in San Juan make a special dress of pink organdy, hand-embroidered with tiny flowers and musical notes. The shoes and socks were also pink, as were the silk ribbons for my hair. But early in the morning, María dressed me in an old white dress and took me to mass. She did not take me in to my family and have breakfast with them. I kept questioning the departure from our daily routine, but María said to be silent and do as I was told.

8   After mass was over, María brought me to an altar over which stood a statue of the Virgin Mary. While I knelt down before the

image, María pulled from her capacious handbag a large wooden rosary, and proceeded to pass the beads. She stood behind me, praying in muted tones, with her hand on my shoulder as if she were introducing me to the Virgin.

9   Even if you don't pray the litanies, a compilation of fifty-three Hail Marys and seven Pater-nosters is a lengthy business if you are a child of five. My stomach was empty. My knees ached and throbbed and threatened to buckle, and I had to keep balancing my weight first on the one knee, then on the other. I must have presented a most unhappy picture to Our Blessed Lady. But not once did I think to complain to María. One did not question her orders; one simply did what one was told.

10   It was already midmorning when we left the church. My knees were functioning again after María rubbed them briskly with her handkerchief, but my stomach was grumbling louder than ever.

11   "María, are we going to the marketplace or back home?"

12   "I know you're tired and hungry," she said evasively, opening her parasol and pulling me under it. "But you must never let your body tell you what to do. It must obey you, not the other way around."

13   I trotted obediently by her side. "But how does my body tell me what to do?"

14   "By making you feel things," she answered. "It makes you feel hungry, so you eat. Tired, so you sit down. Sleepy, so you go to bed. Sometimes it makes you feel angry, so you scream and yell and stomp your feet."

15   My face colored, remembering my occasional temper tantrums.

16   "But, María, then my body isn't good."

17   "Oh yes it is, *florecita* [little flower]. Because of your body, you can see the sky and the sun and the sea. You can smell the perfume of the flowers and sing and play, and love your mother and father."

18   "And you," I added, drawing closer to her.

19   "And me," she laughed her great throaty laugh. "But you see, *florecita*, your body is like a little child. It must be taught good habits and to obey. It must learn we can't always eat when we're hungry or sit down when we're tired or sleep when we're sleepy. And the best way to teach your body these things is by sometimes not doing the things it wants you to do. Not always," she emphasized. "Only sometimes."

20   "Like now?" I asked.

21   "Like now."

22   We reached the bus stop. With delight, I thought we were going home, where I could eat some breakfast and play before my party in the afternoon.

23   "But I will only eat a little," I promised myself, remembering María's words, "and I will play with only one doll."

24   But I was not to eat a little breakfast or play with any dolls that morning.

25   The bus chugged along the country road to our home. Palm trees and banana plants heavy with fruit grew profusely on both sides of the road, as did the brilliant blossoms of the hibiscus, the poinciana, and the bougainvillea. To our left, gently sloping hills alternated with narrow valleys carpeted in a dazzling variety of greens. To our right, the Atlantic melted with the sky in a majestic display of aquamarine and gold. A few peasant huts, known as *bohíos*, were scattered on the hillside, while on the ocean side rose elegant, luxurious *quintas* of white stucco ornamented with costly mosaics and Spanish ironwork.

26   We were still about ten minutes from home when María pulled the cord to get off. Before I knew what was happening I found myself standing by the road, watching the bus disappear in the distance. María opened her parasol and gathered her parcels together.

27   Directly in front of us was a rough path, largely overgrown with vegetation. María and I trudged along this path until we emerged directly onto a part of the beach hidden from the main road by a series of large boulders imbedded in the sand. Among the dunes grew a profusion of tropical sea grapes, their hard, bitter fruit shining like amethysts among their harsh round leaves. Some palm trees bent their trunks so close to the sand one could easily grab the clusters of coconut growing among the fan-shaped leaves.

28   We stopped under the shadow of a palm while María removed my shoes and socks, her own heavy brogans, and the thick cotton stockings she always wore. Thus barefoot we trampled through the warm sand.

29   I did not bother to ask María the reason for our detour, used as I was to being taken along on all her outings. I had the vague feeling this surprise visit to the beach I had always admired from a distance, but never had walked on before, was María's birthday present to me. Intoxicated by the sharp, tangy smell of the sea, I wanted to stay on the shore for the rest of my life.

30   When we finally arrived at the water's edge, María set her parcels down, closed her parasol, and then calmly proceeded to tear the clothes from my body.

31   I felt no shame. María washed and dressed me every day and put me to sleep every night. I had stood naked in front of her many times before. I had not yet learned to be ashamed of my own body. But her action had a certain ominous authority that made me feel destitute and vulnerable beyond description. Deprived of more

than my own clothes, I felt stripped of identity, of a sense of being. It was as if I had died somehow, standing there on the golden sand, with the sun like a halo around me and the taste of salt water on my lips. I stood there in shock and utter humiliation, tears rolling steadily down my cheeks. I did not understand María's actions, but I knew there was always a reason for everything she did. (Many years later I would find an echo of María's teachings, in the philosophies of some of the world's greatest religions, especially Zen Buddhism. When María tore my clothes and left me naked facing the sea, without any sense of ego or identity, she was echoing Zen's concept of the perfect Initiate, who must be "devoid of selfhood, devoid of personality, devoid of identity, and devoid of separate identity.")

32   Out of her handbag's unfathomable depths, María extracted a bottle of sugarcane syrup and the red handkerchief, tied in a knot, where she kept all her loose change. Only then did she turn to look at me, all at once the picture of consternation.

33   "Ah, my little flower, don't cry. You afraid of María? You think María can hurt you?" She rocked me gently against her bosom as she spoke her soothing words. "Why, my *florecita*, María would cut out her heart for you. María could never hurt you."

34   Slowly my tears stopped flowing. I lifted my wet face from her shoulder. I felt I could question her now.

35   "Why, María?" I asked, with still trembling lips. "Why did you do that?"

36   "Because I want you to be protected from all harm. Now that you're going to school, you'll be alone, *florecita*, without María to watch over you. You need protection, and only God and the Blessed Lady can give it to you and give you her blessings. And now I bring you to the Lady and her true power, the sea."

37   As she spoke, María opened the bottle of sugarcane syrup. Tasting it with her forefinger, she anointed my temples, lips, wrists, and ankles with the thick liquid. I automatically licked the heavy, cloying syrup on my lips.

38   "It's too sweet," I grimaced. "I don't like it."

39   "It has to be sweet for the Lady, as sweet as possible. Nothing can be too sweet for her."

40   María undid the knot of her red handkerchief. Counting seven pennies, she pressed them in my hand.

41   "Here, *florecita*," she said, closing my fingers around the coins. "This is the payment, *el derecho*, of the Lady. I give you seven pennies because seven is her number. You remember that. Seven is the number of the Lady, of Yemayá."

42   "Of who?" I asked, staring at the pennies. "What Lady are you talking about, María? The Blessed Lady is in the church and in heaven."

43   "Yes, *florecita*, but her true power is in the sea and the seawater. She stands in heaven, but where the bottom of her mantle touches the earth, it turns into the ocean. The waves and the sea foam are her ruffles and her lace. And here, in the sea, her name is Yemayá."

44   She enunciated the strange name carefully so that I could grasp its melodious rhythm, "Say it, *florecita*. Ye-ma-yá."

45   I repeated it after her. "It is the prettiest name I ever heard, María!"

46   "The prettiest name in the whole world," María laughed delightedly. "It is the name of the Lady in African, in Yoruba. My mammy taught it to me. And now, my little flower, your black mammy teaches it to you." She took my hand gently and guided me to the water. "Come, let me show you how to salute Yemayá."

47   Lifting her voluminous skirts so that the waves would not wet them, she turned her body to the left and forced me to do the same. We both stood ankle-deep in the water, our bodies at right angles to the sea.

48   "See, *florecita*, you never enter into the ocean facing front. To do so is a challenge to Yemayá; it's like saying, 'I'm here, come get me.' So then maybe she does. Always, always enter on your side, better the right side. Then you say, '*Hekua, Yemayá, hekua.*' Say it, little flower."

49   I looked dubiously at the water, then at María. Like most Puerto Rican children I had been raised as a very strict Catholic, and I had the vague feeling that our parish priest would not approve of what María was saying. But my trust in her had been firmly reestablished and I did not want to offend her. "*Hekua, Yemayá, hekua,*" I repeated.

50   As soon as I repeated these words, I felt relieved and relaxed, as if an unseen link had been established between the sea and myself. My soul was overwhelmed by a great love for the sea, that has never stopped growing within me. I have never bathed in the sea again without remembering that incredible feeling of love illuminating my entire being.

51   "See, *florecita*," María said joyously. "Yemayá blesses you, she accepts you. She will always protect you now."

52   I looked up at her with wondering eyes. "Is that what *hekua* means?"

53   "Yes, *hekua* means blessings. And see how Yemayá blesses you?"

54   María pointed to the water frothing softly around my feet. Small whirlpools of foam enveloped my ankles, then my knees. Then suddenly an unexpectedly huge wave rose from the sea like a great green arm. As the wall of water collapsed over my head, I heard María cry out, "The coins! The coins!... Let go the coins!"

55   I felt myself being drawn out to sea inside a glimmering cocoon, with the rushing sound of a thousand crystal bells. I opened my arms to embrace the sea, and the seven pennies fell from my fingers. Almost immediately, the water receded and the waves resumed their usual gentle motion. I stood as before, ankle-deep in foamy water, blinking at the morning sunshine.

56   I recall little of what happened inside the water. The lingering memory is one of silky green depths, of sun rays shining through the water; of softness, warmth and safety. It was almost as if I had returned to the womb of the world, and felt reluctant to be born anew. This episode at the beach was my first initiation in the Yoruba religion known as Santería.

57   María used to tell me that the presence of Yemayá is always much stronger in very deep waters. Off the north coast of Puerto Rico, in an area known as Bronson's Deep, the ocean floor plunges down to 27,000 feet. Measured from this depth, the mountains of Puerto Rico would be among the highest in the world, with an approximate height of 31,500 feet. Anything that falls within these waters is lost forever—says the legend—unless Yemayá is offered a prize in exchange for her bounty. Truly, her demands are modest. Seven shiny copper pennies, a bit of sugarcane syrup, and sometimes a few candles are enough to please her. Perhaps it is not the value of the gift that Yemayá really wants, but the faith with which it is given.

58   In these same waters, on August 16, 1977, off the coast of San Juan, an incident took place which was fully reported in the San Juan *Star*. For several weeks I had been in one of the hotels lining El Condado Avenue, working against a deadline on one of my books. One afternoon, a friend went snorkeling in the deep waters off the San Juan coast. When he returned several hours later, he had a tragic story to tell.

59   A family from nearby Santo Domingo had come to visit Puerto Rico for the first time. Their thirteen-year-old son disregarded the warnings of the dangerous undercurrents surrounding the coast of San Juan, and the great depths of the waters, and he swam out far from shore. Probably too weak to fight against the currents, the boy suddenly sank under the water and did not surface again. Local lifeguards and members of the Police Rescue Squad tried to locate his body, but all their efforts proved fruitless.

60   The story spread throughout El Condado, and all the hotels sent out search parties to find the body. The boy's mother was determined not to leave her son's body in the sea, as she wanted to bring it back to Santo Domingo for proper burial. But late in the afternoon of the following day, the authorities called off the search.

All the desperate entreaties of the boy's mother fell on deaf ears. The police were sure the powerful undercurrents in these waters had driven the body toward the ocean floor or wedged it in one of the reef's many underwater crevices. But the mother asked to go along with a search party—the very last one, she pleaded. If the body was not found during this last search, she would not insist any further.

61   After some consideration, the authorities agreed. As the story unfolded in the San Juan *Star*, she brought along with her four white candles. When the boat had gone sufficiently out to sea, she asked the officers to stop the engines. Here, she felt, they would find her son's body. More to humor her than for any other reason, the Rescue Squad officers stopped the boat's engines.

62   The mother then approached the boat's gunwale and began an impassioned plea to the sea. Kneeling on deck, her hands linked together in prayer, tears streaming down her face, she called out to the sea to return her son's body to her. Reminding the sea that the boy was dead, she proposed that it exchange his body for the candles she had brought along. Since four candles are burned around a coffin, these also represented her dead son.

63   As she spoke, she pulled the candles from her handbag and threw them overboard. A few minutes later, the Rescue Squad officers aboard the boat watched, aghast, as the boy's body surfaced on the same spot where the candles had sunk into the water.

64   Had María been aboard that boat, she would not have been at all surprised. Without any doubts she would have stated that Yemayá, the Great Supernal Mother, had taken pity on another mother and had accepted the exchange willingly, and with her blessings. As to the apparent cruelty of the sea in taking the boy's life, María would have probably answered that the sea had been kind, saving him from a life of suffering and giving him eternal life instead.

65   María held the view that life was an illusion. So, for that matter, was death.

66   "It's just another way of life, *florecita*," she would say. "A far better way of life."

67   I would wrinkle my forehead. "But María, then why do we live this life? Wouldn't it be better to die and live in a better life in the other world instead?"

68   "No, *florecita*, we're here for a reason. We're here to learn to become better so that we can enjoy that other, better life. If we're bad here, we don't go to the better life after this one. Instead, we have to come back, again and again, until we learn to be good."

69   This simple explanation is exactly the same as the theory of reincarnation expressed by Buddha to his disciple Subhuti in the Diamond Sutra:

70   "Furthermore, Subhuti, if it be that good men and good women…are downtrodden, their evil destiny is the inevitable retributive result of sins committed in their mortal lives. By virtue of their present misfortunes, the reacting effects of their past will be thereby worked out, and they will be in a position to attain the Consummation of Incomparable Enlightenment."

71   The Consummation of Incomparable Enlightenment was the same concept expressed by María as a "better life in the other world."

72   After she took me out of the water, María dried me, braided my hair and tied it with pink silk ribbons, and then dressed me, with the pink organdy dress my grandfather had given me for my birthday. She seemed in very high spirits and hummed a popular tune. When I told her I was happy to have come to the sea and hoped that she would bring me back again, she laughed and hugged me.

73   "We'll see, *florecita*, we'll see," she said, putting the finishing touches on a satin bow. "But I'm happy that Yemayá has accepted you. Now you can go to school without María and no harm can come to you."

74   To my lips came a question that was burning in my mind. "María, why did you tear my clothes?"

75   She looked at me briefly. Her smiled widened, and she returned her attention to my hair.

76   "Why? Because you had to be presented to Yemayá without clothes, like a newborn baby. I tore the clothes to tell Yemayá you gave up your old life and wanted to start living again with her as your mother."

77   "And now my mother is not my mother anymore?" I asked in alarm, my eyes filling with tears.

78   María hugged me again, brushing away my tears with expert fingers.

79   "Of course she is, *florecita*. But she's your mother on earth, while Yemayá is your mother in heaven and in the sea."

80   "But who is Yemayá, the sea?" I asked, still confused.

81   "Yemayá is the Yoruba name of the Virgin Mary, *florecita*," explained María patiently. "She's the mother of all, of whites and blacks, of yellows and greens; of everybody. But in Africa she's always black because the people there are black, and she wants them to know she's black too."

82   "But María, the Virgin is not black, she's white. I've seen her in the church."

83   "No, *florecita*, the Virgin is like your ribbons. She has many colors. Sometimes she's white, sometimes yellow, sometimes she's red, sometimes black. It depends on the color of the people who adore her. She does this to tell the world she loves everybody the same, no matter what their color is. To the Yorubas she's always black because they're black."

84   "Who are the Yorubas, María?"

85   María paused in the middle of a braid, her eyes lost in reverie.

86   "The Yorubas were a great black people." She continued her braiding. "My mammy was Yoruba," she said, with evident pride. "She come to Puerto Rico 1872, year before abolition."

87   When she spoke of her mother, which was often, María reverted to broken Spanish, with African words interspersed. "She comes with two hundred fifty Yorubas from Ife, that's the name of Yoruba land in black country," she added. "Come from Africa, they did, in them slave boats. In chains they brought them, the mean slave merchants—*los negreros*. Many of the black people die on boat, of hunger and sickness, but mostly of broken heart. Yorubas is proud people. Don't like white man."

88   "I'm white, María," I reminded her sadly.

89   "No you aren't, *florecita*," María cried, holding me tight against her. "You aren't white, and you aren't black. You're like the sun and the stars—all light, no color."

90   She finished tying the last ribbon and stood up with great efforts from her stooped position. Her usually immaculate clothes were drenched with seawater and covered with sand, but she paid no attention to them.

91   "Old María is not as strong as she used to be," she grunted, flexing her back. "Not like my mammy. My mammy real strong," she said with relish. "She only ten when she come to island. But white man leave my mammy alone. She knew how to talk to the *orishas*."

92   "What is *orisha*, María?" I asked.

93   "*Orisha?*" she mused. "Yemayá is *orisha*. Elegguá is *orisha*. Changó is *orisha*. *Orisha* is a saint, a force of the good God. But come," she added, taking me by the hand. "It's no good to ask too many questions all at once. Later, I'll tell you more."

94   "But María," I insisted, "Are there many…*orishas*?"

95   "As many as the grains of sand on the beach. But I only know a dozen or two. There are too many. Someday you'll know them too. But now is time to get back home, *florecita*, or your mammy will be really worried. And then your cake will be eaten, your presents gone, and the ice cream melted."

96   The thought of the promised birthday party came rushing back to my five-year-old mind, erasing all thoughts about the shadowy *orishas*, the Yorubas, and even the black Virgin known as Yemayá.

97   The pink shoes and socks remained in María's handbag until we emerged from the sand into the path that led back to the road. Free from their confinement, I ran ahead of María toward the bus stop, oblivious of my fine embroidered dress, pigtails dancing in the sun, my small feet encrusted with wet sand. She followed behind me slowly, dragging her heavy brogans, her parcels, and her parasol, tired but always smiling.

● ●

YORUBA

Journal

1. MLA Works Cited *Using this model, record this story here.*

Author's Last Name, First Name. "Title of the Story." *Title of the Book.* 3rd ed. Ed.

First Name Last Name. City: Publisher, year. Page number(s) of this story. Print.

2. Main Character(s) *Describe each main character, and explain why you think each is a main character.*

3. Supporting Characters *Describe each supporting character, and explain why you think each is a supporting character.*

4. Setting and Props *Describe the setting(s) and all relevant prop(s).*

5. Sequence   *Outline the events of the story in order.*

6. Plot   *Tell the story in no more than two sentences.*

7. Conflicts   *Identify and explain all the conflicts involved here.*

8. Significant Quotations   *Explain the importance of each of these quotations completely. Record the page number in the parentheses.*

a. "In the late nineteen forties when I was three years old, my mother hired María [...]" ( ).

b. "I was thrilled at the idea of going to school [...]" ( ).

c. "We both stood ankle-deep in the water, our bodies at right angles to the sea" ( ).

d. "The mother then approached the boat's gunwale and began an impassioned plea to the sea" ( ).

e. "But she's your mother on earth, while Yemayá is your mother in heaven and in the sea" ( ).

9. **Literary Elements**   *Look at this chapter's title and explain why you think this story is placed in this chapter. Explain in which other chapter(s) you might place this story, as relevant to the literary element(s) of the chapter(s).*

10. **Foreshadowing, Irony, and/or Symbolism**   *Explain examples of foreshadowing, irony, and/or symbolism in this story.*

FOLLOW-UP QUESTIONS

10 SHORT QUESTIONS

What is the <u>best</u> answer for each?

_____ 1. María is the narrator's
a. mother.
b. grandmother.
c. nanny.

_____ 2. The narrator's family probably
a. is poor.
b. is well-off.
c. lives on a farm.

_____ 3. María is probably
a. a lively and colorful person.
b. a quiet person.
c. considered usual by the narrator's family.

_____ 4. María is
a. a large woman.
b. a small woman.
c. of unknown size.

_____ 5. María practices and is described as a "devout"
a. Buddhist.
b. Protestant.
c. Catholic.

_____ 6. For the ritual by the water, the narrator
a. is stripped of her old clothes.
b. enters the waterfront first.
c. wears her new clothes.

_____ 7. The narrator is anointed in sugarcane syrup
a. because it is good for her.
b. because she likes it.
c. because it is sweet enough to offer Yemaya.

_____ 8. María takes the narrator to the beach
a. to harm her.
b. to protect her.
c. to drown her.

_____ 9. According to the story, the boy's body
a. is lost forever.
b. is returned in exchange for seven pennies.
c. is returned in exchange for four candles.

_____ 10. The ritual at the beach
a. is an act of revenge.
b. is an act of love.
c. is an act of hatred.

5 SIGNIFICANT QUOTATIONS

What is the importance of each of these quotations?

1. "My mother took a dim view of these escapades, but I was so healthy and so happy in María's care that my mother eventually relented and let her take full charge of me."

2. "I was thrilled at the idea of going to school, which opened the day after I turned five, and talked about it incessantly with María."

3. "As the wall of water collapsed over my head, I heard María cry out, 'The coins! The coins!...Let go the coins.'"

4. "A few minutes later, the Rescue Squad officers aboard the boat watched, aghast, as the boy's body surfaced on the same spot where the candles had sunk into the water."

5. "But I'm happy that Yemayá has accepted you."

2 COMPREHENSION ESSAY QUESTIONS

Use specific details and information from the story to answer these questions as completely as possible.

1. What is the ritual at the beach from María's standpoint? Use specific details and information from the story to support your description.

2. What is the ritual at the beach from the narrator's standpoint? Use specific details and information from the story to support your description.

DISCUSSION QUESTIONS

Be prepared to discuss these questions in class.

1. How is the religion in this story like and unlike Christianity? How does it compare to your own religion?

2. How does foreshadowing help you understand the beach ritual?

WRITING

Use each of these ideas for writing an essay.

1. Many of us have superstitions. Describe a superstition you or someone that you know has, and tell the effects this superstition has had on you or on the person you know.

2. Religion and/or spirituality may also have many effects on us. Tell about a specific time that religion or spirituality affected you or someone you know.

Further Writing

1. This story offers one form of adapted Christianity. Research other forms of adapted Christianity found in the Caribbean.

2. Compare the rituals in this story with the ritual found in Canto XXXI of *Purgatoria* by Dante Alighieri (available in a library).

THE MADMAN

Chinua Achebe

PRE-READING VOCABULARY
CONTEXT

Use context clues to define these words before reading. Use a dictionary as needed.

1. Cheryl was declared to be quite *mad* when the lawyer proved that she had long been insane and could not tell real from unreal. *Mad* means

   _____.

2. Wilson went off to the *market* where he was able to buy fruit at the fruit stand and vegetables at the grocery stand. *Market* means

   _____.

3. Brian got lost on his way home and was found *wandering* around in an entirely different part of campus. *Wandering* means

   _____.

4. The small *hut* looked like the wind would blow it over and certainly would not be a good place to live. *Hut* means

   _____.

5. Ali suffered great *defilement* when the crazy woman wrongly accused him of being a thief. *Defilement* means _____.

6. Having no home and wandering from place to the place, the *vagabond* had to look for a safe place to sleep. *Vagabond* means

   _____.

7. Most societies have a *hierarchy* wherein there is one class that is higher than another and another that is still higher. *Hierarchy* means

   _____.

8. Gert knew that the girls were very nice and followed her own *intuition* that they would make good friends. *Intuition* means

_____.

9. Renée is a very *sensible* person and never leaves home without an umbrella when it looks like it will rain. *Sensible* means

_____.

10. Edmund decided to keep his children together by building each a home next to his in the same *compound*. *Compound* means

_____.

11. Since Santi was hired first, he is considered the *senior* editor while all those hired after him are considered junior. *Senior* means

_____.

12. Sallie is very *sane* and can easily recognize what is real and what is not real. *Sane* means _____.

13. In America, people bathe privately because they want to protect their *modesty* and not be seen by others. *Modesty* means

_____.

14. After Hal planted thirty apple trees in the meadow, it later turned into a beautiful *grove* of trees. *Grove* means _____.

15. Those who believe in magic and ESP are said to believe in the *occult* because magic and ESP are impossible to see. *Occult* means

_____.

16. The poor people suffered great *oppression* at the hands of the nobles who beat and starved them. *Oppression* means

_____.

17. The prisoners were so dangerous that their hands and feet were roped to each other to keep them in secure *bondage*. *Bondage* means

_____.

18. When Jason finished medical school, he joined two other doctors and opened up a *practice* in town. *Practice* means

   _____.

19. Robbie never stayed in any city for too long and was truly a *sojourner* as he moved from apartment to apartment. *Sojourner* means

   _____.

20. Jorge did not like the girl who screamed and yelled all the time and was so *boisterous*. *Boisterous* means _____.

PRE-READING VOCABULARY
STRUCTURAL ATTACK

Define these words by solving the parts. Use the Glossary or a dictionary as needed.

1. engulfing
2. beckoning
3. footpath
4. fat-bottomed
5. menfolk
6. nakedness
7. sideroad
8. admission
9. honored
10. midday
11. palm-wine
12. wickedness
13. soup-pot
14. instinctive
15. maddened
16. careless
17. grief-stricken
18. medicine-man
19. overnight

PRE-READING QUESTIONS

Try answering these as you read.

How does the Madman behave?
How does Nwibe behave?
What happens to Nwibe?

THE MADMAN

CHINUA ACHEBE

Chinua Achebe was born in Ogidi, Nigeria, in 1930. With his father, a teacher at the local mission school, Achebe was prepared well educationally and eventually attended the University College in Ibandan. At 28 years old, Achebe's first novel established him as a serious writer. He later joined the Nigerian Broadcasting Company and then the Biafran Ministry of Information. During the civil war in Biafra, Achebe traveled to raise money for the people and awareness of the wrenching war that resulted in the deaths of over one million people from starvation. His writing often presents philosophical clarity and social anguish. He has received many awards, including the Nigerian National Merit Award and Honorary Fellowship in the American Academy and Institute of Arts and Letters. His writing can be found in novels and short story collections.

He was drawn to markets and straight roads. Not any tiny neighborhood market where a handful of garrulous women might gather at sunset to gossip and buy ogili for the evening's soup, but a huge, engulfing bazaar beckoning people familiar and strange from far and near. And not any dusty, old footpath beginning in this village, and ending in that stream, but broad, black, mysterious highways without beginning or end. After much wandering he had discovered two such markets linked together by such a highway; and so ended his wandering. One market was Afo, the other Eke. The two days between them suited him very well: before setting out for Eke he had ample time to wind up his business properly at Afo. He passed the night there putting right again his hut after a day of defilement by two fat-bottomed market women who said it was their market stall. At first he had put up a fight but the women had gone and brought their menfolk—four hefty beasts of the bush—to whip him out of the hut. After that he always avoided them, moving out on the morning of the market and back in at dusk to pass the night. Then in the morning he rounded off his affairs swiftly and set out on that long, beautiful boa-constrictor of a road to Eke in the distant town of Ogbu. He held his staff and cudgel at the ready in his right hand, and with the left he steadied the basket of his belongings on his head. He had got himself this cudgel lately to deal with little beasts on the way who threw stones at him and made fun of their mothers' nakedness, not his own.

2   He used to walk in the middle of the road, holding it in conversation. But one day the driver of a mammy-wagon and his mate came down on him shouting, pushing and slapping his face. They said their lorry [truck] very nearly ran over their mother, not him. After that he avoided those noisy lorries too, with the vagabonds inside them.

3   Having walked one day and one night he was now close to the Eke market-place. From every little sideroad, crowds of market people poured into the big highway to join the enormous flow to Eke. Then he saw some young ladies with water-pots on their heads coming toward him, unlike all the rest, away from the market. This surprised him. Then he saw two more water-pots rise out of a sloping footpath leading off his side of the highway. He felt thirsty then and stopped to think it over. Then he set down his basket on the roadside and turned into the sloping footpath. But first he begged his highway not to be offended or continue the journey without him. "I'll get some for you too," he said coaxingly with a tender backward glance. "I know you are thirsty."

4   Nwibe was a man of high standing in Ogbu and was rising higher; a man of wealth and integrity. He had just given notice to all the ozo men of the town that he proposed to seek admission into their honored hierarchy in the coming initiation season.

5   "Your proposal is excellent," said the men of title.

6   "When we see we shall believe." Which was their dignified way of telling you to think it over once again and make sure

you have the means to go through with it. For ozo is not a child's naming ceremony; and where is the man to hide his face who begins the ozo dance and then is foot-stuck to the arena? But in this instance the caution of the elders was no more than a formality for Nwibe was such a sensible man that no one could think of him beginning something he was not sure to finish.

7   On that Eke day Nwibe had risen early so as to visit his farm beyond the stream and do some light work before going to the market at midday to drink a horn or two of palm-wine with his peers and perhaps buy that bundle of roofing thatch for the repair of his wives' huts. As for his own hut he had a couple of years back settled it finally by changing his thatch roof to zinc. Sooner or later he would do the same for his wives. He could have done Mgboye's hut right away but decided to wait until he could do the two together, or else Udenkwo would set the entire compound on fire. Udenkwo was the junior wife, by three years, but she never let that worry her. Happily Mgboye was a woman of peace who rarely demanded the respect due to her from the other. She would suffer Udenkwo's provoking tongue sometimes for a whole day without offering a word in reply. And when she did reply at all her words were always few and her voice very low.

8   That very morning Udenkwo had accused her of spite and all kinds of wickedness on account of a little dog.

9   "What has a little dog done to you?" she screamed loud enough for half the village to hear. "I ask you, Mgboye, what is the offense of a puppy this early in the day?"

10   "What your puppy did this early in the day," replied Mgboye, "is that he put his shit-mouth into my soup-pot."

11   "And then?"

12   "And then I smacked him."

13   "You smacked him! Why don't you cover your soup-pot? Is it easier to hit a dog than cover a pot? Is a small puppy to have more sense than a woman who leaves her soup-pot about...?"

14   "Enough from you, Udenkwo."

15   "It is not enough, Mgboye, it is not enough. If that dog owes you any debt I want to know. Everything I have, even a little dog I bought to eat my infant's excrement keeps you awake at nights. You are a bad woman, Mgboye, you are a very bad woman!"

16   Nwibe had listened to all of this in silence in his hut. He knew from the vigor in Udenkwo's voice that she could go on like this till market-time. So he intervened, in his characteristic manner by calling out to his senior wife.

17   "Mgboye! Let me have peace this early morning!"

18   "Don't you hear all the abuses Udenkwo..."

19   "I hear nothing at all from Udenkwo and I want peace in my compound. If Udenkwo is crazy must everybody else go crazy with her? Is one crazy woman not enough in my compound so early in the day?"

20   "The great judge has spoken," sang Udenkwo in a sneering sing-song. "Thank you, great judge. Udenkwo is mad. Udenkwo is always mad, but those of you who are sane let..."

21   "Shut your mouth, shameless woman, or a wild beast will lick your eyes for you this morning. When will you learn to keep your badness within this compound instead of shouting it to all Ogbu to hear? I say shut your mouth!"

22   There was silence then except for Udenkwo's infant whose yelling had up till then been swallowed up by the larger noise of the adults.

23   "Don't cry, my father," said Udenkwo to him. "They want to kill your dog, but our people say the man who decides to chase after a chicken, for him is the fall..."

24   By the middle of the morning Nwibe had done all the work he had to do on his farm and was on his way again to prepare for market. At the little stream he decided as he always did to wash off the sweat of work. So he put his cloth on a huge boulder by the men's bathing section and waded in. There was nobody else around because of the time of day and because it was market day. But from instinctive modesty he turned to face the forest away from the approaches.

25   The madman watched him for quite a while. Each time he bent down to carry water in cupped hands from the shallow stream to his head and body the madman smiled at his parted behind. And then remembered. This was the same hefty man who brought three others like him and whipped me out of my hut in the Afo market. He nodded to himself. And he remembered again: this was the same vagabond who descended on me from the lorry in the middle of my highway. He nodded once more. And then he remembered yet again: this was the same fellow who set his children to throw stones at me and make remarks about their mothers' buttocks, not mine. Then he laughed.

26   Nwibe turned sharply round and saw the naked man laughing, the deep grove of the stream amplifying his laughter. Then he stopped as suddenly as he had begun; the merriment vanished from his face.

27   "I have caught you naked," he said.

28   Nwibe ran a hand swiftly down his face to clear his eyes of water.

29   "I say I have caught you naked, with your thing dangling about."

30   "I can see you are hungry for a whipping," said Nwibe with quiet menace in his voice, for a madman is said to be easily scared

away by the very mention of a whip. "Wait till I get up there.... What are you doing? Drop it at once...I say drop it!"

31   The madman had picked up Nwibe's cloth and wrapped it round his own waist. He looked down at himself and began to laugh again.

32   "I will kill you," screamed Nwibe as he splashed toward the bank, maddened by anger. "I will whip that madness out of you today!"

33   They ran all the way up the steep and rocky footpath hedged in by the shadowy green forest. A mist gathered and hung over Nwibe's vision as he ran, stumbled, fell, pulled himself up again and stumbled on, shouting and cursing. The other, despite his unaccustomed encumbrance steadily increased his lead, for he was spare and wiry, a thing made for speed. Furthermore, he did not waste his breath shouting and cursing; he just ran. Two girls going down to the stream saw a man running up the slope towards them pursued by a stark-naked madman. They threw down their pots and fled, screaming.

34   When Nwibe emerged into the full glare of the highway he could not see his cloth clearly any more and his chest was on the point of exploding from the fire and torment within. But he kept running. He was only vaguely aware of crowds of people on all sides and he appealed to them tearfully without stopping: "Hold the madman, he's got my cloth!" By this time the man with the cloth was practically lost among the much denser crowds far in front so that the link between him and the naked man was no longer clear.

35   Now Nwibe continually bumped against people's backs and then laid flat a frail old man struggling with a stubborn goat on a leash. "Stop the madman," he shouted hoarsely, his heart tearing to shreds, "he's got my cloth!" Everyone looked at him first in surprise and then less surprise because strange sights are common in a great market. Some of them even laughed.

36   "They've got his cloth he says."

37   "That's a new one I'm sure. He hardly looks mad yet. Doesn't he have people, I wonder."

38   "People are so careless these days. Why can't they keep proper watch over their sick relation, especially on the day of the market?"

39   Farther up the road on the very brink of the market-place two men from Nwibe's village recognized him and, throwing down the one his long basket of yams, the other his calabash of palm-wine held on a loop, gave desperate chase, to stop him setting foot irrevocably within the occult territory of the powers of the market. But it was in vain. When finally they caught him it was well inside the crowded square. Udenkwo in tears tore off her top-cloth which

they draped on him and led him home by the hand. He spoke just once about a madman who took his cloth in the stream.

40   "It is all right," said one of the men in the tone of a father to a crying child. They led and he followed blindly, his heavy chest heaving up and down in silent weeping. Many more people from his village, a few of his in-laws and one or two others from his mother's place had joined the grief-stricken party. One man whispered to another that it was the worst kind of madness, deep and tongue-tied.

41   "May it end ill for him who did this," prayed the other.

42   The first medicine-man his relatives consulted refused to take him on, out of some kind of integrity.

43   "I could say yes to you and take your money," he said. "But that is not my way. My powers of cure are known throughout Olu and Igbo but never have I professed to bring back to life a man who has sipped the spirit-waters of ani-mmo. It is the same with a madman who of his own accord delivers himself to the divinities of the market-place. You should have kept better watch over him."

44   "Don't blame us too much," said Nwibe's relative. "When he left home that morning his senses were as complete as yours and mine now. Don't blame us too much."

45   "Yes, I know. It happens that way sometimes. And they are the ones that medicine will not reach. I know."

46   "Can you do nothing at all then, not even to untie his tongue?"

47   "Nothing can be done. They have already embraced him. It is like a man who runs away from the oppression of his fellows to the grove of an alusi and says to him: Take me, oh spirit, I am your osu. No man can touch him thereafter. He is free and yet no power can break his bondage. He is free of men but bonded to a god."

48   The second doctor was not as famous as the first and not so strict. He said the case was bad, very bad indeed, but no one folds his arms because the condition of his child is beyond hope. He must still grope around and do his best. His hearers nodded in eager agreement. And then he muttered into his own inward ear: If doctors were to send away every patient whose cure they were uncertain of, how many of them would eat one meal in a whole week from their practice?

49   Nwibe was cured of his madness. That humble practitioner who did the miracle became overnight the most celebrated mad-doctor of his generation. They called him Sojourner to the Land of the Spirits. Even so it remains true that madness may indeed sometimes depart but never with all his clamorous train. Some of these always remain—the trailers of madness you might call them—to haunt the doorway of the eyes. For how could a man be the same again of whom witnesses from all the lands of Olu and

Igbo have once reported that they saw today a fine, hefty man in his prime, stark naked, tearing through the crowds to answer the call of the market-place? Such a man is marked forever.

50   Nwibe became a quiet, withdrawn man avoiding whenever he could the boisterous side of the life of his people. Two years later, before another initiation season, he made a new inquiry about joining the community of titled men in his town. Had they received him perhaps he might have become at least partially restored, but those ozo men, dignified and polite as ever, deftly steered the conversation away to other matters.

● ●

THE MADMAN

Journal

1. MLA Works Cited   *Using this model, record this story here.*

Author's Last Name, First Name. "Title of the Story." *Title of the Book*. 3rd ed. Ed.

First Name Last Name. City: Publisher, year. Page number(s) of this story. Print.

2. Main Character(s)   *Describe each main character, and explain why you think each is a main character.*

3. Supporting Characters   *Describe each supporting character, and explain why you think each is a supporting character.*

4. Setting and Props   *Describe the setting(s) and all relevant prop(s).*

5. Sequence   *Outline the events of the story in order.*

6. Plot   *Tell the story in no more than two sentences.*

7. Conflicts   *Identify and explain all of the conflicts involved here.*

8. Significant Quotations   *Explain the importance of each quotation completely. Record the page number in the parentheses.*

a. "He used to walk in the middle of the road, holding it in conversation. But one day the driver of a mammy-wagon and his mate came down on him shouting, pushing and slapping his face" (   ).

b. "Nwibe was a man of high standing in Ogbu and was rising higher; a man of wealth and integrity" (   ).

c. "And he remembered again: this was the same vagabond who descended on me from the lorry in the middle of my highway" ( ).

d. "Two girls going down to the stream saw a man running up the slope towards them pursued by a stark-naked madman" ( ).

e. "Even so it remains true that madness may indeed sometimes depart but never with all his clamorous train" ( ).

9. **Literary Elements**   *Look at this chapter's title and explain why you think this story is placed in this chapter. Explain in which other chapter(s) you might place this story, as relevant to the literary element(s) of the chapter(s).*

10. **Foreshadowing, Irony, and/or Symbols**   *Explain examples of foreshadowing, irony, and/or symbols in this story.*

FOLLOW-UP QUESTIONS

10 SHORT QUESTIONS

What is the <u>best</u> answer for each?

____ 1. The madman is probably
     a. a merchant.
     b. a doctor.
     c. a leader.

____ 2. The madman is probably
     a. a social person.
     b. a loner.
     c. a leader.

____ 3. At the beginning, the madman wears
     a. fine clothing.
     b. old clothing.
     c. no clothing.

____ 4. The madman is
     a. loved.
     b. admired.
     c. scorned.

____ 5. Nwibe is probably
     a. a merchant.
     b. a doctor.
     c. a loner.

____ 6. Nwibe is probably
     a. a loner.
     b. a social person.
     c. a single man.

____ 7. The madman
     a. blames Nwibe for his problems.
     b. does not see Nwibe.
     c. is related to Nwibe.

____ 8. The madman
     a. steals Nwibe's clothes.
     b. gives his clothes to Nwibe.
     c. leaves the clothes alone.

____ 9. Nwibe
     a. does not pursue the madman.
     b. appears in the marketplace nude.
     c. does not go to the marketplace.

____ 10. Nwibe
     a. is cared for by a sincere doctor.
     b. is cared for by an insincere doctor.
     c. is accepted into the society.

5 SIGNIFICANT QUOTATIONS

What is the importance of each of these quotations?

1. "He had got himself this cudgel lately to deal with little beasts on the way who threw stones at him and made fun of their mother's nakedness, not his own."

2. "He had just given notice to all the ozo men of the town that he proposed to seek admission into their honored hierarchy in the coming initiation season."

3. "The madman had picked up Nwibe's cloth and wrapped it around his own waist."

4. "When finally they caught him it was well inside the crowded square
   […]. He spoke just once about a madman who took his cloth in the
   stream."

5. "Two years later, before another initiation season, he made a new inquiry
   about joining the community of titled men in his town."

2 Comprehension Essay Questions

*Use specific details and information from the story to answer these questions as
completely as possible.*

1. What is ironic in this story? Use specific details and information from the
   story to support your answer.

2. How is the title relevant to the story? Use specific details and information
   from the story to support your answer.

Discussion Questions

Be prepared to discuss these questions in class.

1. What seem to be magical or supernatural elements here?

2. What actions foreshadow the events to come?

Writing

Use each of these ideas for writing an essay.

1. We have all been frustrated in being misunderstood by others. Discuss
   a time—humorous or serious—that you or someone you know has been
   misunderstood.

2. Much of life is a matter of perception or how we see things. Tell of a time
   that you or someone you know has perceived something or someone to
   appear different than it or s/he really is.

Further Writing

1. Compare the characters and events in this story to those in Leo Tolstoy's
   "God Sees the Truth, but Waits" (page 337).

2. Research "psychosis" and "neurosis." Discuss these terms as they relate
   to the madman and Nwibe.

SWEAT

Zora Neale Hurston

Pre-reading Vocabulary
Context

Use context clues to define these words before reading. Use a dictionary as needed.

1. Bill *soiled* his hands when he was digging in the garden and moving dirt around. *Soiled* means _____.

2. Rudy hitched up the horse, put his vegetables in the *buckboard*, and drove it to town. *Buckboard* means _____.

3. Sender used a chair and a long leather *whip* to train the tigers. *Whip* means _____.

4. Sam *truculently* denied the charges, loudly claiming he was innocent. *Truculently* means _____.

5. The wind blew the leaves *helter-skelter*, and it took hours to rake them up. *Helter-skelter* means _____.

6. Liz found, much to her *dismay*, that the jacket she planned to save money on was no longer on sale. *Dismay* means

    _____.

7. Jacob grew into a strong, *strapping* young man who lettered in football and track. *Strapping* means _____.

8. Akim loved eating and sat down at the dinner table prepared to eat his *vittles*. *Vittles* means _____.

9. The bunny backed up into the protective woods, *cowed* by the large dog's barking. *Cowed* means _____.

10. After the windstorm, Tricia cleared all the broken twigs, leaves, and *debris* that the storm had brought down. *Debris* means _____.

11. Farmers *sow* seeds and *reap* what grows. *Sow* means

_____, and *reap* means _____.

12. Andrew was completely *indifferent* and did not care one way

or the other if he went to the party. *Indifferent* means

_____.

13. Allison *abominates* washing dishes and always refuses to wash them.

Abominate means _____.

14. Josette was in a *fury* when the tax assessor overrated her home by

a hundred percent. *Fury* means _____.

15. Much to Edmund's *amazement*, his son surprised him with a totally

unexpected party. *Amazement* means _____.

16. The escaped tarantula struck *horror* and *terror* into Chris' heart when

he found the spider under the chair. *Horror* means _____

and *terror* means _____.

17. Zach *crouched* under the stairs so his friends would not find him

and he could surprise them. *Crouch* means _____.

18. Matt is such a good *ventriloquist* that he can make it seem like his dog

is talking even though Matt's lips don't move. *Ventriloquist* means

_____.

19. Edgar was so nervous when she won the award that he spoke

gibberish, and no one could understand him. *Gibberish* means

_____.

20. When the fire flared up, the firemen came with water and

extinguished the fire. *Extinguish* means _____.

Pre-reading Vocabulary
Structural Attack

Define these words by solving the parts. Use the Glossary or a dictionary as needed.

1. washwoman
2. mournful
3. washbench
4. scornfully
5. habitual
6. knuckly
7. numerous
8. penniless
9. knotty

10. earthworks
11. biggety
12. swellest
13. work-worn
14. friendliness
15. bloodier
16. underfoot
17. maddened

Pre-reading Questions

Try answering these questions as you read.

What is Delia like?

What is Sykes like?

What does Sykes do?

What is ironic in the story?

SWEAT

ZORA NEALE HURSTON

Zora Neale Hurston was born in 1901 in Eatonville, Florida, the first town in America incorporated by African Americans. Although her mother died when Hurston was young and she was shifted from relative to relative, Hurston enjoyed a childhood relatively free of the discrimination found elsewhere. Marked by creativity and determination throughout her life, she managed to secure scholarships at the Morgan Academy, Howard University, and Barnard College, where she studied under Franz Boaz, the renowned anthropologist. Securing support from the same patron who supported Langston Hughes, Hurston returned to Eatonville to study its stories, melodies, and folkways. She thoroughly believed that the African American experience was both unique and positive, and the small town ways and speech of Eatonville fairly sing through her writing. Her female characters, especially, emerge as intelligent, thoughtful, resourceful, and surviving. However, she was heavily criticized for presenting too much of the positive and too little of the anger in the African American experience, although today many consider her a forerunner in African American self-recognition. A part of the Harlem Renaissance in the 1920s and a thoughtful writer in the 1930s, she was devoted to recreating the Eatonville experience—a devotion that continued throughout her writing. *Their Eyes Were Watching God* is her master work. Hurston died in 1960 in Saint Lucie, Florida, of continuing gastrointestinal problems.

It was eleven o'clock of a Spring night in Florida. It was Sunday. Any other night, Delia Jones would have been in bed for two hours by this time. But she was a washwoman, and Monday morning meant a great deal to her. So she collected the soiled clothes on Saturday when she returned the clean things. Sunday night after church, she sorted them and put the white things to soak. It saved her almost a half day's start. A great hamper in the bedroom held the clothes that she brought home. It was so much neater than a number of bundles lying around.

2   She squatted on the kitchen floor beside the great pile of clothes, sorting them into small heaps according to color, and humming a song in a mournful key, but wondering through it all where Sykes, her husband, had gone with her horse and buckboard.

3   Just then something long, round, limp, and black fell upon her shoulders and slithered to the floor beside her. A great terror took hold of her. It softened her knees and dried her mouth so that it was a full minute before she could cry out or move. Then she saw that it was the big bull whip her husband liked to carry when he drove.

4   She lifted her eyes to the door and saw him standing there bent over with laughter at her fright. She screamed at him.

5   "Sykes, what you throw dat whip on me like dat? You know it would skeer me—looks just like a snake, an' you knows how skeered Ah is of snakes."

6   "Course Ah knowed it! That's how come Ah done it." He slapped his leg with his hand and almost rolled on the ground in his mirth. "If you such a big fool dat you got to have a fit over a earth worm or a string, Ah don't keer how bad Ah skeer you."

7   "You aint got no business doing it. Gawd knows it's a sin. Some day Ah'm gointuh drop dead from some of yo' foolishness. 'Nother thing, where you been wid mah rig? Ah feeds dat pony. He aint fuh you to be drivin' wid no bull whip."

8   "Yo sho is one aggravatin' n——woman!" he declared and stepped into the room. She resumed her work and did not answer him at once. "Ah done tole you time and again to keep them white folks' clothes outa dis house."

9   He picked up the whip and glared down at her. Delia went on with her work. She went out into the yard and returned with a galvanized tub and set it on the washbench. She saw that Sykes had kicked all of the clothes together again, and now stood in her way truculently, his whole manner hoping, praying, for an argument. But she walked calmly around him and commenced to re-sort the things.

10   "Next time, Ah'm gointer to kick 'em outdoors," he threatened as he struck a match along the leg of his corduroy breeches.

11   Delia never looked up from her work, and her thin, stooped shoulders sagged further.

12   "Ah aint for no fuss t'night Sykes. Ah just come from taking sacrament at the church house."

13   He snorted scornfully. "Yeah, you just come from de church house on a Sunday night, but heah you is gone to work on them clothes. You aint nothing but a hypocrite. One of them amen-corner Christians—sing, whoop, shout, then come home and wash white folks clothes on the Sabbath."

14   He stepped roughly upon the whitest pile of things, kicking them helter-skelter as he crossed the room. His wife gave a little scream of dismay, and quickly gathered them together again.

15   "Sykes, you quit grindin' dirt into these clothes! How can Ah git through by Sat'day if Ah don't start on Sunday?"

16   "Ah don't keer if you never git through. Anyhow, Ah done promised Gawd and a couple of other men, Ah aint gointer have it in mah house. Don't gimme no lip neither, else Ah'll throw 'em out and put mah fist up side yo' head to boot."

17   Delia's habitual meekness seemed to slip from her shoulders like a blown scarf. She was on her feet; her poor little body, her bare knuckly hands bravely defying the strapping hulk before her.

18   "Looka heah, Sykes, you done gone too fur. Ah been married to you fur fifteen years, and Ah been takin' in washin' for fifteen years. Sweat, sweat, sweat! Work and sweat, cry and sweat, pray and sweat!"

19   "What's that go to do with me?" he asked brutally.

20   "What's it got to do with you, Sykes? Mah tub of suds is filled yo' belly with vittles more times than yo' hands is filled it. Mah sweat is done paid for this house and Ah reckon Ah kin keep on sweatin' in it."

21   She seized the iron skillet from the stove and struck a defensive pose, which act surprised him greatly, coming from her. It cowed him and he did not strike her as he usually did.

22   "Naw you won't," she panted, "that ole snaggle-toothed black woman you runnin' with aint comin' heah to pile up on *mah* sweat and blood. You aint paid for nothin' on this place, and Ah'm gointer stay right heah till Ah'm toted out foot foremost."

23   "Well, you better quit gittin' me riled up, else they'll be totin' you out sooner than you expect. Ah'm so tired of you Ah don't know whut to do. Gawd! how Ah hates skinny wimmen!"

24   A little awed by this new Delia, he sidled out of the door and slammed the back gate after him. He did not say where he had gone, but she knew too well. She knew very well that he would not return until nearly daybreak also. Her work over, she went on to bed but not to sleep at once. Things had come to a pretty pass!

25   She lay awake, gazing upon the debris that cluttered their matrimonial trail. Not an image left standing along the way. Anything like flowers had long ago been drowned in the salty stream that had been pressed from her heart. Her tears, her sweat, her blood. She had brought love to the union and he had brought a longing for the flesh. Two months after the wedding, he had given her the first brutal beating. She had the memory of numerous trips to Orlando with all of his wages when he had returned to her penniless, even before the first year had passed. She was young and soft then, but now she thought of her knotty, muscled limbs, her harsh knuckly hands, and drew herself up into an unhappy little ball in the middle of the big feather bed. Too late now to hope for love, even if it were not Bertha it would be someone else. This case differed from the others only in that she was bolder than the others. Too late for everything except her little home. She had built it for her old days, and planted one by one the trees and flowers there. It was lovely to her, lovely.

26   Somehow before sleep came, she found herself saying aloud: "Oh well, whatever goes over the Devil's back, is got to come under his belly. Sometime or ruther, Sykes, like everybody else, is gointer reap his sowing." After that she was able to build a spiritual earthworks against her husband. His shells could no longer reach her. *Amen*. She went to sleep and slept until he announced his presence in bed by kicking her feet and rudely snatching the cover away.

27   "Gimme some kivah heah, an' git yo' damn foots over on yo' own side! Ah oughter mash you in yo' mouf fuh drawing dat skillet on me."

28   Delia went clear to the rail without answering him. A triumphant indifference to all that he was or did.

29   The week was as full of work for Delia as all other weeks, and Saturday found her behind her little pony, collecting and delivering clothes.

30   It was a hot, hot day near the end of July. The village men on Joe Clarke's porch even chewed cane listlessly. They did not hurl the cane-knots as usual. They let them dribble over the edge of the porch. Even conversation had collapsed under the heat.

31   "Heah comes Delia Jones," Jim Merchant said, as the shaggy pony came 'round the bend of the road toward them. The rusty buckboard was heaped with baskets of crisp, clean laundry.

32   "Yep," Joe Lindsay agreed. "Hot or col', rain or shine, jes ez reg'lar ez de weeks roll roun' Delia carries 'em an' fetches 'em on Sat'day."

33   "She better if she wanter eat," said Moss. "Syke Jones aint wuth de shot an' powder hit would tek tuh kill 'em. Not to *bub* he aint."

34   "He sho' aint," Walter Thomas chimed in. "It's too bad, too, cause she wuz a right pritty lil trick when he got huh. Ah'd uh mah'ied huh mahseff if he hadnter beat me to it."

35   Delia nodded briefly at the men as she drove past.

36   "Too much knockin' will ruin *any* 'oman. He done beat huh 'nough tuh kill three women, let 'lone change they looks," said Elijah Mosely. "How Syke kin stommuck dat big black greasy Mogul he's layin' roun' wid, gits me. Ah swear dat eight-rock couldn't kiss a sardine can Ah done thowed out de back do' 'way las' yeah."

37   "Aw, she's fat, thass how come. He's allus been crazy 'bout fat women," put in Merchant. "He'd a' been tied up wid one long time ago if he could a' found one tuh have him. Did Ah tell yuh 'bout him come sidlin' roun' *mah* wife—bringin' her a basket uh pee-cans outa his yard fuh a present? Yes-sir, mah wife! She tol' him tuh take 'em right straight back home, cause Delia works so hard ovah dat washtub she reckon everything en de place taste lak sweat an' soapsuds. Ah jus'wisht Ah'd a' caught 'im 'roun' dere! Ah'd a' made his hips ketch on fiah down dat shell road."

38   "Ah know he done it, too. Ah sees 'im grinnin' at every 'oman dat passes," Walter Thomas said. "But even so, he useter eat some mighty big hunks uh humble pie tuh git dat lil' 'oman he got. She wuz *ez pritty* ez a speckled pup! Dat wuz fifteen yeahs ago. He useter be so skeered uh losin' huh, she could make him do some parts of a husband's duty. Dey never wuz de same in de mind."

39   "There oughter be a law about him," said Lindsay. "He aint fit tuh carry guts tuh a bear."

40   Clarke spoke for the first time. "Taint no law on earth dat kin make a man be decent if it aint in 'im. There's plenty men dat takes a wife lak dey do a joint uh sugar-cane. It's round, juicy an' sweet when dey gits it. But dey squeeze an' grind, squeeze an' grind an' wring tell dey wring every drop uh pleasure dat's in 'em out. When dey's satisfied dat dey is wrung dry, dey treats 'em jes lak dey do a cane-chew. Dey thows 'em away. Dey knows whut dey is doin' while dey is at it, an' hates theirselves fuh it but they keeps on hangin' after huh tell she's empty. Den dey hates huh fuh bein' a cane-chew an' in de way."

41   "We oughter take Syke an' dat stray 'oman uh his'n down in Lake Howell swamp an' lay on de rawhide till they cain't say 'Lawd a' mussy.' He allus wuz uh ovahbearin' n——, but since dat white 'oman from up north done teached 'im how to run a automobile, he done got too biggety to live—an' we oughter kill 'im," Old Man Anderson advised.

42   A grunt of approval went around the porch. But the heat was melting their civic virtue and Elijah Moseley began to bait Joe Clarke.

43   "Come on, Joe, git a melon outa dere an' slice it up for yo' customers. We'se all sufferin' wid de heat. De bear's done got *me!*"

44   "Thass right, Joe, a watermelon is jes' whut Ah needs tuh cure de eppizudicks," Walter Thomas joined forces with Moseley. "Come on dere, Joe. We all is steady customers an' you aint set us up in a long time. Ah chooses dat long, bowlegged Floridy favorite."

45   "A god, an' be dough. You all gimme twenty cents and slice away," Clarke retorted. "Ah needs a col' slice m'self. Heah, everybody chip in. Ah'll lend y'll mah meat knife."

46   The money was quickly subscribed and the huge melon brought forth. At that moment, Sykes and Bertha arrived. A determined silence fell on the porch and the melon was put away again.

47   Merchant snapped down the blade of his jackknife and moved toward the store door.

48   "Come on in, Joe, an' gimme a slab uh sow belly an' uh pound uh coffee—almost fuhgot 'twas Sat'day. Got to git on home." Most of the men left also.

49   Just then Delia drove past on her way home, as Sykes was ordering magnificently for Bertha. It pleased him for Delia to see.

50   "Git whutsoever yo' heart desires, Honey. Wait a minute, Joe. Give huh two bottles uh strawberry soda-water, uh quart uh parched groundpeas, an' a block uh chewin' gum."

51   With all this they left the store, with Sykes reminding Bertha that this was his town and she could have it if she wanted it.

52   The men returned soon after they left, and held their watermelon feast. "Where did Syke Jones git dat 'oman from nohow?" Lindsay asked.

53   "Ovah Apopka. Guess dey musta been cleanin' out de town when she lef'. She don't look lak a thing but a hunk uh liver wid hair on it."

54   "Well, she sho' kin squall," Dave Carter contributed. "When she gits ready tuh laff, she jes' opens huh mouf an' latches it back tuh de las' notch. No ole grandpa alligator down in Lake Bell aint got nothin' on huh."

55   Bertha had been in town three months now. Sykes was still paying her room rent at Della Lewis'—the only house in town that would have taken her in. Sykes took her frequently to Winter Park to "stomps." He still assured her that he was the swellest man in the state.

56   "Sho! you kin have dat lil' ole house soon's Ah kin git dat 'oman outa dere. Everything b'longs tuh me an' you sho' kin have it. Ah sho' 'bominates uh skinny 'oman. Lawdy, you sho' is got one portly shape on you! You kin git *anything* you wants. Dis is *mah* town an' you sho' kin have it."

57   Delia's work-worn knees crawled over the earth in Gethsemane and on the rocks of Calvary many, many times during these months. She avoided the villagers and meeting places in her efforts to be blind and deaf. But Bertha nullified this to a degree, by coming to Delia's house to call Sykes out to her at the gate.

58   Delia and Sykes fought all the time now with no peaceful interludes. They slept and ate in silence. Two or three times Delia had attempted a timid friendliness, but she was repulsed each time. It was plain that the breaches must remain agape.

59   The sun had burned July to August. The heat streamed down like a million hot arrows, smiting all things living upon the earth. Grass withered, leaves browned, snakes went blind in shedding and men and dogs went mad. Dog days!

60   Delia came home one day and found Sykes there before her. She wondered, but started to go on into the house without speaking, even though he was standing in the kitchen door and she must either stoop under his arm or ask him to move. He made no room for her. She noticed a soap box beside the steps, but paid no particular attention to it, knowing that he must have brought it there. As she was stooping to pass under his outstretched arm, he suddenly pushed her backward, laughingly.

61   "Look in de box dere Delia, Ah done brung yuh somethin'!"

62   She nearly fell upon the box in her stumbling, and when she saw what it held, she all but fainted outright.

63   "Syke! Syke, mah Gawd! You take dat rattlesnake 'way from heah! You *gottuh*. Oh, Jesus, have mussy!"

64   "Ah aint gut tuh do nuthin' uh de kin'—fact is Ah aint got tuh do nothin' but die. Taint no use uh you puttin' on airs makin' out lak you skeered uh dat snake—he's gointer stay right heah tell he die. He wouldn't bite me cause Ah knows how tuh handle 'im. Nohow he wouldn't risk breakin' out his fangs 'gin yo' skinny laigs."

65   "Naw, now Syke, don't keep dat thing 'roun' heah tuh skeer me tuh death. You knows Ah'm even feared uh earth worms. Thass de biggest snake Ah evah did see. Kill 'im Syke, please."

66   "Doan ast me tuh do nothin' fuh yuh. Goin' 'roun' tryin' to be so damn asterperious. Naw, Ah aint gonna kill it. Ah think uh damn sight mo' uh him dan you! Dat's a nice snake an' anybody doan lak 'im kin jes' hit de grit."

67   The village soon heard that Sykes had the snake, and came to see and ask questions.

68   "How de hen-fire did you ketch dat six-foot rattler, Syke?" Thomas asked.

69   "He's full uh frogs so he caint hardly move, thass how Ah eased up on 'm. But Ah'm a snake charmer an' knows how tuh handle 'em. Shux, dat aint nothin'. Ah could ketch one eve'y day if Ah so wanted tuh."

70   "Whut he needs is a heavy hick'ry club leaned real heavy on his head. Dat's de bes' way tuh charm a rattlesnake."

71   "Naw, Walt, y'll jes' don't understand dese diamon' backs lak Ah do," said Sykes in a superior tone of voice.

72   The village agreed with Walter, but the snake stayed on. His box remained by the kitchen door with its screen wire covering. Two or three days later it had digested its meal of frogs and literally came to life. It rattled at every movement in the kitchen or the yard. One day as Delia came down the kitchen steps she saw his chalky-white fangs curved like scimitars hung in the wire meshes. This time she did not run away with averted eyes as usual. She stood for a long time in the doorway in a red fury that grew bloodier for every second that she regarded the creature that was her torment.

73   That night she broached the subject as soon as Sykes sat down to the table.

74   "Syke, Ah wants you tuh take dat snake 'way fum heah. You done starved me an' Ah put up widcher, you done beat me an Ah took dat, but you done kilt all mah insides bringin' dat varmint heah."

75   Sykes poured out a saucer full of coffee and drank it deliberately before he answered her.

76   "A whole lot Ah keer 'bout how you feels inside uh out. Dat snake aint goin' no damn wheah till Ah gits ready fuh 'im tuh go. So fur as beatin' is concerned, yuh aint took near all dat you gointer take ef yuh stay 'roun' *me*."

77   Delia pushed back her plate and got up from the table, "Ah hates you, Sykes," she said calmly. "Ah hates you tuh de same degree dat Ah useter love yuh. Ah done took an' took till mah belly is full up tuh mah neck. Dat's de reason Ah got mah letter fum de church an' moved mah membership tuh Woodbridge— so Ah don't haftuh take no sacrament wid yuh. Ah don't wantuh see yuh, 'roun' me atall. Lay 'roun' wid dat 'oman all yuh wants tuh, but gwan 'way fum me an' mah house. Ah hates yuh lak uh suck-egg dog."

78   Sykes almost let the huge wad of corn bread and collard greens he was chewing fall out of his mouth in amazement. He had a hard time whipping himself to the proper fury to try to answer Delia.

79   "Well, Ah'm glad you does hate me. Ah'm sho' tiahed uh you hangin' ontuh me. Ah don't want yuh. Look at yuh stringey ole neck! Yo' raw-bony laigs an' arms is enough tuh cut uh man tuh death. You looks jes' lak de devvul's doll-baby tuh *me*. You cain't hate me no worse dan Ah hates you. Ah been hatin' *you* fuh years."

80   "Yo' ole black hide don't look lak nothin' tuh me, but uh passle uh wrinkled up rubber, wid yo' big ole yeahs flappin' on

each side lak up paih uh buzzard wings. Don't think Ah'm gointuh be run 'way fum mah house neither. Ah'm goin' tuh de white folks about *you*, mah young man, de very nex' time you lay yo' han's on me. Mah cup is done run ovah." Delia said this with no signs of fear and Sykes departed from the house, threatening her, but made not the slightest move to carry out any of them.

81　　That night he did not return at all, and the next day being Sunday, Delia was glad that she did not have to quarrel before she hitched up her pony and drove the four miles to Woodbridge.

82　　She stayed to the night service—"love feast"—which was very warm and full of spirit. In the emotional winds her domestic trials were borne far and wide so that she sang as she drove homeward,

83　　　　　　*"Jurden water, black an' col'*
84　　　　　　*Chills de body, not de soul*
85　　　　　　*An' Ah wantah cross Jurden in uh calm time."*

86　　She came from the barn to the kitchen door and stopped.

87　　"Whut's de mattah, ol' satan, you aint kickin' up yo' racket?" She addressed the snake's box. Complete silence. She went on into the house with a new hope in its birth struggles. Perhaps her threat to go to the white folks had frightened Sykes! Perhaps he was sorry! Fifteen years of misery and suppression had brought Delia to the place where she would hope *anything* that looked towards a way over or through her wall of inhibitions.

88　　She felt in the match safe behind the stove at once for a match. There was only one there.

89　　"Dat n—— wouldn't fetch nothin heah tuh save his rotten neck, but he kin run thew whut Ah brings quick enough. Now he done toted off nigh on tuh haff uh box uh matches. He done had dat 'oman heah in mah house, too."

90　　Nobody but a woman could tell how she knew this even before she struck the match. But she did and it put her into a new fury.

91　　Presently she brought in the tubs to put the white things to soak. This time she decided she need not bring the hamper out of the bedroom; she would go in there and do the sorting. She picked up the pot-bellied lamp and went in. The room was small and the hamper stood hard by the foot of the white iron bed. She could sit and reach through the bedposts—resting as she worked.

92　　"Ah wantah cross Jurden in uh calm time." She was singing again. The mood of the "love feast" had returned. She threw back the lid of the basket almost gaily. Then, moved by both horror and terror, she sprang back toward the door. *There lay the snake in the basket!* He moved sluggishly at first, but even as she turned round and round, jumped up and down in an insanity of fear, he began to stir vigorously. She saw him pouring his awful beauty from the basket upon the bed, then she seized the lamp and ran as fast as she could to the kitchen. The wind from the open door blew out the light and the darkness added to her terror. She sped to the darkness of the yard, slamming the door after her before she thought to set down the lamp. She did not feel safe even on the ground, so she climbed up in the hay barn.

93   There for an hour or more she lay sprawled upon the hay a gibbering wreck.

94   Finally she grew quiet, and after that, coherent thought. With this, stalked through her a cold, bloody rage. Hours of this. A period of introspection, a space of retrospection, then a mixture of both. Out of this an awful calm.

95   "Well, Ah done de bes' Ah could. If things aint right, Gawd knows taint mah fault."

96   She went to sleep—a twitchy sleep—and woke up to a faint gray sky. There was a loud hollow sound below. She peered out. Sykes was at the wood-pile, demolishing a wire-covered box.

97   He hurried to the kitchen door, but hung outside there some minutes before he entered, and stood some minutes more inside before he closed it after him.

98   The gray in the sky was spreading. Delia descended without fear now, and crouched beneath the low bedroom window. The drawn shade shut out the dawn, shut in the night. But the thin walls held back no sound.

99   "Dat ol' scratch is woke up now!" She mused at the tremendous whirr inside, which every woodsman knows, is one of the sound illusions. The rattler is a ventriloquist. His whirr sounds to the right, to the left, straight ahead, behind, close under foot—everywhere but where it is. Woe to him who guesses wrong unless he is prepared to hold up his end of the argument! Sometimes he strikes without rattling at all.

100   Inside, Sykes heard nothing until he knocked a pot lid off the stove while trying to reach the match safe in the dark. He had emptied his pockets at Bertha's.

101   The snake seemed to wake up under the stove and Sykes made a quick leap into the bedroom. In spite of the gin he had had, his head was clearing now.

102   "Mah Gawd!" he chattered, "ef Ah could on'y strack uh light!"

103   The rattling ceased for a moment as he stood paralyzed. He waited. It seemed that the snake waited also.

104   "Oh, fuh de light! Ah thought he'd be too sick"—Sykes was muttering to himself when the whirr began again, closer, right underfoot this time. Long before this, Sykes' ability to think had been flattened down to primitive instinct and he leaped—onto the bed.

105   Outside Delia heard a cry that might have come from a maddened chimpanzee, a stricken gorilla. All the terror, all the horror, all the rage that man possibly could express, without a recognizable human sound.

106   A tremendous stir inside there, another series of animal screams, the intermittent whirr of the reptile. The shade torn violently down from the window, letting in the red dawn, a huge brown hand seizing the window stick, great dull blows upon the wooden floor punctuating the gibberish of sound long after the rattle of the snake had abruptly subsided. All this Delia could see and hear from her place beneath the window, and it made her ill. She crept over to the four-o'clocks and stretched herself on the cool earth to recover.

107   She lay there. "Delia, Delia!" She could hear Sykes calling in a most despairing tone as one who expected no answer. The sun crept on up, and he called. Delia could not move—her legs were gone flabby. She never moved, he called, and the sun kept rising.

108   "Mah Gawd!" She heard him moan, "Mah Gawd fum Heben!" She heard him stumbling about and got up from her flower-bed. The sun was growing warm. As she approached the door she heard him call out hopefully, "Delia, is dat you Ah heah?"

109   She saw him on his hands and knees as soon as she reached the door. He crept an inch or two toward her—all that he was able, and she saw his horribly swollen neck and his one open eye shining with hope. A surge of pity too strong to support bore her away from that eye that must, could not, fail to see the tubs. He would see the lamp. Orlando with its doctors was too far. She could scarcely reach the Chinaberry tree, where she waited in the growing heat while inside she knew the cold river was creeping up and up to extinguish that eye which must know by now that she knew.

* *

SWEAT

JOURNAL

1. MLA Works Cited   *Using this model, record this story here.*

Author's Last Name, First Name. "Title of the Story." *Title of the Book.* 3rd ed. Ed.

First Name Last Name. City: Publisher, year. Page number(s) of this story. Print.

2. Main Character(s)   *Describe each main character, and explain why you think each is a main character.*

3. Supporting Characters   *Describe each supporting character, and explain why you think each is a supporting character.*

4. Setting and Props   *Describe the setting(s) and all relevant prop(s).*

5. Sequence   *Outline the events of the story in order.*

6. Plot   *Tell the story in no more than two sentences.*

7. Conflicts   *Identify and explain all the conflicts involved here.*

8. Significant Quotations   *Explain the importance of each quotations. Record the page number in the parentheses.*

a. "Mah sweat is done paid for this house and Ah reckon Ah kin keep on sweatin' in it" ( ).

b. "She had brought love to the union and he had brought a longing after the flesh" ( ).

c. "Taint no use uh you puttin' on airs makin' out lak you skeered uh dat snake—he's gointer stay right heah tell he die. He wouldn't bite me cause Ah knows how tuh handle 'im" ( ).

    d. "'Whut's de mattah, ol' satan, you aint kickin' up yo' racket?' She addressed the snake's box. Complete silence" ( ).

    e. "She lay there. 'Delia, Delia!' She could hear Sykes calling [...]" ( ).

9. Literary Elements *Look at this chapter's title and explain why you think this story is placed in this chapter. Explain in which other chapter(s) you might place this story, as relevant to the literary element(s) of the chapter(s).*

10. Foreshadowing, Irony, and/or Symbolism *Explain examples of foreshadowing, irony, and/or symbolism in this story.*

FOLLOW-UP QUESTIONS

10 SHORT QUESTIONS

What is the <u>best</u> answer for each?

____ 1. Delia
  a. works hard.
  b. seems to have no job.
  c. seems to be up to no good.

____ 2. Sykes
  a. works hard.
  b. is faithful.
  c. has another woman.

____ 3. Sykes
  a. is kind to Delia.
  b. has beaten Delia.
  c. has not beaten Delia.

____ 4. The town
  a. thinks highly of Sykes.
  b. does not think highly of Sykes.
  c. does not know Sykes.

____ 5. Delia
  a. wants a pet snake.
  b. is afraid of snakes.
  c. is not afraid of snakes.

____ 6. Sykes feels he
  a. can handle a rattlesnake.
  b. cannot handle a rattlesnake.
  c. does not want a rattlesnake.

____ 7. Sykes uses the snake because
  a. he likes animals.
  b. he wants Delia to stay.
  c. he wants Delia to leave.

____ 8. Delia plans
  a. to stay.
  b. to leave.
  c. to kill Sykes.

____ 9. When Sykes calls for help, Delia
  a. goes to help him.
  b. does not hear him.
  c. does not help him.

____ 10. In the end, Sykes
  a. lives and leaves Delia.
  b. dies.
  c. lives and pushes Delia out.

5 SIGNIFICANT QUOTATIONS

What is the importance of each of these quotations?

1. "Ah been married to you fur fifteen years, and Ah been takin' in washin' fur fifteen years. Sweat, sweat, sweat! Work and sweat, cry and sweat, pray and sweat!"

2. "Oh well, whatever goes over the Devil's back, is got to come under his belly. Sometime or ruther, Sykes, like everybody else, is gointer reap his sowing."

3. "Syke! Syke, mah Gawd! You take dat rattlesnake 'way from heah! You *gottuh.* Oh, Jesus, have mussy!"

4. "But Ah'm a snake charmer an' knows how tuh handle 'em."

5. "Delia could not move—her legs were gone flabby. She never moved, he called, and the sun kept rising."

2 Comprehension Essay Questions

Use specific details and information from the story to answer these questions as completely as possible.

1. What is the irony in this story? Use specific details and information from the story to support your explanation.

2. What might be another title for this story? Use specific details and information from the story to explain your choice.

Discussion Questions

Be prepared to discuss these questions in class.

1. Do you think Delia should have helped Sykes? Use specific details from the story to support your thinking.

2. What qualities does Hurston see in the survivor? Use specific details from the story to support your ideas.

Writing

Use each of these ideas for writing an essay.

1. Whether younger or older, one often has to face something feared. Write an essay telling the story of something you or someone you know has feared and has had to face.

2. Many of us have found ourselves locked in bad relationships. Describe a poor relationship you or someone you know has been in, and describe how you or your friend got out of it.

Further Writing

1. Compare and contrast Hurston's irony with that in Dorothy Parker's "The Wonderful Old Gentleman" (available in a library).

2. Research spousal abuse, and use Delia's story to offer insight into the question, "Why don't they leave?"

CHAPTER

4

Irony

Irony is found in the difference between what *is* and what *should be*. Irony may be bitter—you work and work, and someone new, who has done nothing, arrives at your job and gets the promotion you deserve. Irony may be humorous—you wake up late and race around knowing you will be late for class, only to get to school and find out that your class has been canceled. Irony may even be providential—you sleep in and miss your bus, only to find out that the bus was in an accident and you are still safe at home. Think of ironies as unexpected twists in time, places, or events.

A story by O. Henry is a good example of irony. In the story, a gentleman treats a poor man to a Thanksgiving feast. In the end, both men end up in the hospital. The reader finds out that the poor man has had a big dinner before this second feast and is overfed. Meanwhile, the proud gentleman has spent his money on feeding this poor man, who does not need more food, and the gentleman is underfed. The irony, of course, is that the man who does not need the food is overfed, while the man who does need the food goes without food.

Although many of the stories in this book present ironic twists, the stories in this chapter focus on irony. Characters' worlds turn upside down in "Ah Bah's Money," "The Necklace," and "The Ransom of Red Chief." Then justice is served and even elevated in "The Adventure of the speckled Band" with the inimitable Sherlock Holmes and in "God Sees the Truth, but Waits."

Enjoy the twists here, and reflect on the ironies you have read in other stories—and on those you have experienced in your own life.

AH BAH'S MONEY

Catherine Lim

Pre-reading Vocabulary
Context

Use context clues to define these words before reading. Use a dictionary as needed.

1. When she felt a sneeze coming on, Lisa looked for a *handkerchief* in her bag to cover up her sneeze. *Handkerchief* means _____.

2. Although it was a hot day, Ashley was *reluctant* to enter the pool after she tested the water and the water was too cold. *Reluctant* means

   _____.

3. When she wanted to take her toys with her, Caitlin took out a cloth and put the toys in it, making a *bundle* she could carry. *Bundle* means _____.

4. When Bonnie graduated from college, she took a job so that she could *earn* enough money to support herself. *Earn* means _____.

5. John was very confident in the electrician he hired and felt *secure* that the electrician did a good job. *Secure* means _____.

6. When she bought new dishes, Jamie also bought a large *cupboard* for the dining room that would show off her new dishes. *Cupboard* means

   _____.

7. When Teddy bought his Mercedes, he treated it like a *treasure*, polishing it and keeping it as good as new. *Treasure* means

   _____.

8. When the fraternity house planned a party, the members bought potato chips to eat and a lot of *beer* to drink. *Beer* means

   _____.

9. Carrie was *terrified* of spiders and would yell for her mother to drop everything and come kill the spider. *Terrified* means _____.

10. Rajan became very *dispirited* when he worked hard to solve a prolem and then his boss stole the credit from Rajan. *Dispirited* means

_____.

11. Chinese people celebrate the New Year by giving children *ang pows*, which are little red bags filled with money. *Ang pow* means

_____.

12. Jess was delighted when she won the lottery and had many ideas on how to spend her newfound *wealth*. *Wealth* means

_____.

13. When Reid's team won the game, his joy was *conspicuous* in the large smile that lit up his entire face. *Conspicuous* means

_____.

14. When Li Qin wadded up all her paper money in a big roll, it made a *bulge* in her pocket that everyone could see. *Bulge* means _____.

15. When Tricia took the little two-year-old to the toy store, the child *bawled* and cried and carried on when he didn't get the toy he wanted. *Bawl* means _____.

16. Not being able to solve a problem can cause a great deal of frustration and *vexation*. *Vexation* means _____.

17. When Xi Ling ruined her shoes by walking in the rain, her mother *scolded* her for ruining her shoes. *Scold* means _____.

18. With no planning and without even thinking first, Margaret bought a lottery ticket on *impulse* and won the big prize. *Impulse* means

_____.

19. Bob showed great *ingenuity* when he cleverly solved the problem that others could not solve. *Ingenuity* means _____.

20. When Ben lost his wallet, it was a great *loss,* not only because of the money he lost but also because of the time he lost trying to find it. *Loss* means _____.

PRE-READING VOCABULARY
STRUCTURAL ATTACK

Define these words by solving the parts. Use the Glossary or a dictionary as needed.

1. greenish
2. thereafter
3. uneasy
4. broken-down
5. endlessly
6. bad-tempered
7. indifferent
8. forefinger
9. expertly
10. immediately
11. frantically
12. feverishly
13. bitterly
14. bedroom
15. miserably
16. successfully
17. triumphantly
18. amazement
19. firewood
20. restless
21. aching
22. quietened

PRE-READING QUESTIONS

Try answering these questions as you read.

How does Ah Bah hide his money?
From whom is he hiding his money?
What is ironic here?

AH BAH'S MONEY

CATHERINE LIM

Catherine Lim was born in Malaya but continued her schooling in Singapore. She first taught and then became an administrator, developing curriculum materials for elementary schoolchildren. She later became a writer, focusing on and even satirizing life in Singapore. More of her stories can be found in *Little Ironies: Stories of Singapore.*

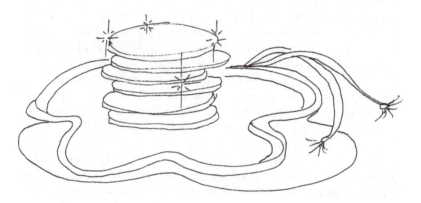

Ah Bah's money, in 2 one-dollar notes and an assortment of coins, lay in a pile on the old handkerchief, but Ah Bah was reluctant to pull up the corners into a bundle to put inside the cigarette tin. Ah Bah was reluctant because the sight of his money gave him so much pleasure. He had already done the following things with his money: spread out the notes and arranged the coins in a row beside them, stacked up the coins according to their denominations, stacked up the coins to make each stack come to a dollar. But still he wanted to go on touching his money. He could tell exactly which coin came from whom or where. The twenty-cent coin with the greenish stain on the edge was given to him by Ah Lam Soh, who was opening her purse when the coin dropped out and he picked it up for her.

"You may keep it," she said, and thereafter Ah Bah watched closely every time Ah Lam Soh opened her purse or put her hand into her blouse pocket. The ten-cent coin, which had a better shine than all the rest, he had actually found near

2

a rubbish dump, almost hidden from sight by an old slipper. And the largest coin of all, the fifty-cent coin, he had earned. He was still rather puzzled about why Kim Heok Soh had given him so much money; he had been required merely to stand in the front portion of the house and to say to any visitor, "Kim Heok Soh has gone to the dry goods shop and will not be back till an hour later. She has asked me to take care of her house for her." But all the time Kim Heok Soh was in the house; he knew because he could hear her in the room and there was somebody with her.

3   He counted his money—five dollars and eighty-five cents, and his heart glowed. Very carefully, he pulled up the corners of the handkerchief at last into a tight bundle which he then put inside the cigarette tin. Then he put the cover on firmly, and his money, now safe and secure, was ready to go back into its hiding place in a corner of the cupboard behind the stacks of old clothes, newspapers and calendars.

4   And now Ah Bah became uneasy, and he watched to see if his father's eyes would rest on the old broken-down cupboard that held his treasure, for once his father had found his money— two dollars in twenty- and ten-cent coins—tied up in a piece of rag and hidden under his pillow, and had taken it away for another bottle of beer. His father drank beer almost every night. Sometimes he was in a good mood after his beer and he would talk endlessly about this or that, smiling to himself. But generally he became sullen and bad-tempered, and he would begin shouting at anyone who came near. Once he threw an empty beer bottle at Ah Bah's mother; it missed her head and went crashing against the wall. Ah Bah was terrified of his father, but his mother appeared indifferent. "The lunatic," she would say, but never in his hearing. Whenever he was not at home, she would slip out and play cards in Ah Lam Soh's house. One evening she returned, flushed with excitement and gave him fifty cents; she said it had been her lucky day. At other times she came back with a dispirited look, and Ah Bah knew she had lost all her money in Ah Lam Soh's house.

5   The New Year was coming and Ah Bah looked forward to it with an intensity that he could barely conceal. New Year meant *ang pows*; Ah Bah's thin little fingers closed round the red packets of money given him by the New Year visitors with such energy that his mother would scold him and shake her head in doleful apology, as she remarked loudly to the visitors, "My Ah Bah, he feels no shame whatever!"

6   His forefinger and thumb feeling expertly through the red paper, Ah Bah could tell immediately how much was in the red

packet; his heart would sink a little if the fingers felt the hard edges of coins, for that would be forty cents or eighty cents at most. But if nothing was felt, then joy of joys! Here was at least a dollar inside.

7   This year Ah Bah had *eight* dollar notes. He could hardly believe it when he took stock of his wealth on the last day of the festive season. Eight new notes, crisp, still smelling new, and showing no creases except where they had been folded to go into the red packets. Eight dollars! And a small pile of coins besides. Ah Bah experienced a thrill such as he had never felt before.

8   And then it was all anxiety and fear, for he realized that his father knew about his *ang pow* money; indeed his father had referred to it once or twice, and would, Ah Bah was certain, be searching the bedding, cupboard and other places in the house for it.

9   Ah Bah's heart beat with the violence of angry defiance at the thought. The total amount in his cigarette tin was now seventeen dollars and twenty-five cents, and Ah Bah was determined to protect his money at all costs. Nobody was going to take his money from him. Frantically, Ah Bah went to the cupboard, took out the bundle of money from the cigarette tin and stuffed it into his trouser pocket. It made a conspicuous bulge. Ah Bah didn't know what to do, and his little mind worked feverishly to find a way out of this very direful situation.

10   He was wandering about in the village the next day as usual, and when he returned home, he was crying bitterly. His pocket was empty. When his mother came to him and asked him what the matter was, he bawled. He told her, between sobs, that a rough-looking Indian had pushed him to the ground and taken away his money. His father who was in the bedroom rushed out, and made Ah Bah tell again what had happened. When Ah Bah had finished, sniffling miserably, his father hit him on the head, snarling, "You idiot! Why were you so anxious to show off your *ang pow* money? Now you've lost it all!" And when he was told that the sum was seventeen dollars and twenty-five cents, his vexation was extreme, so that he would not be contented till he had hit the boy again.

11   Ah Bah's mother cleaned the bruise on the side of his face where he had been pushed to the ground, and led him away from his father.

12   "You are a silly boy," she scolded. "Why did you carry so much money around with you? Someone was sure to rob you!" And feeling sorry for him, she felt about in her blouse pocket and found she could spare fifty cents, so she gave it to him, saying, "Next time, don't be so silly, son."

13   He took the coin from her, and he was deeply moved. And then, upon impulse, he took her by the hand, and led her outside their house to the old hen-house, near the well, under the trees, and he whispered to her, his heart almost bursting with the excitement of a portentous secret successfully kept, "It's there! In the cigarette tin, behind that piece of wood!" To prove it, he squeezed into the hen house and soon emerged, reeking of hen house odors, triumphantly clutching the tin. He took off the lid and showed her the money inside.

14   She was all amazement. Then she began to laugh and to shake her head over the ingenuity of it all, while he stood looking up at her, his eyes bright and bold with victory.

15   "You're a clever boy," she said, "but take care that you don't go near the hen house often. Your father's pocket is empty again, and he's looking around to see whose money he can get hold of, that devil."

16   Ah Bah earned twenty cents helping Ah Lau Sim to scrape coconut, and his mother allowed him to have the ten cents which he found on a shelf, under a comb. Clutching his money, he stole out of the house; he was just in time to back out of the hen house, straighten himself and pretend to be looking for dried twigs for firewood, for his father stood at the doorway, looking at him. His father was in a restless mood again, pacing the floor with a dark look on his face, and this was the sign that he wanted his beer very badly but had no money to pay for it. Ah Bah bent low, assiduously looking for firewood, and then through the corner of his eye, he saw his father go back into the house.

17   That night Ah Bah dreamt that his father had found out the hiding place in the hen house, and early next morning, his heart beating wildly, he stole out and went straight to the hen house. He felt about in the darkness for his cigarette tin; his hand touched the damp of the hen droppings and caught on a nail, and still he searched—but the cigarette tin was not there.

18   He ran sniffling to his mother, and she began to scold him, "I told you not to go there too often, but you wouldn't listen to me. Didn't you know your father has been asking for money? The devil's found you out again!"

19   The boy continued to sniff, his little heart aching with the terrible pain of the loss.

20   "Never mind," his mother said, "you be a good boy and don't say anything about it; otherwise your father's sure to rage like a mad man." She led him inside the house and gave him a slice of bread with some sugar.

21   She was glad when he quietened down at last, for she didn't want to keep Ah Lam Soh and the others waiting. The seventeen dollars and twenty-five cents (she had hurriedly hidden the handkerchief and the cigarette tin) was secure in her blouse pocket, and she slipped away with eager steps for, as the fortune teller had told her, this was the beginning of a period of good luck for her.

• •

AH BAH'S MONEY

JOURNAL

1. MLA Works Cited *Using this model, record this story here.*

Author's Last Name, First Name. "Title of the Story." *Title of the Book.* 3rd ed. Ed.

First Name Last Name. City: Publisher, year. Page number(s) of this story. Print.

2. Main Character(s) *Describe each main character, and explain why you think each is a main character.*

3. Supporting Characters *Describe each supporting character, and explain why you think each is a supporting character.*

4. Setting and Props *Describe the setting(s) and all relevant prop(s).*

5. Sequence   *Outline the events of the story in order.*

6. Plot   *Tell the story in no more than two sentences.*

7. Conflicts   *Identify and explain all the conflicts involved here.*

8. Significant Quotations   *Explain the importance of each quotation completely. Record the page number in the parentheses.*

a. "Ah Bah was reluctant because the sight of his money gave him so much pleasure" (   ).

b. "And now Ah Bah became uneasy, and he watched to see if his father's eyes would rest on the old broken-down cupboard that held his treasure, for once his father had found his money—[…]" (   ).

    c. "Frantically, Ah Bah went to the cupboard, took out the bundle of money from cigarette tin and stuffed it into his trouser pocket" (   ).

    d. "To prove it, he squeezed into the hen house and soon emerged, reeking of hen house odors, triumphantly clutching the tin" (   ).

    e. "She was glad when he quietened down at last, for she didn't want to keep Ah Lam Soh and the others waiting" (   ).

9. Literary Elements   *Look at this chapter's title and explain why you think this story is placed in this chapter. Explain in which other chapter(s) you might place this story, as relevant to the literary element(s) of the chapter(s).*

10. Foreshadowing, Irony, and/or Symbols   *Explain examples of foreshadowing, irony, and/or symbols in this story.*

Follow-up Questions

10 Short Questions

What is the <u>best</u> answer for each?

____ 1. Ah Bah's money
    a. is very important to him.
    b. does not concern him.
    c. is easy for him to hide.

____ 2. Ah Bah's money
    a. is all earned by him.
    b. comes from gifts and earnings.
    c. all comes from gifts.

____ 3. Ah Bah
    a. always keeps his money behind the cupboard.
    b. works hard at hiding his money.
    c. always keeps his money in the same place.

____ 4. Ah Bah
    a. is never sure how much money he has.
    b. sometimes is not sure how much money he has.
    c. almost always knows exactly how much money he has.

____ 5. Ah Bah's father
    a. gives Ah Bah money.
    b. wants Ah Bah's money.
    c. does not know about Ah Bah's money.

____ 6. Ah Bah's father
    a. is a drinker.
    b. is kind to Ah Bah.
    c. is generous to Ah Bah.

____ 7. Ah Bah
    a. always keeps his money behind the cupboard.
    b. is sure his father does not know about his money.
    c. tries to hide his money in the hen house.

____ 8. Ah Bah tells
    a. no one about the hen house.
    b. his mother about the hen house.
    c. his father about the hen house.

____ 9. Ah Bah's mother
    a. warns Ah Bah against his father.
    b. gives Ah Bah a safe hiding place.
    c. deserves Ah Bah's trust.

____ 10. In the end, Ah Bah's money
    a. is safe.
    b. is taken by his father.
    c. is taken by his mother.

5 Significant Quotations

What is the importance of each of these quotations?

1. "He could tell exactly which coin came from whom or where."

2. "Then he put the cover on firmly, and his money, now safe and secure, was ready to go back into its hiding place in a corner of the cupboard [...]."

3. "His father drank beer almost every night."

4. "And then, upon impulse, he took her by the hand, and led her outside their house to the old hen house […]."

5. "He ran sniffling to his mother, and she began to scold him, 'I told you not to go there too often […]. Didn't you know your father has been asking for money?'"

2 COMPREHENSION ESSAY QUESTIONS

Use specific details and information from the story to answer these questions as completely as possible.

1. What characteristics mark Ah Bah? His father? His mother? Use specific details and information from the story to support your descriptions.

2. What is the irony in this story? Use specific details and information from the story to support your answer.

DISCUSSION QUESTIONS

Be prepared to discuss these questions in class.

1. How would you describe Ah Bah? His father? His mother?

2. What is ironic here?

WRITING

Use each of these ideas for writing an essay.

1. Certainly, Ah Bah has a problem with people he trusts. Tell of a time that you or someone you know has been cheated by someone you or your friend trusted.

2. Ah Bah treasures his money, yet we all have things we especially treasure. Focus on some special thing that you or someone you know truly treasures. Tell the story of what makes this object so special.

Further Writing

1. Although this story is told with a very light touch, it brings up the very serious topic of addiction. Research alcoholism, drug abuse, and/or gambling addiction and apply your research to this story.

2. This story also demonstrates some of the dysfunctional dynamics found in families impacted by addiction. Research the psychosocial dynamics of addictive families and relate your research to this story.

THE NECKLACE

GUY DE MAUPASSANT

PRE-READING VOCABULARY
CONTEXT

Use context clues to define these words before reading. Use a dictionary as needed.

1. When Francine lost her business, she was forced to take a job as a *clerk,* filing papers and making much less money. *Clerk* means

   _____.

2. Pierre is a very *petty* person who always worries about stupid little things while other people have real problems. *Petty* means

   _____.

3. Georgiana lives in true *luxury* in a spacious home surrounded by lush gardens and tended by a butler and maids. *Luxury* means

   _____.

4. Evelyn learned that her family was part of the *aristocracy* and that her uncle had been a duke and her aunt a duchess. *Aristocracy* means

   _____.

5. Pascal lived in *poverty* without a roof over his head or enough food to eat, until he graduated college and got a good job. *Poverty* means

   _____.

6. The king was very aware of his family's *station* in life and would not let his children marry any commoner who was beneath them. *Station* means _____.

7. Kristin chose a beautiful, blue silk *frock* with puffy, white sleeves and lacy hem to wear to the formal party. *Frock* means

   _____.

8. Sarah loved *jewels* and selected a diamond and ruby necklace to wear around her neck for her birthday. *Jewel* means

_____.

9. Shirley enjoyed listening to the morning song of the little brown *larks* that built a nest outside her kitchen window. *Lark* means

_____.

10. Lisa is a very *chic* woman who only wears the finest and most refined clothing from the best designers. *Chic* means

_____.

11. Libby has a *superb* sense of humor and can see humor in almost anything that occurs in her life. *Superb* means

_____.

12. Mike was in sheer *ecstasy* when Judy surprised him with a new Corvette, exactly the car he had always wanted. *Ecstasy* means

_____.

13. One can become as *intoxicated* with power as another becomes drunk by drinking alcohol. *Intoxicated* means

_____.

14. Susan met with important people in her beautifully furnished *salon* that overlooked Park Avenue. *Salon* means

_____.

15. Marna ordered a horse-drawn *coupe* with a chauffeur to take her and Buz to the theater. *Coupe* means _____.

16. When people visited Pedro, they first had to remove their wet shoes and leave them in the *vestibule* before entering the living room. *Vestibule* means _____.

17. When Roger lost his dog, he offered a $500 *reward* for anyone who returned his dog. *Reward* means _____.

18. In France, Meredith had to change her dollars and pay for everything she bought with *francs, louises,* or *sous. Franc, louis,* or *sou* means

_____.

19. Frank decided to buy a new car and took out a loan from the bank, which left him $10,000 in *debt. Debt* means

_____.

20. Elizabeth was in a state of *astonishment* when her lazy son cleaned his room, cut the lawn, and cooked dinner. *Astonishment* means

_____.

PRE-READING VOCABULARY
STRUCTURAL ATTACK

Define these words by solving the parts. Use the Glossary or a dictionary as needed.

1. inborn	**12.** poverty-laden
2. instinctive	**13.** humiliating
3. incessantly	**14.** admirable
4. antechamber	**15.** workmanship
5. footmen	**16.** immoderate
6. inestimable	**17.** bewilderment
7. peopling	**18.** jeweler
8. personage	**19.** frightful
9. spitefully	**20.** grocer
10. impatiently	**21.** fruiterer
11. economical	**22.** decently

PRE-READING QUESTIONS

Try answering these questions as you read.

What does Monsieur Loisel do?

What does Madame Loisel do?

What happens?

THE NECKLACE

Guy de Maupassant

Guy de Maupassant was born in Normandy, France in 1850 and died in Paris in 1893, institutionalized with the effects of chronic headaches and extended medications. Thanks to familial ties on his mother's side, de Maupassant shared a close relationship with Gustave Flaubert. However, it was de Maupassant's accurate memory and life experiences that shaped his writing. Life in Normandy gave him understanding and sympathy toward these people. Army service during the Franco-Prussian War and brief service as a clerk in the government gave him more people to study. In contrast, his later associations with Parisian salons and sophistication left him with little caring for the urbane. Although he published multiple novels and plays, de Maupassant's genius is in his incisive irony and his short stories have made him a French master of irony. His writings can be found in novels, plays, and short story collections.

She was one of those pretty, charming young ladies, born, as if through an error of destiny, into a family of clerks. She had no dowry, no hopes, no means of becoming known, appreciated, loved, and married by a man either rich or distinguished; and she allowed herself to marry a petty clerk in the office of the Board of Education.

She was simple, not being able to adorn herself; but she was unhappy, as one out of her class; for women belong to no caste, no race; their grace, their beauty, and their charm serving them in the place of birth and family. Their inborn finesse, their instinctive elegance, their suppleness of wit are their only aristocracy, making some daughters of the people the equal of great ladies.

3   She suffered incessantly, feeling herself born for all delicacies and luxuries. She suffered from the poverty of her apartment, the shabby walls, the worn chair, and the faded stuffs. All these things, which another woman of her station would not have noticed, tortured and angered her. The sight of the little Breton, who made this humble home, awoke in her sad regrets and desperate dreams. She thought of quiet antechambers, with their Oriental hangings, lighted by high, bronze torches, and of the two great footmen in short trousers who sleep in the large armchairs, made sleepy by the heavy air from the heating apparatus. She thought of large drawing-rooms, hung in old silks, of graceful pieces of furniture carrying bric-a-brac of inestimable value, and of the little perfumed coquettish apartments, made for five o'clock chats with most intimate friends, men known and sought after, whose attention all women envied and desired.

4   When she seated herself for dinner, before the round table where the tablecloth had been used three days, opposite her husband, who uncovered the tureen with a delighted air, saying: "Oh! the good potpie! I know nothing better than that—" she would think of elegant dinners, of the shining silver, of the tapestries peopling the walls with ancient personages and rare birds in the midst of fairy forests; she thought of the exquisite food served on marvelous dishes, of the whispered gallantries, listened to with the smile of the sphinx, while eating the rose-colored flesh of the trout or a chicken's wing.

5   She had neither frocks nor jewels, nothing. And she loved only those things. She felt that she was made for them. She had such a desire to please, to be sought after, to be clever, and courted.

6   She had a rich friend, a schoolmate at the convent, whom she did not like to visit, she suffered so much when she returned. And she wept for whole days from chagrin, from regret, from despair, and disappointment.

7   One evening her husband returned elated, bearing in his hand a large envelope.

8   "Here," he said, "here is something for you."

9   She quickly tore open the wrapper and drew out a printed card on which were inscribed these words:

10   *The Minister of Public Instruction and Madame George Ramponneau ask the honor of Monsieur and Madame Loisel's company Monday evening, January 18, at the Minister's residence.*

11   Instead of being delighted, as her husband had hoped, she threw the invitation spitefully upon the table murmuring:

12   "What do you suppose I want with that?"

13   "But, my dearie, I thought it would make you happy. You never go out, and this is an occasion, and a fine one! I had a great deal of trouble to get it. Everybody wishes one, and it is very select; not many are given to employees. You will see the whole official world there."

14   She looked at him with an irritated eye and declared impatiently:

15   "What do you suppose I have to wear to such a thing as that?"

16   He had not thought of that; he stammered:

17   "Why, the dress you wear when we go to the theater. It seems very pretty to me—"

18   He was silent, stupefied, in dismay, at the sight of his wife weeping. Two great tears fell slowly from the corners of her eyes toward the corners of her mouth; he stammered:

19   "What is the matter? What is the matter?"

20   By a violent effort, she had controlled her vexation and responded in a calm voice, wiping her moist cheeks:

21   "Nothing. Only I have no dress and consequently I cannot go to this affair. Give your card to some colleague whose wife is better fitted out than I."

22   He was grieved, but answered:

23   "Let us see, Matilda. How much would a suitable costume cost, something that would serve for other occasions, something very simple?"

24   She reflected for some seconds, making estimates and thinking of a sum that she could ask for without bringing with it an immediate refusal and a frightened exclamation from the economical clerk.

25   Finally she said, in a hesitating voice:

26   "I cannot tell exactly, but it seems to me that four hundred francs ought to cover it."

27   He turned a little pale, for he had saved just this sum to buy a gun that he might be able to join some hunting parties the next summer, on the plains of Nanterre, with some friends who went to shoot larks up there on Sunday. Nevertheless, he answered:

28   "Very well. I will give you four hundred francs. But try to have a pretty dress."

29   The day of the ball approached and Madame Loisel seemed sad, disturbed, anxious. Nevertheless, her dress was nearly ready. Her husband said to her one evening:

30   "What is the matter with you? You have acted strangely for two or three days."

31   And she responded: "I am vexed not to have a jewel, not one stone, nothing to adorn myself with. I shall have such a poverty-laden look. I would prefer not to go to this party."

32   He replied: "You can wear some natural flowers. At this season they look very *chic*. For ten francs you can have two or three magnificent roses."

33   She was not convinced. "No," she replied, "there is nothing more humiliating than to have a shabby air in the midst of rich women."

34   Then her husband cried out: "How stupid we are! Go and find your friend Madame Forestier and ask her to lend you her jewels. You are well enough acquainted with her to do this."

35   She uttered a cry of joy: "It is true!" she said. "I had not thought of that."

36   The next day she took herself to her friend's house and related her story of distress. Madame Forestier went to her closet with the glass doors, took out a large jewel-case, brought it, opened it, and said: "Choose, my dear."

37   She saw at first some bracelets, then a collar of pearls, then a Venetian cross of gold and jewels and of admirable workmanship. She tried the jewels before the glass, hesitated, but could neither decide to take them nor leave them. Then she asked:

38   "Have you nothing more?"

39   "Why, yes. Look for yourself. I do not know what will please you."

40   Suddenly she discovered, in a black satin box, a superb necklace of diamonds, and her heart beat fast with an immoderate desire. Her hands trembled as she took them up. She placed them about her throat against her dress, and remained in ecstasy before them. Then she asked, in a hesitating voice, full of anxiety:

41   "Could you lend me this? Only this?"

42   "Why, yes, certainly."

43   She fell upon the neck of her friend, embraced her with passion, then went away with her treasure.

44   The day of the ball arrived. Madame Loisel was a great success. She was the prettiest of all, elegant, gracious, smiling, and full of joy. All the men noticed her, asked her name, and wanted to be presented. All the members of the Cabinet wished to waltz with her. The Minister of Education paid her some attention.

45   She danced with enthusiasm, with passion, intoxicated with pleasure, thinking of nothing, in the triumph of her beauty, in the glory of her success, in a kind of cloud of happiness that came of all this homage, and all this admiration, of all these awakened desires, and this victory so complete and sweet to the heart of woman.

46   She went home toward four o'clock in the morning. Her husband had been half asleep in one of the little salons since midnight, with three other gentlemen whose wives were enjoying themselves very much.

47   He threw around her shoulders the wraps they had carried for the coming home, modest garments of everyday wear, whose poverty clashed with the elegance of the ball costume. She felt this and wished to hurry away in order not to be noticed by the other women who were wrapping themselves in rich furs.

48   Loisel retained her: "Wait," said he. "You will catch cold out there. I am going to call a cab."

49   But she would not listen and descended the steps rapidly. When they were in the street, they found no carriage; and they began to seek for one, hailing the coachmen whom they saw at a distance.

50   They walked along toward the Seine, hopeless and shivering. Finally they found on the dock one of those old, nocturnal *coupés* that one sees in Paris after nightfall, as if they were ashamed of their misery by day.

51   It took them as far as their door in Martyr Street, and they went wearily up to their apartment. It was all over for her. And on his part, he remembered that he would have to be at the office by ten o'clock.

52   She removed the wraps from her shoulders before the glass, for a final view of herself in her glory. Suddenly she uttered a cry. Her necklace was not around her neck.

53   Her husband, already half undressed, asked: "What is the matter?"

54   She turned toward him excitedly:

55   "I have—I have—I no longer have Madame Forestier's necklace."

56   He arose in dismay: "What! How is that? It is not possible."

57   And they looked in the folds of the dress, in the folds of the mantle, in the pockets, everywhere. They could not find it.

58   He asked: "You are sure you still had it when we left the house?"

59   "Yes, I felt it in the vestibule as we came out."

60   "But if you had lost it in the street, we should have heard it fall. It must be in the cab."

61   "Yes. It is probably. Did you take the number?"

62   "No. And you, did you notice what it was?"

63   "No."

64   They looked at each other utterly cast down. Finally, Loisel dressed himself again.

65   "I am going," said he, "over the track where we went on foot, to see if I can find it."

66   And he went. She remained in her evening gown, not having the force to go to bed, stretched upon a chair, without ambition or thoughts.

67   Toward seven o'clock her husband returned. He had found nothing.

68   He went to the police and to the cab offices, and put an advertisement in the newspapers, offering a reward; he did everything that afforded them a suspicion of hope.

69   She waited all day in a state of bewilderment before this frightful disaster. Loisel returned at evening with his face harrowed and pale; and had discovered nothing.

70   "It will be necessary," said he, "to write to your friend that you have broken the clasp of the necklace and that you will have it repaired. That will give us time to turn around."

71   She wrote as he dictated.

72   At the end of a week, they had lost all hope. And Loisel, older by five years, declared:

73   "We must take measures to replace this jewel."

74   The next day they took the box which had inclosed it, to the jeweler whose name was on the inside. He consulted his books:

75   "It is not I, Madame," said he, "who sold this necklace; I only furnished the casket."

76   Then they went from jeweler to jeweler seeking a necklace like the other one, consulting their memories, and ill, both of them, with chagrin and anxiety.

77   In a shop of the Palais-Royal, they found a chaplet of diamonds which seemed to them exactly like the one they had lost. It was valued at forty thousand francs. They could get it for thirty-six thousand.

78   They begged the jeweler not to sell it for three days. And they made an arrangement by which they might return it for thirty-four thousand francs if they found the other one before the end of February.

79   Loisel possessed eighteen thousand francs which his father had left him. He borrowed the rest.

80   He borrowed it, asking for a thousand francs of one, five hundred of another, five louis of this one, and three louis of that one. He gave notes, made ruinous promises, took money of usurers and the whole race of lenders. He compromised his whole existence, in fact, risked his signature, without even knowing whether he could make it good or not, and, harassed by anxiety for the future, by the black misery which surrounded him, and by the prospect of all physical privations and moral torture, he went to get the new necklace, depositing on the merchant's counter thirty-six thousand francs.

81   When Madame Loisel took back the jewels to Madame Forestier, the latter said to her in a frigid tone:

82   "You should have returned them to me sooner, for I might have needed them."

83   She did not open the jewel-box as her friend feared she would. If she should perceive the substitution, what would she think? What should she say? Would she take her for a robber?

84   Madame Loisel now knew the horrible life of necessity. She did her part, however, completely, heroically. It was necessary to pay this frightful debt. She would pay it. They sent away the maid; they changed their lodgings; they rented some rooms under a mansard roof.

85   She learned the heavy cares of a household, the odious work of a kitchen. She washed the dishes, using her rosy nails upon the greasy pots and the bottoms of the stewpans. She washed the soiled linen, the chemises and dishcloths, which she hung on the line to dry; she took down the refuse to the street each morning and brought up the water, stopping at each landing to breathe. And, clothed like a woman of the people, she went to the grocer's, the butcher's, and the fruiterer's, with her basket on her arm, shopping, haggling over the last sou of her miserable money.

86   Every month it was necessary to renew some notes, thus obtaining time, and to pay others.

87   The husband worked evenings, putting the books of some merchants in order, and nights he often did copying at five sous a page.

88   And this life lasted for ten years.

89   At the end of ten years, they had restored all, all, with interest of the usurer, and accumulated interest besides.

90   Madame Loisel seemed old now. She had become a strong, hard woman, the crude woman of the poor household. Her hair badly dressed, her skirts awry, her hands red, she spoke in a loud tone, and washed the floors with large pails of water. But sometimes, when her husband was at the office, she would seat herself before the window and think of that evening party of former times, of that ball where she was so beautiful and so flattered.

91   How would it have been if she had not lost that necklace? Who knows? Who knows? How singular is life, and how full of changes! How small a thing will ruin or save one!

92   One Sunday, as she was taking a walk in the Champs-Elysées, to rid herself of the cares of the week, she suddenly perceived a woman walking with a child. It was Madame Forestier, still young,

still pretty, still attractive. Madame Loisel was affected. Should she speak to her? Yes, certainly. And now that she had paid, she would tell her all. Why not?

93   She approached her. "Good morning, Jeanne."

94   Her friend did not recognize her and was astonished to be so familiarly addressed by this common personage. She stammered:

95   "But, Madame—I do not know—You must be mistaken——"

96   "No, I am Matilda Loisel."

97   Her friend uttered a cry of astonishment: "Oh! my poor Matilda! How you have changed—"

98   "Yes, I have had some hard days since I saw you; and some miserable ones—and all because of you—"

99   "Because of me? How is that?"

100   "You recall the diamond necklace that you loaned me to wear to the Commissioner's ball?"

101   "Yes, very well."

102   "Well, I lost it."

103   "How is that, since you returned it to me?"

104   "I returned another to you exactly like it. And it has taken us ten years to pay for it. You can understand that it was not easy for us who have nothing. But it is finished and I am decently content."

105   Madame Forestier stopped short. She said:

106   "You say that you bought a diamond necklace to replace mine?"

107   "Yes. You did not perceive it then? They were just alike."

108   And she smiled with a proud and simple joy. Madame Forestier was touched and took both her hands as she replied:

109   "Oh! my poor Matilda! Mine were false. They were not worth over five hundred francs!"

● ●

THE NECKLACE

JOURNAL

1. MLA Works Cited   *Using this model, record this story here.*

Author's Last Name, First Name. "Title of the Story." *Title of the Book.* 3rd ed. Ed.

First Name Last Name. City: Publisher, year. Page number(s) of this story. Print.

2. Main Character(s)   *Describe each main character, and explain why you think each is a main character.*

3. Supporting Characters   *Describe each supporting character, and explain why you think each is a supporting character.*

4. Setting and Props   *Describe the setting(s) and all relevant prop(s).*

5. Sequence   *Outline the events of the story in order.*

6. Plot   *Tell the story in no more than two sentences.*

7. Conflicts   *Identify and explain all the conflicts involved here.*

8. Significant Quotations   *Explain the importance of each quotation completely. Record the page number in the parentheses.*

a. "She suffered incessantly, feeling herself born for all delicacies and luxuries" (   ).

b. "One evening her husband returned elated, bearing in his hand a large envelope" (   ).

   c. "Suddenly she discovered, in a black satin box, a superb necklace of diamonds, and her heart beat fast with an immoderate desire" (   ).

   d. "Suddenly she uttered a cry. Her necklace was not around her neck" (   ).

   e. "Oh! my dear Matilda! Mine were false. They were not worth over five hundred francs!" (   ).

9. Literary Elements   *Look at this chapter's title and explain why you think this story is placed in this chapter. Explain in which other chapter(s) you might place this story, as relevant to the literary element(s) of the chapter(s).*

10. Foreshadowing, Irony, and/or Symbols   *Explain examples of foreshadowing, irony, and/or symbols in this story.*

FOLLOW-UP QUESTIONS

10 SHORT QUESTIONS

What is the <u>best</u> answer for each?

_____ 1. Matilda Loisel is
  a. a vain woman.
  b. a shy woman.
  c. an unattractive woman.

_____ 2. Matilda Loisel
  a. is happy in her marriage.
  b. feels she has married well.
  c. feels she has married beneath her.

_____ 3. Matilda Loisel
  a. is content at home.
  b. wishes she had a richer life.
  c. wishes she had a simpler life.

_____ 4. Monsieur Loisel
  a. tries to please his wife.
  b. does not care about his wife.
  c. is a selfish man.

_____ 5. Mme. Forestier is
  a. a poor relative.
  b. a wealthy relative.
  c. a wealthy friend.

_____ 6. Mme. Forestier is
  a. a generous woman.
  b. a nasty woman.
  c. a poor woman.

_____ 7. Matilda Loisel
  a. enjoys the ball.
  b. hates the ball.
  c. does not attend the ball.

_____ 8. Matilda Loisel replaces the necklace
  a. immediately.
  b. after much searching and trouble.
  c. never.

_____ 9. The Loisels' lifestyle
  a. changes for the better.
  b. changes for the worse.
  c. stays the same.

_____ 10. The irony is that the necklace is
  a. a good luck charm that brings good luck.
  b. broken and unfixable.
  c. a fake worth much less than expected.

5 SIGNIFICANT QUOTATIONS

What is the importance of each of these quotations?

1. "When she seated herself for dinner, the round table where the tablecloth had been used three days, opposite her husband, who uncovered the tureen with a delighted air, saying: 'Oh! the good potpie! I know nothing better than that—' she would think of elegant dinners, of the shining silver, of the tapestries peopling the walls with ancient personages and rare birds in the midst of fairy forests [...]."

2. *"The Minister of Public Instruction and Madame George Ramponneau ask the honor of Monsieur and Madame Loisel's company Monday evening, January 18, at the Minister's residence."*

3. "Then her husband cried out: 'How stupid we are! Go and find your friend Madame Forestier and ask her to lend you her jewels.'"

4. "Madame Loisel now knew the horrible life of necessity."

5. "Oh, my poor Matilda! Mine were false. They were not worth over five hundred francs."

2 COMPREHENSION ESSAY QUESTIONS

Use specific details and information from the story to answer these questions as completely as possible.

1. What is the irony in this story? Use specific details and information from the story to support your answer.

2. Why has de Maupassant named this "The Necklace"? Use specific details and information from the story to support your answer.

DISCUSSION QUESTIONS

Be prepared to discuss these questions in class.

1. The Loisels live on Martyr Street. What is ironic about this?

2. What is the role of pride in this story?

WRITING

Use each of these ideas for writing an essay.

1. Pride has often caused many of us trouble. Tell of a time you or someone you know has been prideful and the trouble this pride has caused.

2. Telling lies has often gotten many of us into trouble. Tell of a time you or someone you know suffered consequences because of telling a lie. Relate the lie and the consequences that resulted.

Further Writing

1. Read O. Henry's "Gifts of the Magi" (available in a library) and compare and contrast the characters in that story with those in "The Necklace."

2. Compare and contrast the irony in Leo Tolstoy's "God Sees the Truth, but Waits" (page 337) with the irony in "The Necklace."

THE RANSOM OF RED CHIEF

O. Henry

Pre-reading Vocabulary
Context

Use context clues to define these words before reading. Use a dictionary as needed.

1. *Kidnapping*, or the taking of someone against her or his will, is a federal offense. *Kidnapping* means _____.

2. When Kelli climbed to the very top of the hill, she had reached the *summit*. *Summit* means _____.

3. Scott is a very honest person and refuses to be part of anything that is *fraudulent*. *Fraudulent* means _____.

4. Vernie had a *scheme* to make a fortune; she would buy old houses, fix them up, and sell them for a profit. *Scheme* means

_____.

5. Dennis is a *prominent* citizen who has served as mayor, senator, and governor. *Prominent* means _____.

6. In order to get back his rare bird that was stolen, José had to pay a *ransom* of five hundred dollars. *Ransom* means

_____.

7. Janet decided to drive across the flat fields of Oklahoma and Nebraska, which are part of the American *plains*. *Plains* means

_____.

8. When Ajay had his head shaved, he looked as if the top of his head was gone and he had been *scalped*. *Scalped* means

_____.

9. When Rudy bought a new boat, he *christened* it "Weekends" and had this name painted on the back. *Christen* means _____.

10. When Purvi lost her wallet with all her money in it, she was *desperate* to get it back. *Desperate* means _____.

11. After getting lost, Artie had to get out the map and *reconnoiter* to figure out where he was. *Reconnoiter* means _____.

12. Courtney loved the many trees that were around her home and that gave her a rich, *sylvan* view. *Sylvan* means _____.

13. JoAnne *complies* with the law and always obeys the speed limit. *Comply* means _____.

14. Patrick looked at Meredith *suspiciously* when he saw Meredith's face was covered with chocolate and the new cake was missing. *Suspicious* means _____.

15. Old cowboys in the West sometimes referred to a horse as a *"hoss."* *Hoss* means _____.

16. Carrie thought Reid was trying to cheat her, but then she decided he was being fair and *square*. *Square* means _____.

17. Hal offered a thousand dollars for the car, but the seller offered a *counter-proposition* of two thousand dollars. *Counter-proposition* means _____.

18. The people who live around you are called your *neighbors*. *Neighbor* means _____.

19. Mary was so *liberal* in spreading the jelly that the bread fell apart because of the sheer weight of the jelly. *Liberal* means

_____.

20. After walking on the old wooden boardwalk, Missy had to *abstract* a splinter from her foot. *Abstract* means _____.

Pre-reading Vocabulary
Structural Attack

Define these words by solving the parts. Use the Glossary or a dictionary as needed.

1. self-satisfied
2. semi-rural
3. bloodhound
4. fancier
5. forecloser
6. welter-weight
7. tail-feathers
8. magic-lantern
9. warpath
10. during-dinner
11. war-whoop
12. outlaw
13. indecent
14. terrifying
15. sun-up

16. sleepiness
17. lambkin
18. disappearance
19. earthquake
20. skyrocket
21. parental
22. wildcat
23. hereinafter
24. fence-post
25. postmaster
26. mail-carrier
27. self-defense
28. mad-house
29. counterplot
30. spend-thrift

Pre-reading Questions

Try answering these questions as you read.

What is the plan?

How does the boy react?

What goes wrong?

What is the irony in the story?

THE RANSOM OF RED CHIEF

O. Henry

William Sydney Porter was born in 1862 to an educated and comfortable family living in Greensboro, North Carolina, and he grew up in the Reconstruction South. As a result of his mother's early death and his father's alcoholism, he was raised by his aunt, who gave him a love for narration. Like his father, he became a pharmacist's apprentice, and although he did not like the work, his uncle's drugstore provided him with a good vantage point from which to observe the townspeople. In 1882 he married Athol Estes Roach, settled into work at the National Bank of Texas, and bought a printing press to publish his stories in the short-lived weekly newspaper *The Rolling Stone*. He was charged and cleared of embezzlement—a charge he consistently denied. Later, faced with retrial, he fled to New Orleans and then to Honduras, all the while observing others. Returning to Texas because of his wife's failing health and subsequent death, he was retried and sent to the Ohio state penitentiary, where he served three years of a five-year sentence. Although it was a dark period in his life, he was again observing and, perhaps, gained his compassion for the underdog, as well as the pen name "O. Henry." In 1902 he moved to New York City to produce weekly stories for the *New York Sunday World*, and at the turn of the century and amid the streets of New York, which were largely filled with immigrants, he found endless stock for his stories. O. Henry died in 1910.

His stories are marked by concise characterizations, concern for working women and the poor, adroit wit, and succinct irony. His many stories and selected sketches are largely based on kernels from his real-life observations and are available in many collections.

It looked like a good thing: but wait till I tell you. We were down South, in Alabama—Bill Driscoll and myself—when this kidnapping idea struck us. It was, as Bill afterward expressed it, "during a moment of temporary mental apparition"; but we didn't find that out till later.

2   There was a town down there, as flat as a flannel-cake, and called Summit, of course. It contained inhabitants of as undeleterious and self-satisfied a class of peasantry as ever clustered around a Maypole.

3   Bill and me had a joint capital of about six hundred dollars, and we needed just two thousand dollars more to pull off a fraudulent town-lot scheme in Western Illinois with. We talked it over on the front steps of the hotel. Philoprogenitoveness, says we, is strong in semi-rural communities; therefore, and for other reasons, a kidnapping project ought to do better there than in the radius of newspapers that send reporters out in plain clothes to stir up talk about such things. We knew that Summit couldn't get after us with anything stronger than constables and, maybe, some lackadaisical bloodhounds and a diatribe or two in the *Weekly Farmers' Budget*. So, it looked good.

4   We selected for our victim the only child of a prominent citizen named Ebenezer Dorset. The father was respectable and tight, a mortgage fancier and a stern, upright collection-plate passer and forecloser. The kid was a boy of ten, with bas-relief freckles, and hair the color of the cover of the magazine you buy at the newsstand when you want to catch a train. Bill and me figured that Ebenezer would melt down for a ransom of two thousand dollars to a cent. But wait till I tell you.

5   About two miles from Summit was a little mountain, covered with a dense cedar brake. On the rear elevation of this mountain was a cave. There we stored provisions.

6   One evening after sundown, we drove in a buggy past old Dorset's house. The kid was in the street, throwing rocks at a kitten on the opposite fence.

7   "Hey, little boy!" says Bill, "would you like to have a bag of candy and a nice ride?"

8   The boy catches Bill neatly in the eye with a piece of brick.

9   "That will cost the old man an extra five hundred dollars," says Bill, climbing over the wheel.

10   That boy put up a fight like a welter-weight cinnamon bear; but, at last, we got him down in the bottom of the buggy and drove away. We took him up to the cave, and I hitched the horse in the cedar brake. After dark I drove the buggy to the little village, three miles away, where we had hired it, and walked back to the mountain.

11   Bill was pasting court-plaster over the scratches and bruises on his features. There was a fire burning behind the big rock at the

entrance of the cave, and the boy was watching a pot of boiling coffee, with two buzzard tail-feathers stuck in his red hair. He points a stick at me when I come up, and says:

12   "Ha! cursed paleface, do you dare to enter the camp of Red Chief, the terror of the plains?"

13   "He's all right now," says Bill, rolling up his trousers and examining some bruises on his shins. "We're playing Indian. We're making Buffalo Bill's show look like magic-lantern views of Palestine in the town hall. I'm Old Hank, the Trapper, Red Chief's captive, and I'm to be scalped at daybreak. By Geronimo! that kid can kick hard."

14   Yes, sir, that boy seemed to be having the time of his life. The fun of camping out in a cave had made him forget that he was a captive himself. He immediately christened me Snake-eye, the Spy, and announced that, when his braves returned from the warpath, I was to be broiled at the stake at the rising of the sun.

15   Then we had supper; and he filled his mouth full of bacon and bread and gravy, and began to talk. He made a during-dinner speech something like this:

16   "I like this fine. I never camped out before; but I had a pet 'possum once, and I was nine last birthday. I hate to go to school. Rats ate up sixteen of Jimmy Talbot's aunt's speckled hen's eggs. Are there any real Indians in these woods? I want some more gravy. Does the trees moving make the wind blow? We had five puppies. What makes your nose so red, Hank? My father has lots of money. Are the stars hot? I whipped Ed Walker twice, Saturday. I don't like girls. You dassent catch toads unless with a string. Do oxen make any noise? Why are oranges round? Have you got beds to sleep on in this cave? Amos Murray has got six toes. A parrot can talk, but a monkey or a fish can't. How many does it take to make twelve?"

17   Every few minutes he would remember that he was a pesky Indian, and pick up his stick rifle and tiptoe to the mouth of the cave to rubber for the scouts of the hated paleface. Now and then he would let out a war-whoop that made Old Hank the Trapper shiver. That boy had Bill terrorized from the start.

18   "Red Chief," says I to the kid, "would you like to go home?"

19   "Aw, what for?" says he. "I don't have any fun at home. I hate to go to school. I like to camp out. You won't take me back home again, Snake-eye, will you?"

20   "Not right away," says I. "We'll stay here in the cave awhile."

21   "All right!" says he. "That'll be fine. I never had such fun in all my life."

22   We went to bed about eleven o'clock. We spread down some wide blankets and quilts and put Red Chief between us. We weren't afraid he'd run away. He kept us awake for three hours, jumping up and reaching for his rifle and screeching: "Hist! pard," in mine

and Bill's ears, as the fancied crackle of a twig or the rustle of a leaf revealed to his young imagination the stealthy approach of the outlaw band. At last, I fell into a troubled sleep, and dreamed that I had been kidnapped and chained to a tree by a ferocious pirate with red hair.

23   Just at daybreak, I was awakened by a series of awful screams from Bill. They weren't yells, or howls, or shouts, or whoops, or yawps, such as you'd expect from a manly set of vocal organs— they were simply indecent, terrifying, humiliating screams, such as women emit when they see ghosts or caterpillars. It's an awful thing to hear a strong, desperate, fat man scream incontinently in a cave at daybreak.

24   I jumped up to see what the matter was. Red Chief was sitting on Bill's chest, with one hand twined in Bill's hair. In the other he had the sharp case-knife we used for slicing bacon; and he was industriously and realistically trying to take Bill's scalp, according to the sentence that had been pronounced upon him the evening before.

25   I got the knife away from the kid and made him lie down again. But, from that moment, Bill's spirit was broken. He laid down on his side of the bed, but he never closed an eye again in sleep as long as that boy was with us. I dozed off for a while, but along toward sun-up I remembered that Red Chief had said I was to be burned at the stake at the rising of the sun. I wasn't nervous or afraid; but I sat up and lit my pipe and leaned against a rock.

26   "What you getting up so soon for, Sam?" asked Bill.

27   "Me?" says I. "Oh, I got a kind of pain in my shoulder. I thought sitting up would rest it."

28   "You're a liar!" says Bill. "You're afraid. You was to be burned at sunrise, and you was afraid he'd do it. And he would, too, if he could find a match. Ain't it awful, Sam? Do you think anybody will pay out money to get a little imp like that back home?"

29   "Sure," said I. "A rowdy kid like that is just the kind that parents dote on. Now, you and the Chief get up and cook breakfast, while I go up on the top of this mountain and reconnoiter."

30   I went up on the peak of the little mountain and ran my eye over the contiguous vicinity. Over towards Summit I expected to see the sturdy yeomanry of the village armed with scythes and pitchforks beating the countryside for the dastardly kidnappers. But what I saw was a peaceful landscape dotted with one man ploughing with a dun mule. Nobody was dragging the creek; no couriers dashed hither and yon, bringing tidings of no news to the distracted parents. There was a sylvan attitude of somnolent sleepiness pervading that section of the external outward surface of Alabama that lay exposed to my view. "Perhaps," says I to myself, "it has not yet been discovered that the wolves have borne away the

tender lambkin from the fold. Heaven help the wolves!" says I, and I went down the mountain to breakfast.

31   When I got to the cave I found Bill backed up against the side of it, breathing hard, and the boy threatening to smash him with a rock half as big as a cocoanut.

32   "He put a red-hot boiled potato down my back," explained Bill, "and then mashed it with his foot; and I boxed his ears. Have you got a gun about you, Sam?"

33   I took the rock away from the boy and kind of patched up the argument. "I'll fix you," says the kid to Bill. "No man ever yet struck the Red Chief but he got paid for it. You better beware!"

34   After breakfast the kid takes a piece of leather with strings wrapped around it out of his pocket and goes outside the cave unwinding it.

35   "What's he up to now?" says Bill, anxiously. "You don't think he'll run away, do you, Sam?"

36   "No fear of it," says I. "He don't seem to be much of a home body. But we've got to fix up some plan about the ransom. There don't seem to be much excitement around Summit on account of his disappearance; but maybe they haven't realized yet that he's gone. His folks may think he's spending the night with Aunt Jane or one of the neighbors. Anyhow, he'll be missed to-day. To-night we must get a message to his father demanding the two thousand dollars for his return."

37   Just then we heard a kind of war-whoop, such as David might have emitted when he knocked out the champion Goliath. It was a sling that Red Chief had pulled out of his pocket, and he was whirling it around his head.

38   I dodged, and heard a heavy thud and a kind of a sigh from Bill, like a horse gives out when you take his saddle off. A rock the size of an egg had caught Bill just behind his left ear. He loosened himself all over and fell in the fire across the frying pan of hot water for washing the dishes. I dragged him out and poured cold water on his head for half an hour.

39   By and by, Bill sits up and feels behind his ear and says: "Sam, do you know who my favorite Biblical character is?"

40   "Take it easy," says I. "You'll come to your senses presently."

41   "King Herod," says he. "You won't go away and leave me here alone, will you, Sam?"

42   I went out and caught that boy and shook him until his freckles rattled.

43   "If you don't behave," says I, "I'll take you straight home. Now, are you going to be good, or not?"

44   "I was only funning," says he, sullenly. "I didn't mean to hurt Old Hank. But what did he hit me for? I'll behave, Snake-eye, if you won't send me home, and if you'll let me play the Black Scout to-day."

45   "I don't know the game," says I. "That's for you and Mr. Bill to decide. He's your playmate for the day. I'm going away for a while, on business. Now, you come in and make friends with him and say you are sorry for hurting him, or home you go, at once."

46   I made him and Bill shake hands, and then I took Bill aside and told him I was going to Poplar Grove, a little village three miles from the cave, and find out what I could about how the kidnapping had been regarded in Summit. Also, I thought it best to send a peremptory letter to old man Dorset that day, demanding the ransom and dictating how it should be paid.

47   "You know, Sam," says Bill, "I've stood by you without batting an eye in earthquakes, fire and flood—in poker games, dynamite outrages, police raids, train robberies, and cyclones. I never lost my nerve yet till we kidnapped that two-legged skyrocket of a kid. He's got me going. You won't leave me long with him, will you, Sam?"

48   "I'll be back some time this afternoon," says I. "You must keep the boy amused and quiet till I return. And now we'll write the letter to old Dorset."

49   Bill and I got paper and pencil and worked on the letter while Red Chief, with a blanket wrapped around him, strutted up and down, guarding the mouth of the cave. Bill begged me tearfully to make the ransom fifteen hundred dollars instead of two thousand. "I ain't attempting," says he, "to decry the celebrated moral aspect of parental affection, but we're dealing with humans, and it ain't human for anybody to give up two thousand dollars for that forty-pound chunk of freckled wildcat. I'm willing to take a chance at fifteen hundred dollars. You can charge the difference up to me."

50   So, to relieve Bill, I acceded, and we collaborated a letter that ran this way:

51   *Ebenezer Dorset, Esq.:*

52   *We have your boy concealed in a place far from Summit. It is useless for you or the most skilful detectives to attempt to find him. Absolutely, the only terms on which you can have him restored to you are these: We demand fifteen hundred dollars in large bills for his return; the money to be left at midnight to-night at the same spot and in the same box as your reply—as hereinafter described. If you agree to these terms, send your answer in writing by a solitary messenger to-night at half-past eight o'clock. After crossing Owl Creek on the road to Poplar Grove, there are three large trees about a hundred yards apart, close to the fence of the wheat field on the right-hand side. At the bottom of the fence-post, opposite the third tree, will be found a small pasteboard box.*

53   *The messenger will place the answer in this box and return immediately to Summit.*

54   *If you attempt any treachery or fail to comply with our demand as stated, you will never see your boy again.*

55   *If you pay the money as demanded, he will be returned to you safe and well within three hours. These terms are final, and if you do not accede to them no further communication will be attempted.*

56   TWO DESPERATE MEN

57   I addressed this letter to Dorset, and put it in my pocket. As I was about to start, the kid comes up to me and says:

58   "Aw, Snake-eye, you said I could play the Black Scout while you was gone."

59   "Play it, of course," says I. "Mr. Bill will play with you. What kind of a game is it?"

60   "I'm the Black Scout," says Red Chief, "and I have to ride to the stockade to warn the settlers that the Indians are coming. I'm tired of playing Indian myself. I want to be the Black Scout."

61   "All right," says I. "It sounds harmless to me. I guess Mr. Bill will help you foil the pesky savages."

62   "What am I to do?" asks Bill, looking at the kid suspiciously.

63   "You are the hoss," says Black Scout. "Get down on your hands and knees. How can I ride to the stockade without a hoss?"

64   "You'd better keep him interested," said I, "till we get the scheme going. Loosen up."

65   Bill gets down on his all fours, and a look comes in his eye like a rabbit's when you catch it in a trap.

66   "How far is it to the stockade, kid?" he asks, in a husky manner of voice.

67   "Ninety miles," says the Black Scout. "And you have to hump yourself to get there on time. Whoa, now!"

68   The Black Scout jumps on Bill's back and digs his heels in his side.

69   "For Heaven's sake," says Bill, "hurry back, Sam, as soon as you can. I wish we hadn't made the ransom more than a thousand. Say, you quit kicking me or I'll get up and warm you good."

70   I walked over to Poplar Grove and sat around the post-office and store, talking with the chaw-bacons that came in to trade. One whiskerando says that he hears Summit is all upset on account of Elder Ebenezer Dorset's boy having been lost or stolen. That was all I wanted to know. I bought some smoking tobacco, referred casually to the price of blackeyed peas, posted my letter surreptitiously, and came away. The postmaster said the mail-carrier would come by in an hour to take the mail to Summit.

71   When I got back to the cave Bill and the boy were not to be found. I explored the vicinity of the cave, and risked a yodel or two, but there was no response.

72   So I lighted my pipe and sat down on a mossy bank to await developments.

73   In about half an hour I heard the bushes rustle, and Bill wabbled out into the little glade in front of the cave. Behind him was the kid, stepping softly like a scout, with a broad grin on his face. Bill stopped, took off his hat, and wiped his face with a red handkerchief. The kid stopped about eight feet behind him.

74   "Sam," says Bill, "I suppose you'll think I'm a renegade, but I couldn't help it. I'm a grown person with masculine proclivities and habits of self-defense, but there is a time when all systems of egotism and predominance fall. The boy is gone. I sent him home. All is off. There was martyrs in old times," goes on Bill, "that suffered death rather than give up the particular graft they enjoyed. None of 'em ever was subjugated to such supernatural tortures as I have been. I tried to be faithful to our articles of depredation; but there came a limit."

75   "What's the trouble, Bill?" I asks him.

76   "I was rode," says Bill, "the ninety miles to the stockade, not barring an inch. Then, when the settlers was rescued, I was given oats. Sand ain't a palatable substitute. And then, for an hour I had to try to explain to him why there was nothin' in holes, how a road can run both ways, and what makes the grass green. I tell you, Sam, a human can only stand so much. I takes him by the neck of his clothes and drags him down the mountain. On the way he kicks my legs black and blue from the knees down; and I've got to have two or three bites on my thumb and hand cauterized.

77   "But he's gone"—continues Bill—"gone home. I showed him the road to Summit and kicked him about eight feet nearer there at one kick. I'm sorry we lose the ransom; but it was either that or Bill Driscoll to the madhouse."

78   Bill is puffing and blowing, but there is a look of ineffable peace and growing content on his rose-pink features.

79   "Bill," says I, "there isn't any heart disease in your family, is there?"

80   "No," says Bill, "nothing chronic except malaria and accidents. Why?"

81   "Then you might turn around," says I, "and have a look behind you."

82   Bill turns and sees the boy, and loses his complexion and sits down plump on the ground and begins to pluck aimlessly at grass and little sticks. For an hour I was afraid of his mind. And then I told him that my scheme was to put the whole job through immediately and that we would get the ransom and be off with it by midnight if old Dorset fell in with our proposition. So Bill braced up enough to give the kid a weak sort of a smile and a promise to play the Russian in a Japanese war with him as soon as he felt a little better.

83   I had a scheme for collecting that ransom without danger of being caught by counterplots that ought to commend itself to professional kidnappers. The tree under which the answer was to be left—and the money later on—was close to the road fence with big, bare fields on all sides. If a gang of constables should be watching for any one to come for the note, they could see him a long way off crossing the fields or in the road. But no, sirree! At half-past eight I was up in that tree as well hidden as a tree toad, waiting for the messenger to arrive.

84   Exactly on time, a half-grown boy rides up the road on a bicycle, locates the pasteboard box at the foot of the fence-post, slips a folded piece of paper into it, and pedals away again back toward Summit.

85   I waited an hour and then concluded the thing was square. I slid down the tree, got the note, slipped along the fence till I struck the woods, and was back at the cave in another half an hour. I opened the note, got near the lantern, and read it to Bill. It was written with a pen in a crabbed hand, and the sum and substance of it was this:

86   *Two Desperate Men.*

87   *Gentlemen: I received your letter to-day by post, in regard to the ransom you ask for the return of my son. I think you are a little high in your demands, and I hereby make you a counter-proposition, which I am inclined to believe you will accept. You bring Johnny home and pay me two hundred and fifty dollars in cash, and I agree to take him off your hands. You had better come at night, for the neighbors believe he is lost, and I couldn't be responsible for what they would do to anybody they saw bringing him back. Very respectfully,*

88   *Ebenezer Dorset*

89   "Great pirates of Penzance," says I; "of all the impudent—"

90   But I glanced at Bill, and hesitated. He had the most appealing look in his eyes I ever saw on the face of a dumb or a talking brute.

91   "Sam," says he, "what's two hundred and fifty dollars, after all? We've got the money. One more night of this kid will send me to a bed in Bedlam. Besides being a thorough gentleman, I think Mr. Dorset is a spendthrift for making us such a liberal offer. You ain't going to let the chance go, are you?"

92   "Tell you the truth, Bill," says I, "this little he ewe lamb has somewhat got on my nerves too. We'll take him home, pay the ransom, and make our getaway."

93   We took him home that night. We got him to go by telling him that his father had bought a silver-mounted rifle and a pair of moccasins for him, and we were to hunt bears the next day.

94   It was just twelve o'clock when we knocked at Ebenezer's front door. Just at the moment when I should have been abstracting the fifteen hundred dollars from the box under the tree, according to the original proposition, Bill was counting out two hundred and fifty dollars into Dorset's hand.

95   When the kid found out we were going to leave him at home he started up a howl like a calliope and fastened himself as tight as a leech to Bill's leg. His father peeled him away gradually, like a porous plaster.

96   "How long can you hold him?" asks Bill.

97   "I'm not as strong as I used to be," says old Dorset, "but I think I can promise you ten minutes."

98   "Enough," says Bill. "In ten minutes I shall cross the Central, Southern, and Middle Western States, and be legging it trippingly for the Canadian border."

99   And, as dark as it was, and as fat as Bill was, and as good a runner as I am, he was a good mile and a half out of Summit before I could catch up with him.

● ●

THE RANSOM OF RED CHIEF

JOURNAL

1. MLA Works Cited   *Using this model, record this story here.*

Author's Last Name, First Name. "Title of the Story." *Title of the Book.* 3rd ed. Ed.

First Name Last Name. City: Publisher, year. Page number(s) of this story. Print.

2. Main Character(s)   *Describe each main character, and explain why you think each is a main character.*

3. Supporting Characters   *Describe each supporting character, and explain why you think each is a supporting character.*

4. Setting and Props   *Describe the setting(s) and all relevant prop(s).*

5. Sequence *Outline the events of the story in order.*

6. Plot *Tell the story in no more than two sentences.*

7. Conflicts *Identify and explain all the conflicts involved here.*

8. Significant Quotations *Explain the importance of each of these quotations. Record the page number in the parentheses.*

a. "Bill and me had a joint capital of about six hundred dollars, and we needed just two thousand dollars more to pull off a fraudulent town-lot scheme in Western Illinois with" ( ).

b. " 'For Heaven's sake,' says Bill, 'hurry back, Sam, as soon as you can. I wish we hadn't made the ransom more than a thousand' " ( ).

   c. "'Then you might turn around,' says I, 'and have a look behind you'" ( ).

   d. "You bring Johnny home and pay me two hundred and fifty dollars in cash, and I agree to take him off your hands" ( ).

   e. "[A]ccording to the original proposition, Bill was counting out two hundred and fifty dollars into Dorset's hand" ( ).

9. **Literary Elements** *Look at this chapter's title and explain why you think this story is placed in this chapter. Explain in which other chapter(s) you might place this story, as relevant to the literary element(s) of the chapter(s).*

10. **Foreshadowing, Irony, and/or Symbolism** *Explain examples of foreshadowing, irony, and/or symbolism in this story.*

FOLLOW-UP QUESTIONS

10 SHORT QUESTIONS

What is the __best__ answer for each?

_____ 1. Bill and Sam probably
   a. are rich.
   b. are comfortable.
   c. need money.

_____ 2. Johnny Dorset
   a. stays at camp.
   b. has to be forced to stay.
   c. decides to stay home.

_____ 3. When Johnny is with Bill and Sam, he feels
   a. that he is suffering.
   b. as if he is out camping.
   c. homesick.

_____ 4. Bill
   a. pays no attention to Johnny.
   b. enjoys playing with Johnny.
   c. does not enjoy playing with Johnny.

_____ 5. The one who seems to plan the scheme is
   a. Sam.
   b. Bill.
   c. Johnny.

_____ 6. When Sam goes to Poplar Grove, he thinks Summit
   a. is happy or, at least, relieved.
   b. is deeply concerned and upset.
   c. has not yet heard the news.

_____ 7. In fact, Summit probably
   a. is happy or, at least, relieved.
   b. is deeply concerned and upset.
   c. has not yet heard the news.

_____ 8. Bill and Sam ask for a ransom of
   a. $2,000.
   b. $1,500.
   c. $250.

_____ 9. Ebenezer Dorset
   a. rapidly pays the ransom.
   b. sends out the sheriff.
   c. sends a counter-proposition.

_____ 10. In the end, Bill and Sam
   a. gain $2,000.
   b. gain $1,500.
   c. pay out $250.

5 SIGNIFICANT QUOTATIONS

What is the importance of each of these quotations?

1. "We selected for our victim the only child of a prominent citizen named Ebenezer Dorset."

2. " 'You're a liar!' says Bill. '[…]. You was to be burned at sunrise, and you was afraid he'd do it.' "

3. *"We demand fifteen hundred dollars in large bills for his return […]."*

4. "One whiskerando says that he hears Summit is all upset on account of Elder Ebenezer Dorset's boy having been lost or stolen."

5. *"I think you are a little high in your demands, and I hereby make you a counter-proposition, which I am inclined to believe you will accept."*

2 COMPREHENSION ESSAY QUESTIONS

Use specific details and information from the story to answer these questions as completely as possible.

1. What is the irony in this story? Use specific details and information from the story to support your explanation.

2. What are Sam and Bill's mistakes? Use specific details and information from the story to support your explanation.

DISCUSSION QUESTIONS

Be prepared to discuss these questions in class.

1. How does the illustration demonstrate this story? Use specific details from the story to support your ideas.

2. How many ironies can you find in this story? Be prepared to discuss each.

WRITING

Use each of these ideas for writing an essay.

1. The irony here is based on a series of misunderstandings and wrong assumptions. Write about a time that you or someone you know had problems because of misunderstandings or wrong assumptions.

2. The irony in this story is a series of humorous twists. Write about a humorous twist in your life or in the life of someone you know.

Further Writing

1. Compare and contrast Johnny Dorset in this story with Tom Sawyer in the selection by Mark Twain (page 132).

2. Compare and contrast the society in the stories of Mark Twain and O. Henry, which are set in simpler times, with American society today.

THE ADVENTURE OF THE SPECKLED BAND

Arthur Conan Doyle

Pre-reading Vocabulary
Context

Use context clues to define these words before reading. Use a dictionary as needed.

1. The snake's skin was *speckled* with dots of colors in reds and browns and blues. *Speckled* means _____.

2. By putting two and two together from little hints he sees, Sherlock Holmes is able to make *deductions* about a person. *Deduction* means _____.

3. The people watched in *horror* as the boat began to sink off-shore and they were too far away to help. *Horror* means

   _____.

4. Vernie had a *suspicion* that Bill was planning a surprise party for her when he would not let her look in the closets. *Suspicion* means

   _____.

5. Sandy was absolutely thrilled when she was able to purchase a large *estate* with forty rooms and acres of gardens. *Estate* means

   _____.

6. Because he is an only child, Albert is the only *heir* to his father's estate and, therefore, will receive all his father's money. *Heir* means

   _____.

7. When Helena bought a new home, she had to go to the bank and take out a *mortgage* to pay for the house. *Mortgage* means

   _____.

8. After Brendan spent all his money, he ended up living on the streets like a *pauper*. *Pauper* means _____.

9. Before she died, Lena *bequeathed* all her jewelry to her daughters so that the jewelry would stay in the family. *Bequeath* means

_____.

10. Wanting to be the first or the best can drive someone crazy and can become a *mania*. *Mania* means _____.

11. The wandering *gypsy* led a *vagabond's* life, living in the trailer he traveled in from town to town. *Gypsy* and/or *vagabond* means

_____.

12. The spotted *cheetah* is faster than the lion or tiger and is a mighty hunter. *Cheetah* means _____.

13. Justin gave Lauren a ring to let everyone know about their *engagement* to be married. *Engagement* means _____.

14. Drinking poison is generally *fatal* and results in death. *Fatal* means

_____.

15. To call his dog, Keith bought a small, silver *whistle* that made a sound when he put the whistle up to his mouth and blew on it. *Whistle* means _____.

16. When someone dies, it is normal to call the *coroner* so that he can medically determine the cause of death. *Coroner* means

_____.

17. The heat in the room comes through a small grate in the top of the wall that allows for *ventilation* and movement air. *Ventilation* means _____.

18. Although there really was no window there, the artist painted a *dummy* window on the wall to pretend there was one. *Dummy* means _____.

19. When Lucille wanted to walk the dog, she took out his narrow *lash* that she would hold and attached it to the dog's collar. *Lash* means

_____.

20. The *adder* is a nasty snake and one of the most dangerous of all poisonous serpents. *Adder* means _____.

PRE-READING VOCABULARY
STRUCTURAL ATTACK

Define these words by solving the parts. Use the Glossary or a dictionary as needed.

1. commonplace	17. wasteful	33. recovered
2. acquirement	18. aristocratic	34. beloved
3. unusual	19. imprisonment	35. metallic
4. fantastic	20. remarriage	36. lonelier
5. untimely	21. ancestral	37. housekeeper
6. widespread	22. overjoyed	38. agricultural
7. logical	23. disgraceful	39. unapproachable
8. unravelled	24. uncontrollable	40. whitewashed
9. veiled	25. hospitality	41. country-house
10. frightened	26. occasionally	42. stepdaughter
11. all-comprehensive	27. inhabited	43. unrepaired
12. soothingly	28. awakened	44. noiselessly
13. forearm	29. impending	45. open-eyed
14. dog-cart	30. terrified	46. night-blind
15. wickedness	31. horror-stricken	47. usually
16. stepfather	32. unconscious	48. schemer

PRE-READING QUESTIONS

Try answering these questions as you read.

What has happened to Helen Stoner's sister?

What is Doctor Roylott like?

What does Holmes discover?

THE ADVENTURE OF THE SPECKLED BAND

Arthur Conan Doyle

Arthur Conan Doyle was born in Edinburgh, Scotland, in 1859. After studying under the Jesuits at Stonehurst College in Britain and Feldkirch College in Austria, he secured his M.D. at Edinburgh University. He eventually became a practicing ophthalmologist in London, but within a short time he largely left his medical practice and turned to writing. In 1902, he was knighted and became Sir Arthur Conan Doyle for his service to Britain during the Boer War. He died in Sussex in 1930.

Since his character, Sherlock Holmes, took up residence at 221b Baker Street, Holmes has become one of the most enduring detectives in the English language. With the curious Dr. Watson, Holmes sets off to solve mysteries with extraordinary deductive skills. At one point, Doyle became tired of Holmes and killed him off, but then brought him back to life due to popular demand. Today, Holmes remains the quintessential sleuth and can be found in many novels and short story collections.

On glancing over my notes of the seventy odd cases in which I have during the last eight years studied the methods of my friend Sherlock Holmes, I find many tragic, some comic, a large number merely strange, but none commonplace; for, working as he did rather for the love of his art than for the acquirement of wealth, he refused to associate himself with any investigation which did not tend towards the unusual, and even the fantastic. Of all these varied cases, however, I cannot recall any which presented more singular features than that which was associated with the well-known Surrey family of the Roylotts of Stoke Moran. The events in question occurred in the early days of my association with Holmes, when we were sharing rooms as bachelors in Baker Street. It is possible that I might have placed them upon record before, but a promise of secrecy was made at the time, from which I have only been freed during the last month by the untimely death of the lady to whom the pledge was given. It is perhaps as well that the facts should now come to light, for I have reasons to know that there are widespread rumours as to the death of Dr. Grimesby Roylott which tend to make the matter even more terrible than the truth.

2   It was early in April in the year '83 that I woke one morning to find Sherlock Holmes standing, fully dressed, by the side of my bed. He was a late riser, as a rule, and as the clock on the mantel-piece showed me that it was only a quarter-past seven, I blinked up at him in some surprise, and perhaps just a little resentment, for I was myself regular in my habits.

3   "Very sorry to knock you up, Watson," said he, "but it's the common lot this morning. Mrs. Hudson has been knocked up, she retorted upon me, and I on you."

4   "What is it, then—a fire?"

5   "No; a client. It seems that a young lady has arrived in a considerable state of excitement, who insists upon seeing me. She is waiting now in the sitting-room. Now, when young ladies wander about the metropolis at this hour of the morning, and knock sleepy people up out of their beds, I presume that it is something very pressing which they have to communicate. Should it prove to be an interesting case, you would, I am sure, wish to follow it from the outset. I thought, at any rate, that I should call you and give you the chance."

6   "My dear fellow, I would not miss it for anything."

7   I had no keener pleasure than in following Holmes in his professional investigations, and in admiring the rapid deductions, as swift as intuitions, and yet always founded on a logical basis, with which he unravelled the problems which were submitted to him. I rapidly threw on my clothes and was ready in a few minutes to accompany my friend down to the sitting-room. A lady dressed in black and heavily veiled, who had been sitting in the window, rose as we entered.

8   "Good-morning, madam," said Holmes cheerily. "My name is Sherlock Holmes. This is my intimate friend and associate, Dr. Watson, before whom you can speak as freely as before myself. Ha! I am glad to see that Mrs. Hudson has had the good sense to light the fire. Pray draw up to it, and I shall order you a cup of hot coffee, for I observe that you are shivering."

9   "It is not cold which makes me shiver," said the woman in a low voice, changing her seat as requested.

10   "What, then?"

11   "It is fear, Mr. Holmes. It is terror." She raised her veil as she spoke, and we could see that she was indeed in a pitiable state of agitation, her face all drawn and gray, with restless, frightened eyes, like those of some hunted animal. Her features and figure were those of a woman of thirty, but her hair was shot with premature gray, and her expression was weary and haggard. Sherlock Holmes ran her over with one of his quick, all-comprehensive glances.

12   "You must not fear," said he soothingly, bending forward and patting her forearm. "We shall soon set matters right, I have no doubt. You have come in by train this morning, I see."

13   "You know me, then?"

14   "No, but I observe the second half of a return ticket in the palm of your left glove. You must have started early, and yet you had a good drive in a dog-cart, along heavy roads, before you reached the station."

15   The lady gave a violent start and stared in bewilderment at my companion.

16   "There is no mystery, my dear madam," said he, smiling. "The left arm of your jacket is spattered with mud in no less than seven places. The marks are perfectly fresh. There is no vehicle save a dog-cart which throws up mud in that way, and then only when you sit on the left-hand side of the driver."

17   "Whatever your reasons may be, you are perfectly correct," said she. "I started from home before six, reached Leatherhead at twenty past, and came in by the first train to Waterloo. Sir, I can stand this strain no longer; I shall go mad if it continues. I have no one to turn to—none, save only one, who cares for me, and he, poor fellow, can be of little aid. I have heard of you, Mr. Holmes; I have heard of you from Mrs. Farintosh, whom you helped in the hour of her sore need. It was from her that I had your address. Oh, sir, do you not think that you could help me, too, and at least throw a little light through the dense darkness which surrounds me? At present it is out of my power to reward you for your services, but in a month or six weeks I shall be married, with the control of my own income, and then at least you shall not find me ungrateful."

18   Holmes turned to his desk and, unlocking it, drew out a small case-book, which he consulted.

19   "Farintosh," said he. "Ah yes, I recall the case; it was concerned with an opal tiara. I think it was before your time, Watson. I can only say, madam, that I shall be happy to devote the same care to your case as I did to that of your friend. As to reward, my profession is its own reward; but you are at liberty to defray

whatever expenses I may be put to, at the time which suits you best. And now I beg that you will lay before us everything that may help us in forming an opinion upon the matter."

20   "Alas!" replied the visitor, "the very horror of my situation lies in the fact that my fears are so vague, and my suspicions depend so entirely upon small points, which might seem trivial to another, that even he to whom of all others I have a right to look for help and advice looks upon all that I tell him about it as the fancies of a nervous woman. He does not say so, but I can read it from his soothing answers and averted eyes. But I have heard, Mr. Holmes, that you can see deeply into the manifold wickedness of the human heart. You may advise me how to walk amid the dangers which encompass me."

21   "I am all attention, madam."

22   "My name is Helen Stoner, and I am living with my stepfather, who is the last survivor of one of the oldest Saxon families in England, the Roylotts of Stoke Moran, on the western border of Surrey."

23   Holmes nodded his head. "The name is familiar to me," said he.

24   "The family was at one time among the richest in England, and the estates extended over the borders into Berkshire in the north, and Hampshire in the west. In the last century, however, four successive heirs were of a dissolute and wasteful disposition, and the family ruin was eventually completed by a gambler in the days of the Regency. Nothing was left save a few acres of ground, and the two-hundred-year-old house, which is itself crushed under a heavy mortgage. The last squire dragged out his existence there, living the horrible life of an aristocratic pauper; but his only son, my stepfather, seeing that he must adapt himself to the new conditions, obtained an advance from a relative, which enabled him to take a medical degree and went out to Calcutta, where, by his professional skill and his force of character, he established a large practice. In a fit of anger, however, caused by some robberies which had been perpetrated in the house, he beat his native butler to death and narrowly escaped a capital sentence. As it was, he suffered a long term of imprisonment and afterwards returned to England a morose and disappointed man.

25   "When Dr. Roylott was in India he married my mother, Mrs. Stoner, the young widow of Major-General Stoner, of the Bengal Artillery. My sister Julia and I were twins, and we were only two years old at the time of my mother's remarriage. She had a considerable sum of money—not less than £1000 a year—and this she bequeathed to Dr. Roylott entirely while we resided with him, with a provision that a certain annual sum should be allowed to each of us in the event of our marriage. Shortly after

our return to England my mother died—she was killed eight years ago in a railway accident near Crewe. Dr. Roylott then abandoned his attempts to establish himself in practice in London and took us to live with him in the old ancestral house at Stoke Moran. The money which my mother had left was enough for all our wants, and there seemed to be no obstacle to our happiness.

26   "But a terrible change came over our stepfather about this time. Instead of making friends and exchanging visits with our neighbors, who had at first been overjoyed to see a Roylott of Stoke Moran back in the old family seat, he shut himself up in his house and seldom came out save to indulge in ferocious quarrels with whoever might cross his path. Violence of temper approaching mania has been hereditary in the men of the family, and in my stepfather's case it had, I believe, been intensified by his long residence in the tropics. A series of disgraceful brawls took place, two of which ended in the police-court, until at last he became the terror of the village, and the folks would fly at his approach, for he is a man of immense strength, and absolutely uncontrollable in his anger.

27   "Last week he hurled the local blacksmith over a parapet into a stream, and it was only by paying over all the money which I could gather together that I was able to avert another public exposure. He had no friends at all save the wandering gypsies, and he would give these vagabonds leave to encamp upon the few acres of bramble-covered land which represent the family estate, and would accept in return the hospitality of their tents, wandering away with them sometimes for weeks on end. He has a passion also for Indian animals, which are sent over to him by a correspondent, and he has at this moment a cheetah and a baboon, which wander freely over his grounds and are feared by the villagers almost as much as their master.

28   "You can imagine from what I say that my poor sister Julia and I had no great pleasure in our lives. No servant would stay with us, and for a long time we did all the work of the house. She was but thirty at the time of her death, and yet her hair had already begun to whiten, even as mine has."

29   "Your sister is dead, then?"

30   "She died just two years ago, and it is of her death that I wish to speak to you. You can understand that, living the life which I have described, we were little likely to see anyone of our own age and position. We had, however, an aunt, my mother's maiden sister, Miss Honoria Westphail, who lives near Harrow, and we were occasionally allowed to pay short visits at this lady's house. Julia went there at Christmas two years ago, and met there a half-pay major of marines, to whom she became engaged. My stepfather learned of the engagement when my sister returned

and offered no objection to the marriage; but within a fortnight of the day which had been fixed for the wedding, the terrible event occurred which has deprived me of my only companion."

31   Sherlock Holmes had been leaning back in his chair with his eyes closed and his head sunk in a cushion, but he half opened his lids now and glanced across at his visitor.

32   "Pray be precise as to details," said he.

33   "It is easy for me to be so, for every event of that dreadful time is seared into my memory. The manor-house is, as I have already said, very old, and only one wing is now inhabited. The bedrooms in this wing are on the ground floor, the sitting-rooms being in the central block of the buildings. Of these bedrooms the first is Dr. Roylott's, the second my sister's, and the third my own. There is no communication between them, but they all open out into the same corridor. Do I make myself plain?"

34   "Perfectly so."

35   "The windows of the three rooms open out upon the lawn. That fatal night Dr. Roylott had gone to his room early, though we knew that he had not retired to rest, for my sister was troubled by the smell of the strong Indian cigars which it was his custom to smoke. She left her room, therefore, and came into mine, where she sat for some time, chatting about her approaching wedding. At eleven o'clock she rose to leave me, but she paused at the door and looked back.

36   " 'Tell me, Helen,' said she, 'have you ever heard anyone whistle in the dead of the night?'

37   " 'Never,' said I.

38   " 'I suppose that you could not possibly whistle, yourself, in your sleep?'

39   " 'Certainly not. But why?'

40   " 'Because during the last few nights I have always, about three in the morning, heard a low, clear whistle. I am a light sleeper, and it has awakened me. I cannot tell where it came from—perhaps from the next room, perhaps from the lawn. I thought that I would just ask you whether you had heard it.'

41   " 'No, I have not. It must be those wretched gypsies in the plantation.'

42   " 'Very likely. And yet if it were on the lawn, I wonder that you did not hear it also.'

43   " 'Ah, but I sleep more heavily than you.'

44   " 'Well, it is of no great consequence, at any rate.' She smiled back at me, closed my door, and a few moments later I heard her key turn in the lock."

45   "Indeed," said Holmes. "Was it your custom always to lock yourselves in at night?"

46   "Always."

47   "And why?"

48   "I think that I mentioned to you that the doctor kept a cheetah and a baboon. We had no feeling of security unless our doors were locked."

49   "Quite so. Pray proceed with your statement."

50   "I could not sleep that night. A vague feeling of impending misfortune impressed me. My sister and I, you will recollect, were twins, and you know how subtle are the links which bind two souls which are so closely allied. It was a wild night. The wind was howling outside, and the rain was beating and splashing against the windows. Suddenly, amid all the hubbub of the gale, there burst forth the wild scream of a terrified woman. I knew that it was my sister's voice. I sprang from my bed, wrapped a shawl round me, and rushed into the corridor. As I opened my door I seemed to hear a low whistle, such as my sister described, and a few moments later a clanging sound, as if a mass of metal had fallen. As I ran down the passage, my sister's door was unlocked, and revolved slowly upon its hinges. I stared at it horror-stricken, not knowing what was about to issue from it. By the light of the corridor-lamp I saw my sister appear at the opening, her face blanched with terror, her hands groping for help, her whole figure swaying to and fro like that of a drunkard. I ran to her and threw my arms round her, but at that moment her knees seemed to give way and she fell to the ground. She writhed as one who is in terrible pain, and her limbs were dreadfully convulsed. At first I thought that she had not recognized me, but as I bent over her she suddenly shrieked out in a voice which I shall never forget, 'Oh, my God! Helen! It was the band! The speckled band!' There was something else which she would fain have said, and she stabbed with her finger into the air in the direction of the doctor's room, but a fresh convulsion seized her and choked her words. I rushed out, calling loudly for my stepfather, and I met him hastening from his room in his dressing-gown. When he reached my sister's side she was unconscious, and though he poured brandy down her throat and sent for medical aid from the village, all efforts were in vain, for she slowly sank and died without having recovered her consciousness. Such was the dreadful end of my beloved sister."

51   "One moment," said Holmes; "are you sure about this whistle and metallic sound? Could you swear to it?"

52   "That was what the county coroner asked me at the inquiry. It is my strong impression that I heard it, and yet, among the crash of the gale and the creaking of an old house, I may possibly have been deceived."

53   "Was your sister dressed?"

54   "No, she was in her night-dress. In her right hand was found the charred stump of a match, and in her left a matchbox."

55   "Showing that she had struck a light and looked about her when the alarm took place. That is important. And what conclusions did the coroner come to?"

56   "He investigated the case with great care, for Dr. Roylott's conduct had long been notorious in the county, but he was unable to find any satisfactory cause of death. My evidence showed that the door had been fastened upon the inner side, and the windows were blocked by old-fashioned shutters with broad iron bars, which were secured every night. The walls were carefully sounded, and were shown to be quite solid all round, and the flooring was also thoroughly examined, with the same result. The chimney is wide, but is barred up by four large staples. It is certain, therefore, that my sister was quite alone when she met her end. Besides, there were no marks of any violence upon her."

57   "How about poison?"

58   "The doctors examined her for it, but without success."

59   "What do you think that this unfortunate lady died of, then?"

60   "It is my belief that she died of pure fear and nervous shock, though what it was that frightened her I cannot imagine."

61   "Were there gypsies in the plantation at the time?"

62   "Yes, there are nearly always some there."

63   "Ah, and what did you gather from this allusion to a band—a speckled band?"

64   "Sometimes I have thought that it was merely the wild talk of delirium, sometimes that it may have referred to some band of people, perhaps to these very gypsies in the plantation. I do not know whether the spotted handkerchiefs which so many of them wear over their heads might have suggested the strange adjective which she used."

65   Holmes shook his head like a man who is far from being satisfied.

66   "These are very deep waters," said he; "pray go on with your narrative."

67   "Two years have passed since then, and my life has been until lately lonelier than ever. A month ago, however, a dear friend, whom I have known for many years, has done me the honour to ask my hand in marriage. His name is Armitage—Percy Armitage—the second son of Mr. Armitage, of Crane Water, near Reading. My stepfather has offered no opposition to the match, and we are to be married in the course of the spring. Two days ago some repairs were started in the west wing of the building, and my bedroom wall has been pierced, so that I have had to move into the chamber in which my sister died, and to sleep in the very bed in which she slept. Imagine, then, my thrill of terror when last night, as I lay awake, thinking over her terrible fate, I suddenly heard in the silence of the night the low whistle which had been the herald

of her own death. I sprang up and lit the lamp, but nothing was to be seen in the room. I was too shaken to go to bed again, however, so I dressed, and as soon as it was daylight I slipped down, got a dog-cart at the 'Crown Inn,' which is opposite, and drove to Leatherhead, from whence I have come on this morning with the one object of seeing you and asking your advice."

68   "You have done wisely," said my friend. "But have you told me all?"

69   "Yes, all."

70   "Miss Stoner, you have not. You are screening your stepfather."

71   "Why, what do you mean?"

72   For answer Holmes pushed back the frill of black lace which fringed the hand that lay upon our visitor's knee. Five little livid spots, the marks of four fingers and a thumb, were printed upon the white wrist.

73   "You have been cruelly used," said Holmes.

74   The lady colored deeply and covered over her injured wrist. "He is a hard man," she said, "and perhaps he hardly knows his own strength."

75   There was a long silence, during which Holmes leaned his chin upon his hands and stared into the crackling fire.

76   "This is a very deep business," he said at last. "There are a thousand details which I should desire to know before I decide upon our course of action. Yet we have not a moment to lose. If we were to come to Stoke Moran to-day, would it be possible for us to see over these rooms without the knowledge of your stepfather?"

77   "As it happens, he spoke of coming into town to-day upon some most important business. It is probable that he will be away all day, and that there would be nothing to disturb you. We have a housekeeper now, but she is old and foolish, and I could easily get her out of the way."

78   "Excellent. You are not averse to this trip, Watson?"

79   "By no means."

80   "Then we shall both come. What are you going to do yourself?"

81   "I have one or two things which I would wish to do now that I am in town. But I shall return by the twelve o'clock train, so as to be there in time for your coming."

82   "And you may expect us early in the afternoon. I have myself some small business matters to attend to. Will you not wait and breakfast?"

83   "No, I must go. My heart is lightened already since I have confided my trouble to you. I shall look forward to seeing you again this afternoon." She dropped her thick black veil over her face and glided from the room.

84   "And what do you think of it all, Watson?" asked Sherlock Holmes, leaning back in his chair.

85   "It seems to me to be a most dark and sinister business."

86   "Dark enough and sinister enough."

87   "Yet if the lady is correct in saying that the flooring and walls are sound, and that the door, window, and chimney are impassable, then her sister must have been undoubtedly alone when she met her mysterious end."

88   "What becomes, then, of these nocturnal whistles and what of the very peculiar words of the dying woman?"

89   "I cannot think."

90   "When you combine the ideas of whistles at night, the presence of a band of gypsies who are on intimate terms with this old doctor, the fact that we have every reason to believe that the doctor has an interest in preventing his stepdaughter's marriage, the dying allusion to a band, and finally, the fact that Miss Helen Stoner heard a metallic clang, which might have been caused by one of those metal bars that secured the shutters falling back into place, I think that there is good ground to think that the mystery may be cleared along those lines."

91   "But what, then, did the gypsies do?"

92   "I cannot imagine."

93   "I see many objections to any such theory."

94   "And so do I. It is precisely for that reason that we are going to Stoke Moran this day. I want to see whether the objections are fatal, or if they may be explained away. But what in the name of the devil!"

95   The ejaculation had been drawn from my companion by the fact that our door had been suddenly dashed open, and that a huge man had framed himself in the aperture. His costume was a peculiar mixture of the professional and of the agricultural, having a black top-hat, a long frock-coat, and a pair of high gaiters, with a hunting-crop swinging in his hand. So tall was he that his hat actually brushed the cross bar of the doorway, and his breadth seemed to span it across from side to side. A large face, seared with a thousand wrinkles, burned yellow with the sun, and marked with every evil passion, was turned from one to the other of us, while his deep-set, bile-shot eyes, and his high, thin, fleshless nose, gave him somewhat the resemblance to a fierce old bird of prey.

96   "Which of you is Holmes?" asked this apparition.

97   "My name, sir; but you have the advantage of me," said my companion quietly.

98   "I am Dr. Grimesby Roylott, of Stoke Moran."

99   "Indeed, Doctor," said Holmes blandly. "Pray take a seat."

100   "I will do nothing of the kind. My stepdaughter has been here. I have traced her. What has she been saying to you?"

101   "It is a little cold for the time of the year," said Holmes.

102   "What has she been saying to you?" screamed the old man furiously.

103   "But I have heard that the crocuses promise well," continued my companion imperturbably.

104   "Ha! You put me off, do you?" said our new visitor, taking a step forward and shaking his hunting-crop. "I know you, you scoundrel! I have heard of you before. You are Holmes, the meddler."

105   My friend smiled.

106   "Holmes, the busybody!"

107   His smile broadened.

108   "Holmes, the Scotland Yard Jack-in-office!"

109   Holmes chuckled heartily. "Your conversation is most entertaining," said he. "When you go out close the door, for there is a decided draught."

110   "I will go when I have said my say. Don't you dare to meddle with my affairs. I know that Miss Stoner has been here. I traced her! I am a dangerous man to fall foul of! See here." He stepped swiftly forward, seized the poker, and bent it into a curve with his huge brown hands.

111   "See that you keep yourself out of my grip," he snarled, and hurling the twisted poker into the fireplace he strode out of the room.

112   "He seems a very amiable person," said Holmes, laughing. "I am not quite so bulky, but if he had remained I might have shown him that my grip was not much more feeble than his own." As he spoke he picked up the steel poker and, with a sudden effort, straightened it out again.

113   "Fancy his having the insolence to confound me with the official detective force! This incident gives zest to our investigation, however, and I only trust that our little friend will not suffer from her imprudence in allowing this brute to trace her. And now, Watson, we shall order breakfast, and afterwards I shall walk down to Doctors' Commons, where I hope to get some data which may help us in this matter."

114   It was nearly one o'clock when Sherlock Holmes returned from his excursion. He held in his hand a sheet of blue paper, scrawled over with notes and figures.

115   "I have seen the will of the deceased wife," said he. "To determine its exact meaning I have been obliged to work out the present prices of the investments with which it is concerned. The total income, which at the time of the wife's death was little short of £1100, is now, through the fall in agricultural prices, not more than £750. Each daughter can claim an income of £250, in case of marriage. It is evident, therefore, that if both girls had married, this

beauty would have had a mere pittance, while even one of them would cripple him to a very serious extent. My morning's work has not been wasted, since it has proved that he has the very strongest motives for standing in the way of anything of the sort. And now, Watson, this is too serious for dawdling, especially as the old man is aware that we are interesting ourselves in his affairs; so if you are ready, we shall call a cab and drive to Waterloo. I should be very much obliged if you would slip your revolver into your pocket. An Eley's No. 2 is an excellent argument with gentlemen who can twist steel pokers into knots. That and a tooth-brush are, I think, all that we need."

116   At Waterloo we were fortunate in catching a train for Leatherhead, where we hired a trap at the station inn and drove for four or five miles through the lovely Surrey lanes. It was a perfect day, with a bright sun and a few fleecy clouds in the heavens. The trees and wayside hedges were just throwing out their first green shoots, and the air was full of the pleasant smell of the moist earth. To me at least there was a strange contrast between the sweet promise of the spring and this sinister quest upon which we were engaged. My companion sat in the front of the trap, his arms folded, his hat pulled down over his eyes, and his chin sunk upon his breast, buried in the deepest thought. Suddenly, however, he started, tapped me on the shoulder, and pointed over the meadows.

117   "Look there!" said he.

118   A heavily timbered park stretched up in a gentle slope, thickening into a grove at the highest point. From amid the branches there jutted out the gray gables and high roof-tree of a very old mansion.

119   "Stoke Moran?" said he.

120   "Yes, sir, that be the house of Dr. Grimesby Roylott," remarked the driver.

121   "There is some building going on there," said Holmes; "that is where we are going."

122   "There's the village," said the driver, pointing to a cluster of roofs some distance to the left; "but if you want to get to the house, you'll find it shorter to get over this stile, and so by the foot-path over the fields. There it is, where the lady is walking."

123   "And the lady, I fancy, is Miss Stoner," observed Holmes, shading his eyes. "Yes, I think we had better do as you suggest."

124   We got off, paid our fare, and the trap rattled back on its way to Leatherhead.

125   "I thought it as well," said Holmes as we climbed the stile, "that this fellow should think we had come here as architects, or on some definite business. It may stop his gossip. Good-afternoon, Miss Stoner. You see that we have been as good as our word."

126   Our client of the morning had hurried forward to meet us with a face which spoke her joy. "I have been waiting so eagerly for you," she cried, shaking hands with us warmly. "All has turned out splendidly. Dr. Roylott has gone to town, and it is unlikely that he will be back before evening."

127   "We have had the pleasure of making the doctor's acquaintance," said Holmes, and in a few words he sketched out what had occurred. Miss Stoner turned white to the lips as she listened.

128   "Good heavens!" she cried, "he has followed me, then."

129   "So it appears."

130   "He is so cunning that I never know when I am safe from him. What will he say when he returns?"

131   "He must guard himself, for he may find that there is someone more cunning than himself upon his track. You must lock yourself up from him to-night. If he is violent, we shall take you away to your aunt's at Harrow. Now, we must make the best use of our time, so kindly take us at once to the rooms which we are to examine."

132   The building was of gray, lichen-blotched stone, with a high central portion and two curving wings, like the claws of a crab, thrown out on each side. In one of these wings the windows were broken and blocked with wooden boards, while the roof was partly caved in, a picture of ruin. The central portion was in little better repair, but the right-hand block was comparatively modern, and the blinds in the windows, with the blue smoke curling up from the chimneys, showed that this was where the family resided. Some scaffolding had been erected against the end wall, and the stonework had been broken into, but there were no signs of any workmen at the moment of our visit. Holmes walked slowly up and down the ill-trimmed lawn and examined with deep attention the outsides of the windows.

133   "This, I take it, belongs to the room in which you used to sleep, the centre one to your sister's, and the one next to the main building to Dr. Roylott's chamber?"

134   "Exactly so. But I am now sleeping in the middle one."

135   "Pending the alterations, as I understand. By the way, there does not seem to be any very pressing need for repairs at that end wall."

136   "There were none. I believe that it was an excuse to move me from my room."

137   "Ah! that is suggestive. Now, on the other side of this narrow wing runs the corridor from which these three rooms open. There are windows in it, of course?"

138   "Yes, but very small ones. Too narrow for anyone to pass through."

139   "As you both locked your doors at night, your rooms were unapproachable from that side. Now, would you have the kindness to go into your room and bar your shutters?"

140   Miss Stoner did so, and Holmes, after a careful examination through the open window, endeavored in every way to force the shutter open, but without success. There was no slit through which a knife could be passed to raise the bar. Then with his lens he tested the hinges, but they were of solid iron, built firmly into the massive masonry. "Hum!" said he, scratching his chin in some perplexity, "my theory certainly presents some difficulties. No one could pass these shutters if they were bolted. Well, we shall see if the inside throws any light upon the matter."

141   A small side door led into the whitewashed corridor from which the three bedrooms opened. Holmes refused to examine the third chamber, so we passed at once to the second, that in which Miss Stoner was now sleeping, and in which her sister had met with her fate. It was a homely little room, with a low ceiling and a gaping fireplace, after the fashion of old country-houses. A brown chest of drawers stood in one corner, a narrow white-counterpaned bed in another, and a dressing-table on the left-hand side of the window. These articles with two small wicker-work chairs made up all the furniture in the room save for a square of Wilton carpet in the centre. The boards round and the panelling of the walls were of brown, worm-eaten oak, so old and discolored that it may have dated from the original building of the house. Holmes drew one of the chairs into a corner and sat silent, while his eyes travelled round and round and up and down, taking in every detail of the apartment.

142   "Where does that bell communicate with?" he asked at last, pointing to a thick bell-rope which hung down beside the bed, the tassel actually lying upon the pillow.

143   "It goes to the housekeeper's room."

144   "It looks newer than the other things?"

145   "Yes, it was only put there a couple of years ago."

146   "Your sister asked for it, I suppose?"

147   "No, I never heard of her using it. We used always to get what we wanted for ourselves."

148   "Indeed, it seemed unnecessary to put so nice a bell-pull there. You will excuse me for a few minutes while I satisfy myself as to this floor." He threw himself down upon his face with his lens in his hand and crawled swiftly backward and forward, examining minutely the cracks between the boards. Then he did the same with the woodwork with which the chamber was panelled. Finally he walked over to the bed and spent some time in staring at it and in running his eye up and down the wall. Finally he took the bell-rope in his hand and gave it a brisk tug.

149   "Why, it's a dummy," said he.

150   "Won't it ring?"

151   "No, it is not even attached to a wire. This is very interesting. You can see now that it is fastened to a hook just above where the little opening for the ventilator is."

152   "How very absurd! I never noticed that before."

153   "Very strange!" muttered Holmes, pulling at the rope. "There are one or two very singular points about this room. For example, what a fool a builder must be to open a ventilator into another room, when, with the same trouble, he might have communicated with the outside air!"

154   "That is also quite modern," said the lady.

155   "Done about the same time as the bell-rope?" remarked Holmes.

156   "Yes, there were several little changes carried out about that time."

157   "They seem to have been of a most interesting character— dummy bell-ropes, and ventilators which do not ventilate. With your permission, Miss Stoner, we shall now carry our researches into the inner apartment."

158   Dr. Grimesby Roylott's chamber was larger than that of his stepdaughter, but was as plainly furnished. A campbed, a small wooden shelf full of books, mostly of a technical character, an armchair beside the bed, a plain wooden chair against the wall, a round table, and a large iron safe were the principal things which met the eye. Holmes walked slowly round and examined each and all of them with the keenest interest.

159   "What's in here?" he asked, tapping the safe.

160   "My stepfather's business papers."

161   "Oh! you have seen inside, then?"

162   "Only once, some years ago. I remember that it was full of papers."

163   "There isn't a cat in it, for example?"

164   "No. What a strange idea!"

165   "Well, look at this!" He took up a small saucer of milk which stood on the top of it.

166   "No; we don't keep a cat. But there is a cheetah and a baboon."

167   "Ah, yes, of course! Well, a cheetah is just a big cat, and yet a saucer of milk does not go very far in satisfying its wants, I daresay. There is one point which I should wish to determine." He squatted down in front of the wooden chair and examined the seat of it with the greatest attention.

168   "Thank you. That is quite settled," said he, rising and putting his lens in his pocket. "Hello! Here is something interesting!"

169   The object which had caught his eye was a small dog lash hung on one corner of the bed. The lash, however, was curled upon itself and tied so as to make a loop of whipcord.

170   "What do you make of that, Watson?"

171   "It's a common enough lash. But I don't know why it should be tied."

172   "That is not quite so common, is it? Ah, me! it's a wicked world, and when a clever man turns his brains to crime it is the worst of all. I think that I have seen enough now, Miss Stoner, and with your permission we shall walk out upon the lawn."

173   I had never seen my friend's face so grim or his brow so dark as it was when we turned from the scene of this investigation. We had walked several times up and down the lawn, neither Miss Stoner nor myself liking to break in upon his thoughts before he roused himself from his reverie.

174   "It is very essential, Miss Stoner," said he, "that you should absolutely follow my advice in every respect."

175   "I shall most certainly do so."

176   "The matter is too serious for any hesitation. Your life may depend upon your compliance."

177   "I assure you that I am in your hands."

178   "In the first place, both my friend and I must spend the night in your room."

179   Both Miss Stoner and I gazed at him in astonishment.

180   "Yes, it must be so. Let me explain. I believe that that is the village inn over there?"

181   "Yes, that is the 'Crown.'"

182   "Very good. Your windows would be visible from there?"

183   "Certainly."

184   "You must confine yourself to your room, on pretence of a headache, when your stepfather comes back. Then when you hear him retire for the night, you must open the shutters of your window, undo the hasp, put your lamp there as a signal to us, and then withdraw quietly with everything which you are likely to want into the room which you used to occupy. I have no doubt that, in spite of the repairs, you could manage there for one night."

185   "Oh, yes, easily."

186   "The rest you will leave in our hands."

187   "But what will you do?"

188   "We shall spend the night in your room, and we shall investigate the cause of this noise which has disturbed you."

189   "I believe, Mr. Holmes, that you have already made up your mind," said Miss Stoner, laying her hand upon my companion's sleeve.

190   "Perhaps I have."

191   "Then, for pity's sake, tell me what was the cause of my sister's death."

192   "I should prefer to have clearer proofs before I speak."

193   "You can at least tell me whether my own thought is correct, and if she died from some sudden fright."

194   "No, I do not think so. I think that there was probably some more tangible cause. And now, Miss Stoner, we must leave you, for if Dr. Roylott returned and saw us our journey would be in vain. Good-bye, and be brave, for if you will do what I have told you you may rest assured that we shall soon drive away the dangers that threaten you."

195   Sherlock Holmes and I had no difficulty in engaging a bedroom and sitting-room at the "Crown Inn." They were on the upper floor, and from our window we could command a view of the avenue gate, and of the inhabited wing of Stoke Moran Manor House. At dusk we saw Dr. Grimesby Roylott drive past, his huge form looming up beside the little figure of the lad who drove him. The boy had some slight difficulty in undoing the heavy iron gates, and we heard the hoarse roar of the doctor's voice and saw the fury with which he shook his clinched fists at him. The trap drove on, and a few minutes later we saw a sudden light spring up among the trees as the lamp was lit in one of the sitting-rooms.

196   "Do you know, Watson," said Holmes as we sat together in the gathering darkness, "I have really some scruples as to taking you to-night. There is a distinct element of danger."

197   "Can I be of assistance?"

198   "Your presence might be invaluable."

199   "Then I shall certainly come."

200   "It is very kind of you."

201   "You speak of danger. You have evidently seen more in these rooms than was visible to me."

202   "No, but I fancy that I may have deduced a little more. I imagine that you saw all that I did."

203   "I saw nothing remarkable save the bell-rope, and what purpose that could answer I confess is more than I can imagine."

204   "You saw the ventilator, too?"

205   "Yes, but I do not think that it is such a very unusual thing to have a small opening between two rooms. It was so small that a rat could hardly pass through."

206   "I knew that we should find a ventilator before ever we came to Stoke Moran."

207   "My dear Holmes!"

208   "Oh, yes, I did. You remember in her statement she said that her sister could smell Dr. Roylott's cigar. Now, of course that suggested at once that there must be a communication between the two rooms. It could only be a small one, or it would have been remarked upon at the coroner's inquiry. I deduced a ventilator."

209   "But what harm can there be in that?"

210   "Well, there is at least a curious coincidence of dates. A ventilator is made, a cord is hung, and a lady who sleeps in the bed dies. Does not that strike you?"

211   "I cannot as yet see any connection."

212   "Did you observe anything peculiar about that bed?"

213   "No."

214   "It was clamped to the floor. Did you ever see a bed fastened like that before?"

215   "I cannot say that I have."

216   "The lady could not move her bed. It must always be in the same relative position to the ventilator and to the rope—or so we may call it, since it was clearly never meant for a bell-pull."

217   "Holmes," I cried, "I seem to see dimly what you are hinting at. We are only just in time to prevent some subtle and horrible crime."

218   "Subtle enough and horrible enough. When a doctor does go wrong, he is the first of criminals. He has nerve and he has knowledge. Palmer and Pritchard were among the heads of their profession. This man strikes even deeper, but I think, Watson, that we shall be able to strike deeper still. But we shall have horrors enough before the night is over; for goodness' sake let us have a quiet pipe and turn our minds for a few hours to something more cheerful."

219   About nine o'clock the light among the trees was extinguished, and all was dark in the direction of the Manor House. Two hours passed slowly away, and then, suddenly, just at the stroke of eleven, a single bright light shone out right in front of us.

220   "That is our signal," said Holmes, springing to his feet; "it comes from the middle window."

221   As we passed out he exchanged a few words with the landlord, explaining that we were going on a late visit to an acquaintance, and that it was possible that we might spend the night there. A moment later we were out on the dark road, a chill wind blowing in our faces, and one yellow light twinkling in front of us through the gloom to guide us on our sombre errand.

222   There was little difficulty in entering the grounds, for unrepaired breaches gaped in the old park wall. Making our way among the trees, we reached the lawn, crossed it, and were about to enter through the window when out from a clump of laurel bushes there darted what seemed to be a hideous and distorted child, who threw itself upon the grass with writhing limbs and then ran swiftly across the lawn into the darkness.

223   "My God!" I whispered; "did you see it?"

224   Holmes was for a moment as startled as I. His hand closed like a vise upon my wrist in his agitation. Then he broke into a low laugh and put his lips to my ear.

225   "It is a nice household," he murmured. "That is the baboon."

226   I had forgotten the strange pets which the doctor affected. There was a cheetah, too; perhaps we might find it upon our

shoulders at any moment. I confess that I felt easier in my mind when, after following Holmes's example and slipping off my shoes, I found myself inside the bedroom. My companion noiselessly closed the shutters, moved the lamp onto the table, and cast his eyes round the room. All was as we had seen it in the daytime. Then creeping up to me and making a trumpet of his hand, he whispered into my ear again so gently that it was all that I could do to distinguish the words:

227   "The least sound would be fatal to our plans."

228   I nodded to show that I had heard.

229   "We must sit without light. He would see it through the ventilator."

230   I nodded again.

231   "Do not go asleep; your very life may depend upon it. Have your pistol ready in case we should need it. I will sit on the side of the bed, and you in that chair."

232   I took out my revolver and laid it on the corner of the table.

233   Holmes had brought up a long thin cane, and this he placed upon the bed beside him. By it he laid the box of matches and the stump of a candle. Then he turned down the lamp, and we were left in darkness.

234   How shall I ever forget that dreadful vigil? I could not hear a sound, not even the drawing of a breath, and yet I knew that my companion sat open-eyed, within a few feet of me, in the same state of nervous tension in which I was myself. The shutters cut off the least ray of light, and we waited in absolute darkness. From outside came the occasional cry of a night-bird, and once at our very window a long drawn catlike whine, which told us that the cheetah was indeed at liberty. Far away we could hear the deep tones of the parish clock, which boomed out every quarter of an hour. How long they seemed, those quarters! Twelve struck, and one and two and three, and still we sat waiting silently for whatever might befall.

235   Suddenly there was the momentary gleam of a light up in the direction of the ventilator, which vanished immediately, but was succeeded by a strong smell of burning oil and heated metal. Someone in the next room had lit a dark-lantern. I heard a gentle sound of movement, and then all was silent once more, though the smell grew stronger. For half an hour I sat with straining ears. Then suddenly another sound became audible—a very gentle, soothing sound, like that of a small jet of steam escaping continually from a kettle. The instant that we heard it, Holmes sprang from the bed, struck a match, and lashed furiously with his cane at the bell-pull.

236   "You see it Watson?" he yelled. "You see it?"

237   But I saw nothing. At the moment when Holmes struck the light I heard a low, clear whistle, but the sudden glare flashing into

my weary eyes made it impossible for me to tell what it was at which my friend lashed so savagely. I could, however, see that his face was deadly pale and filled with horror and loathing.

238   He had ceased to strike and was gazing up at the ventilator when suddenly there broke from the silence of the night the most horrible cry to which I have ever listened. It swelled up louder and louder, a hoarse yell of pain and fear and anger all mingled in the one dreadful shriek. They say that away down in the village, and even in the distant parsonage, that cry raised the sleepers from their beds. It struck cold to our hearts, and I stood gazing at Holmes, and he at me, until the last echoes of it had died away into the silence from which it rose.

239   "What can it mean?" I gasped.

240   "It means that it is all over," Holmes answered. "And perhaps, after all, it is for the best. Take your pistol, and we will enter Dr. Roylott's room."

241   With a grave face he lit the lamp and led the way down the corridor. Twice he struck at the chamber door without any reply from within. Then he turned the handle and entered, I at his heels, with the cocked pistol in my hand.

242   It was a singular sight which met our eyes. On the table stood a dark-lantern with the shutter half open, throwing a brilliant beam of light upon the iron safe, the door of which was ajar. Beside his table, on the wooden chair, sat Dr. Grimesby Roylott, clad in a long gray dressing gown, his bare ankles protruding beneath, and his feet thrust into red heelless Turkish slippers. Across his lap lay the short stock with the long lash which we had noticed during the day. His chin was cocked upward and his eyes were fixed in a dreadful, rigid stare at the corner of the ceiling. Round his brow he had a peculiar yellow band, with brownish speckles, which seemed to be bound tightly round his head. As we entered he made neither sound nor motion.

243   "The band! the speckled band!" whispered Holmes.

244   I took a step forward. In an instant his strange headgear began to move, and there reared itself from among his hair the squat diamond-shaped head and puffed neck of a loathsome serpent.

245   "It is a swamp adder!" cried Holmes; "the deadliest snake in India. He has died within ten seconds of being bitten. Violence does, in truth, recoil upon the violent, and the schemer falls into the pit which he digs for another. Let us thrust this creature back into its den, and we can then remove Miss Stoner to some place of shelter and let the county police know what has happened."

246   As he spoke he drew the dog-whip swiftly from the dead man's lap, and throwing the noose round the reptile's neck he drew it from its horrid perch and, carrying it at arm's length, threw it into the iron safe, which he closed upon it.

247   Such are the true facts of the death of Dr. Grimesby Roylott, of Stoke Moran. It is not necessary that I should prolong a narrative which has already run to too great a length by telling how we broke the sad news to the terrified girl, how we conveyed her by the morning train to the care of her good aunt at Harrow, of how the slow process of official inquiry came to the conclusion that the doctor met his fate while indiscreetly playing with a dangerous pet. The little which I had yet to learn of the case was told me by Sherlock Holmes as we travelled back next day.

248   "I had," said he, "come to an entirely erroneous conclusion which shows, my dear Watson, how dangerous it always is to reason from insufficient data. The presence of the gypsies, and the use of the word 'band,' which was used by the poor girl, no doubt to explain the appearance which she had caught a hurried glimpse of by the light of her match, were sufficient to put me upon an entirely wrong scent. I can only claim the merit that I instantly reconsidered my position when, however, it became clear to me that whatever danger threatened an occupant of the room could not come either from the window or the door. My attention was speedily drawn, as I have already remarked to you, to this ventilator, and to the bell-rope which hung down to the bed. The discovery that this was a dummy, and that the bed was clamped to the floor, instantly gave rise to the suspicion that the rope was there as a bridge for something passing through the hole and coming to the bed. The idea of a snake instantly occurred to me, and when I coupled it with my knowledge that the doctor was furnished with a supply of creatures from India, I felt that I was probably on the right track. The idea of using a form of poison which could not possibly be discovered by any chemical test was just such a one as would occur to a clever and ruthless man who had had an Eastern training. The rapidity with which such a poison would take effect would also, from his point of view, be an advantage. It would be a sharp-eyed coroner, indeed, who could distinguish the two little dark punctures which would show where the poison fangs had done their work. Then I thought of the whistle. Of course he must recall the snake before the morning light revealed it to the victim. He had trained it, probably by the use of the milk which we saw, to return to him when summoned. He would put it through this ventilator at the hour he thought best, with the certainty that it would crawl down the rope and land on the bed. It might or might not bite the occupant, perhaps she might escape every night for a week, but sooner or later she must fall a victim.

249   "I had come to these conclusions before ever I had entered his room. An inspection of his chair showed me that he had been in the habit of standing on it, which of course would be necessary in order that he should reach the ventilator. The sight of the

safe, the saucer of milk, and the loop of whipcord were enough to finally dispel any doubts which may have remained. The metallic clang heard by Miss Stoner was obviously caused by her stepfather hastily closing the door of his safe upon its terrible occupant. Having once made up my mind, you know the steps which I took in order to put the matter to the proof. I heard the creature hiss as I have no doubt that you did also, and I instantly lit the light and attacked it."

250   "With the result of driving it through the ventilator."

251   "And also with the result of causing it to turn upon its master at the other side. Some of the blows of my cane came home and roused its snakish temper, so that it flew upon the first person it saw. In this way I am no doubt indirectly responsible for Dr. Grimesby Roylott's death, and I cannot say that it is likely to weigh very heavily upon my conscience."

● ●

THE ADVENTURE OF THE SPECKLED BAND

JOURNAL

1. MLA Works Cited   *Using this model, record this story here.*

Author's Last Name, First Name. "Title of the Story." *Title of the Book*. 3rd ed. Ed.

First Name Last Name. City: Publisher, year. Page number(s) of this story. Print.

2. Main Character(s)   *Describe each main character, and explain why you think each is a main character.*

3. Supporting Characters   *Describe each supporting character, and explain why you think each is a supporting character.*

4. Setting and Props   *Describe the setting(s) and all relevant prop(s).*

5. Sequence   *Outline the events of the story in order.*

6. Plot   *Tell the story in no more than three sentences.*

7. Conflicts   *Identify and explain all the conflicts involved here.*

8. Significant Quotations   *Explain the importance of each quotation completely. Record the page number in the parentheses.*

a. "She had a considerable sum of money—not less than £1000 a year—and this she bequeathed to Dr. Roylott entirely while we resided with him, with a provision that a certain annual sum should be allowed to each of us in the event of our marriage" ( ).

b. "Your sister is dead, then?" ( ).

   c. "Because during the last few nights I have always, about three in the morning, heard a low, clear whistle" ( ).

   d. "It was clamped to the floor. Did you ever see a bed fastened like that before?" ( ).

   e. "'The band! The speckled band!' whispered Holmes" ( ).

9. Literary Elements *Look at this chapter's title and explain why you think this story is placed in this chapter. Explain in which other chapter(s) you might place this story, as relevant to the literary element(s) of the chapter(s).*

10. Foreshadowing, Irony, and/or Symbols *Explain examples of foreshadowing, irony, and/or symbols in this story.*

———

FOLLOW-UP QUESTIONS

10 SHORT QUESTIONS

What is the <u>best</u> answer for each?

____ 1. Helen's sister has
   a. died out of fear.
   b. been killed.
   c. gotten married.

____ 2. Helen's sister is no longer
   here because
   a. she was afraid.
   b. she ran away.
   c. she was getting
      married.

____ 3. Roylott is not
   a. a kind man.
   b. an evil man.
   c. an aristocrat.

____ 4. Roylott is the son of
   a. a poor, farming family.
   b. an old but now poor
      family.
   c. an old and still wealthy
      family.

____ 5. The gypsies
   a. serve to add confusion to
      the situation.
   b. are the murderers.
   c. are long since gone.

____ 6. The bell-rope
   a. rings a bell for the
      housekeeper.
   b. does not work.
   c. is old and in bad shape.

____ 7. The ventilator
   a. brings in fresh air.
   b. is old and unusable.
   c. serves as a bridge between
      the rooms.

____ 8. Helen is in danger because
   a. she goes to town.
   b. Roylott goes to town.
   c. she is getting married.

____ 9. Roylott wants
   a. Helen's share of the
      money.
   b. Helen to get married.
   c. to fix the old house.

____ 10. In the end, Roylott
   a. gives Helen away in
      marriage.
   b. is destroyed by his
      own evil.
   c. goes back to India.

5 SIGNIFICANT QUOTATIONS

What is the importance of each of these quotations?

1. "In the last century, however, four successive heirs were of a dissolute
   and wasteful disposition, and the family ruin was eventually completed
   by a gambler in the days of the Regency."

2. "There was something else which she would fain have said, and she
   stabbed with her fingers into the air in the direction of the doctor's room,
   but a fresh convulsion seized her and choked her words."

3. "A month ago, however, a dear friend, whom I have known for many years, has done me the honour to ask my hand in marriage."

4. "The lady could not move her bed. It must always be in the same relative position to the ventilator and to the rope—or so we may call it, since it was clearly never meant for a bell-pull."

5. " 'The band! The speckled band!' whispered Holmes."

2 COMPREHENSION ESSAY QUESTIONS

Use specific details and information from the story to answer these questions as completely as possible.

1. How is the title relevant to the story? Use specific details and information from the story to support your answer.

2. What are specific examples of Holmes' deductive power that he uses to solve the mystery? Use specific details and information from the story to support your examples.

DISCUSSION QUESTIONS

Be prepared to discuss these questions in class.

1. What are specific examples of Sherlock Holmes' deduction?

2. Foreshadowing is a technique used by authors to predict events to come. What specific clues foreshadow events in this story?

WRITING

Use each of these ideas for writing an essay.

1. We often use things we observe to form opinions. Tell of an incident that occurred when you or someone you know used observations to form deductions about someone or something. Comment on how well you or someone you know used the power of deduction.

2. Sometime or another, we have all been involved in a mystery—a person who is mysteriously late, a missing article, and so forth. Relate the events in order and narrate a mystery that has involved you or someone you know.

Further Writing

1. Read an Agatha Christie mystery that involves Miss Jane Marple or Hercule Poirot (available in a library). Compare and contrast the deductive abilities of Sherlock Holmes with Miss Marple or Hercule Poirot.

2. Edgar Allan Poe is generally considered the inventor of the modern mystery form. Compare and contrast the characters in "The Cask of Amontillado" (available in a library) with those in "The Adventure of the Speckled Band."

3. Compare and contrast the characters in "Sweat" (page 239) with those in "The Adventure of the Speckled Band."

GOD SEES THE TRUTH, BUT WAITS
Leo Tolstoy

Pre-reading Vocabulary
Context

Use context clues to define these words before reading. Use a dictionary as needed.

1. Debbie is an accomplished *merchant* and makes a great deal of money through the sales in her store. *Merchant* means _____.

2. Johnny hired a *tróyka* drawn by three horses for him and his date to ride in to the prom. *Tróyka* means _____.

3. When Ivan was appointed the head of the police department, he became an important *official*. *Official* means _____.

4. The *thief* was very sneaky and, while everyone was at dinner, no one noticed that he stole the jewelry in the safe. *Thief* means

    _____.

5. The butcher used a sharp *knife* to cut up all the meat that needed to be wrapped in smaller pieces. *Knife* means _____.

6. The criminal became a *convict* when the jury found him guilty of the crimes he was accused of committing. *Convict* means

    _____.

7. Derived from the Latin word "caesar" (pronounced ky-zar), the Russian word *"tsar"* came to mean the ruler of all the Russians. *Tsar*

    means _____.

8. The murderer was *condemned* to twenty years in a solitary prison cell for the horrible crimes he committed. *Condemned* means

    _____.

9. In some cultures, criminals are hit across the back with a whip in the hopes that being *flogged* will make them better people. *Flogged* means

   _____.

10. Rachel felt great *mirth* and smiled from ear to ear at the wonderful surprise party her family held for her. *Mirth* means

    _____.

11. In Russia, criminals may be sent to *Siberia*, a northern area that is frigidly cold and barren. *Siberia* means

    _____.

12. Laura and Missy and Carrie are great *companions* and are always together whether they are in school or on vacation. *Companion* means

    _____.

13. Before he was to behead the prisoner, the *executioner* put on a mask to hide his face. *Executioner* means _____.

14. The poor often live *wretched* lives, having to live in rat-infested homes and never having enough food to eat. *Wretched* means

    _____.

15. The good guy is usually referred to as the "hero," while the bad guy is usually referred to as the *"villain." Villain* means

    _____.

16. When the teens vandalized Doug's new car, Doug sought *vengeance* by suing each one for thousands of dollars. *Vengeance* means

    _____.

17. In order to get a road under the river, the engineers designed a large *tunnel* that would be dug in stone under the river. *Tunnel* means

    _____.

18. Although Dave knew the right answers to the questions, he remained *silent* and did not say a word. *Silent* means _____.

19. Even though Allison sometimes messes up Jacob's toys, he always *forgives* her because she is his sister and he loves her. *Forgive* means

_____.

20. The prisoner received an early *release* from prison because he obeyed all the rules and demonstrated he had changed. *Release* means

_____.

PRE-READING VOCABULARY
STRUCTURAL ATTACK

Define these words by solving the parts. Use the Glossary or a dictionary as needed.

1. riotous
2. adjoin
3. robber
4. unstrapped
5. suddenly
6. blood-stained
7. imprisoned
8. inhabitant
9. downcast
10. meekness
11. fellow-prisoner
12. misfortune
13. unjustly
14. premature
15. frightened
16. emptied
17. unconcerned
18. trembled
19. wrongly
20. bed-shelf
21. forgotten
22. sobbing

PRE-READING QUESTIONS

Try answering these questions as you read.

What does Aksënov do?

What happens to Aksënov?

Who is Makár?

What are the ironies here?

GOD SEES THE TRUTH, BUT WAITS

Leo Tolstoy

Leo Tolstoy was born in the Tula Province of Russia in 1828. Born to great wealth and the title of Count, Tolstoy suffered the loss of his parents when he was very young. He was raised by female relatives and educated by private tutors. He left the family estate to study at Kazar University and was an able student, but he took more interest in the privileged social life, a life he would eventually find empty. He left the university to manage his estate with benevolence and reformist ideals, but again he gave this up for more interest in the social life in Moscow and St. Petersburg. After volunteering to serve in the Russian army and serving during the Crimean War, Tolstoy returned to his estate and finally settled home, where both his estate and his family would prosper. He married Sofya Bers and they produced thirteen children, while he personally attended to his estate and founded a school that let him apply his new ideas about education. During this happy time, he produced his masterworks, *War and Peace* and *Anna Karenina*. However, in time he came to seek a simpler life, searching to find meaning in life and a higher understanding of good and evil. Although he had now become a celebrated writer and an influential thinker and although he continued to write prolifically, he found emptiness in his rich surroundings. Ultimately seeking solitude in order to become closer to God, he and a trusted friend secretly left his home. Within days, he died in a tiny railroad station in 1910.

His artfully drawn characters, his social and philosophical concerns, and his epic overview make Tolstoy an enduring giant. His masterworks are *War and Peace* and *Anna Karenina*, but his writings can also be found in numerous novels, plays, and short story collections.

In the town of Vladimir lived a young merchant named Iván Dmítrich Aksënov. He had two shops and a house of his own.

2   Aksënov was a handsome, fair-haired, curly-headed fellow, full of fun and very fond of singing. When quite a young man he had been given to drink and was riotous when he had had too much; but after he married he gave up drinking except now and then.

3   One summer Aksënov was going to the Nízhny Fair, and as he bade good-bye to his family his wife said to him, "Iván Dmítrich, do not start to-day; I have had a bad dream about you."

4   Aksënov laughed, and said, "You are afraid that when I get to the fair I shall go on the spree."

5   His wife replied: "I do not know what I am afraid of; all I know is that I had a bad dream. I dreamt you returned from the town, and when you took off your cap I saw that your hair was quite grey."

6   Aksënov laughed. "That's a lucky sign," said he. "See if I don't sell out all my goods and bring you some presents from the fair."

7   So he said good-bye to his family and drove away.

8   When he had travelled half-way, he met a merchant whom he knew, and they put up at the same inn for the night. They had some tea together, and then went to bed in adjoining rooms.

9   It was not Aksënov's habit to sleep late, and, wishing to travel while it was still cool, he aroused his driver before dawn and told him to put in the horses.

10   Then he made his way across to the landlord of the inn (who lived in a cottage at the back), paid his bill, and continued his journey.

11   When he had gone about twenty-five miles he stopped for the horses to be fed. Aksënov rested awhile in the passage of the inn, then he stepped out into the porch and, ordering a samovár to be heated, got out his guitar and began to play.

12   Suddenly a *tróyka* drove up with tinkling bells, and an official alighted, followed by two soldiers. He came to Aksënov and began to question him, asking him who he was and whence he came. Aksënov answered him fully, and said, "Won't you have some tea with me?" But the official went on cross-questioning him and asking him, "Where did you spend last night? Were you alone, or with

a fellow-merchant? Did you see the other merchant this morning? Why did you leave the inn before dawn?"

13   Aksënov wondered why he was asked all these questions, but he described all that had happened, and then added, "Why do you cross-question me as if I were a thief or a robber? I am travelling on business of my own, and there is no need to question me."

14   Then the official, calling the soldiers, said, "I am the police-officer of this district, and I question you because the merchant with whom you spent last night has been found with his throat cut. We must search your things."

15   They entered the house. The soldiers and the police-officer unstrapped Aksënov's luggage and searched it. Suddenly the officer drew a knife out of a bag, crying, "Whose knife is this?"

16   Aksënov looked, and seeing a blood-stained knife taken from his bag, he was frightened.

17   "How is it there is blood on this knife?"

18   Aksënov tried to answer, but could hardly utter a word, and only stammered: "I—don't know—not mine."

19   Then the police-officer said, "This morning the merchant was found in bed with his throat cut. You are the only person who could have done it. The house was locked from inside, and no one else was there. Here is this blood-stained knife in your bag, and your face and manner betray you! Tell me how you killed him and how much money you stole?"

20   Aksënov swore he had not done it; that he had not seen the merchant after they had had tea together; that he had no money except eight thousand rúbles of his own, and that the knife was not his. But his voice was broken, his face pale, and he trembled with fear as though he were guilty.

21   The police-officer ordered the soldiers to bind Aksënov and to put him in the cart. As they tied his feet together and flung him into the cart, Aksënov crossed himself and wept. His money and goods were taken from him, and he was sent to the nearest town and imprisoned there. Enquiries as to his character were made in Vladímir. The merchants and other inhabitants of that town said that in former days he used to drink and waste his time, but that he was a good man. Then the trial came on: he was charged with murdering a merchant from Ryazán and robbing him of twenty thousand rúbles.

22   His wife was in despair, and did not know what to believe. Her children were all quite small; one was a baby at the breast. Taking them all with her, she went to the town where her husband was in jail. At first she was not allowed to see him; but, after much begging, she obtained permission from the officials and was taken to him. When she saw her husband in prison-dress and in chains,

shut up with thieves and criminals, she fell down and did not come to her senses for a long time. Then she drew her children to her, and sat down near him. She told him of things at home, and asked about what had happened to him. He told her all, and she asked, "What can we do now?"

23   "We must petition the Tsar not to let an innocent man perish."

24   His wife told him that she had sent a petition to the Tsar, but that it had not been accepted.

25   Askënov did not reply, but only looked downcast.

26   Then his wife said, "It was not for nothing I dreamt your hair had turned grey. You remember? You should not have started that day." And passing her fingers through his hair she said: "Ványa dearest, tell your wife the truth; was it not you who did it?"

27   "So you, too, suspect me!" said Aksënov, and, hiding his face in his hands, he began to weep. Then a soldier came to say that the wife and children must go away, and Aksënov said good-bye to his family for the last time.

28   When they were gone, Aksënov recalled what had been said, and when he remembered that his wife also had suspected him, he said to himself, "It seems that only God can know the truth; it is to Him alone we must appeal and from Him alone expect mercy."

29   And Aksënov wrote no more petitions, gave up all hope, and only prayed to God.

30   Aksënov was condemned to be flogged and sent to the mines. So he was flogged with a knout, and when the wounds caused by the knout were healed, he was driven to Siberia with other convicts.

31   For twenty-six years Aksënov lived as a convict in Siberia. His hair turned white as snow, and his beard grew long, thin, and grey. All his mirth went; he stooped; he walked slowly, spoke little, and never laughed, but he often prayed.

32   In prison Aksënov learnt to make boots, and earned a little money, with which he bought *The Lives of the Saints*. He read this book when it was light enough in the prison; and on Sundays in the prison-church he read the epistle and sang in the choir, for his voice was still good.

33   The prison authorities liked Aksënov for his meekness, and his fellow-prisoners respected him: they called him "Grandfather," and "The Saint." When they wanted to petition the prison authorities about anything, they always made Aksënov their spokesman, and when there were quarrels among the prisoners they came to him to put things right, and to judge the matter.

34   No news reached Aksënov from his home, and he did not even know if his wife and children were still alive.

35   One day a fresh gang of convicts came to the prison. In the evening the old prisoners collected round the new ones and asked them what towns or villages they came from, and what they

were sentenced for. Among the rest Aksënov sat down near the new-comers, and listened with downcast air to what was said.

36   One of the new convicts, a tall, strong man of sixty, with a closely-cropped grey beard, was telling the others what he had been arrested for.

37   "Well, friends," he said, "I only took a horse that was tied to a sledge, and I was arrested and accused of stealing. I said I had only taken it to get home quicker, and had then let it go; besides, the driver was a personal friend of mine. So I said, 'it's all right.' 'No,' said they, 'you stole it.' But how or where I stole it they could not say. I once really did something wrong, and ought by rights to have come here long ago, but that time I was not found out. Now I have been sent here for nothing at all … Eh, but it's lies I'm telling you; I've been to Siberia before, but I did not stay long."

38   "Where are you from?" asked some one.

39   "From Vladímir. My family are of that town. My name is Makár, and they also call me Semënich."

40   Aksënov raised his head and said: "Tell me, Semënich, do you know anything of the merchants Aksënov, of Vladímir? Are they still alive?"

41   "Know them? Of course I do. The Aksënovs are rich, though their father is in Siberia: a sinner like ourselves, it seems! As for you, Gran'dad, how did you come here?"

42   Aksënov did not like to speak of his misfortune. He only sighed, and said, "For my sins I have been in prison these twenty-six years."

43   "What sins?" asked Makár Semënich.

44   But Aksënov only said, "Well, well—I must have deserved it!" He would have said no more, but his companions told the new-comer how Aksënov came to be in Siberia: how some one had killed a merchant and had put a knife among Aksënov's things, and he had been unjustly condemned.

45   When Makár Semënich heard this he looked at Aksënov, slapped his own knee, and exclaimed, "Well, this is wonderful! Really wonderful! But how old you've grown, Gran'dad!"

46   The others asked him why he was so surprised, and where he had seen Aksënov before; but Makár Semënich did not reply. He only said: "It's wonderful that we should meet here, lads!"

47   These words made Aksënov wonder whether this man knew who had killed the merchant; so he said, "Perhaps, Semënich, you have heard of that affair, or maybe you've seen me before?"

48   "How could I help hearing? The world's full of rumours. But it's long ago, and I've forgotten what I heard."

49   "Perhaps you heard who killed the merchant?" asked Aksënov.

50   Makár Semënich laughed, and replied, "It must have been him in whose bag the knife was found! If some one else hid the knife there—'He's not a thief till he's caught,' as the saying is. How could any one put a knife into your bag while it was under your head? It would surely have woke you up?"

51   When Aksënov heard these words he felt sure this was the man who had killed the merchant. He rose and went away. All that night Aksënov lay awake. He felt terribly unhappy, and all sorts of images rose in his mind. There was the image of his wife as she was when he parted from her to go to the fair. He saw her as if she were present; her face and her eyes rose before him, he heard her speak and laugh. Then he saw his children, quite little, as they were at that time: one with a little cloak on, another at his mother's breast. And then he remembered himself as he used to be—young and merry. He remembered how he sat playing the guitar in the porch of the inn where he was arrested, and how free from care he had been. He saw in his mind the place where he was flogged, the executioner, and the people standing around; the chains, the convicts, all the twenty-six years of his prison life, and his premature old age. The thought of it all made him so wretched that he was ready to kill himself.

52   "And it's all that villain's doing!" thought Aksënov. And his anger was so great against Makár Semënich that he longed for vengeance, even if he himself should perish for it. He kept saying prayers all night, but could get no peace. During the day he did not go near Makár Semënich, nor even look at him.

53   A fortnight passed in this way. Aksënov could not sleep at nights and was so miserable that he did not know what to do.

54   One night as he was walking about the prison he noticed some earth that came rolling out from under one of the shelves on which the prisoners slept. He stopped to see what it was. Suddenly Makár Semënich crept out from under the shelf, and looked up at Aksënov with a frightened face. Aksënov tried to pass without looking at him, but Makár seized his hand and told him that he had dug a hole under the wall, getting rid of the earth by putting it into his high boots and emptying it out every day on the road when the prisoners were driven to their work.

55   "Just you keep quiet, old man, and you shall get out too. If you blab they'll flog the life out of me, but I will kill you first."

56   Aksënov trembled with anger as he looked at his enemy. He drew his hand away, saying, "I have no wish to escape, and you have no need to kill me; you killed me long ago! As to telling of you—I may do so or not, as God shall direct."

57   Next day, when the convicts were led out to work, the convoy soldiers noticed that one or other of the prisoners emptied some earth out of his boots. The prison was searched

and the tunnel found. The Governor came and questioned all the prisoners to find out who had dug the hole. They all denied any knowledge of it. Those who knew would not betray Makár Semënich, knowing he would be flogged almost to death. At last the Governor turned to Aksënov, whom he knew to be a just man, and said:

58   "You are a truthful old man; tell me, before God, who dug the hole?"

59   Makár Semënich stood as if he were quite unconcerned, looking at the Governor and not so much as glancing at Aksënov. Aksënov's lips and hands trembled, and for a long time he could not utter a word. He thought, "Why should I screen him who ruined my life? Let him pay for what I have suffered. But if I tell, they will probably flog the life out of him, and maybe I suspect him wrongly. And, after all, what good would it be to me?"

60   "Well, old man," repeated the Governor, "tell us the truth; who has been digging under the wall?"

61   Aksënov glanced at Makár Semënich and said, "I cannot say, your honour. It is not God's will that I should tell! Do what you like with me; I am in your hands."

62   However much the Governor tried, Aksënov would say no more, and so the matter had to be left.

63   That night, when Aksënov was lying on his bed and just beginning to doze, some one came quietly and sat down on his bed. He peered through the darkness and recognized Makár.

64   "What more do you want of me?" asked Aksënov. "Why have you come here?"

65   Makár Semënich was silent. So Aksënov sat up and said, "What do you want? Go away or I will call the guard!"

66   Makár Semënich bent close over Aksënov, and whispered, "Iván Dmítrich, forgive me!"

67   "What for?" asked Aksënov.

68   "It was I who killed the merchant and hid the knife among your things. I meant to kill you too, but I heard a noise outside; so I hid the knife in your bag and escaped through the window."

69   Aksënov was silent and did not know what to say. Makár Semënich slid off the bed-shelf and knelt upon the ground. "Iván Dmítrich," said he, "forgive me! For the love of God, forgive me! I will confess that it was I who killed the merchant, and you will be released and can go to your home."

70   "It is easy for you to talk," said Aksënov, "but I have suffered for you these twenty-six years. Where could I go to now?...My wife is dead, and my children have forgotten me. I have nowhere to go...."

71   Makár Semënich did not rise, but beat his head on the floor. "Iván Dmítrich, forgive me!" he cried. "When they flogged me with

the knout it was not so hard to bear as it is to see you now … yet you had pity on me and did not tell. For Christ's sake forgive me, wretch that I am!" And he began to sob.

72   When Aksënov heard him sobbing he, too, began to weep.

73   "God will forgive you!" said he. "Maybe I am a hundred times worse than you." And at these words his heart grew light and the longing for home left him. He no longer had any desire to leave the prison, but only hoped for his last hour to come.

74   In spite of what Aksënov had said, Makár Semënich confessed his guilt. But when the order for his release came, Aksënov was already dead.

GOD SEES THE TRUTH, BUT WAITS

JOURNAL

1. MLA Works Cited   *Using this model, record this story here.*

Author's Last Name, First Name. "Title of the Story." *Title of the Book.* 3rd ed. Ed.

First Name Last Name. City: Publisher, year. Page number(s) of this story. Print.

2. Main Character(s)   *Describe each main character, and explain why you think each is a main character.*

3. Supporting Characters   *Describe each supporting character, and explain why you think each is a supporting character.*

4. Setting and Props   *Describe the setting(s) and all relevant prop(s).*

5. Sequence   *Outline the events of the story in order.*

6. Plot   *Tell the story in no more than three sentences.*

7. Conflicts   *Identify and explain all the conflicts involved here.*

8. Significant Quotations   *Explain the importance of each quotation completely. Record the page number in the parentheses.*

a. "Suddenly the officer drew a knife out of the bag, crying, 'Whose knife is this?' " (   ).

b. " 'So you, too, suspect me!' said Aksënov [...] and Aksënov said good-bye to his family for the last time" (   ).

c. "Aksënov raised his head and said: 'Tell me, Semënich, do you know anything of the merchants Aksënov, of Vladimir?'" ( ).

d. "You are a truthful old man; tell me, before God, who dug the hole" ( ).

e. "When they flogged me with the knout it was not so hard to bear as it is to see you now…yet you had pity on me and did not tell" ( ).

9. **Literary Elements**   *Look at this chapter's title and explain why you think this story is placed in this chapter. Explain in which other chapter(s) you might place this story, as relevant to the literary element(s) of the chapter(s).*

10. **Foreshadowing, Irony, and/or Symbols**   *Explain examples of foreshadowing, irony, and/or symbols in this story.*

FOLLOW-UP QUESTIONS

10 SHORT QUESTIONS

What is the <u>best</u> answer for each?

_____ 1. As a young man, Aksënov is
   a. a lively young man.
   b. a quiet young man.
   c. not described.

_____ 2. As a married man, Aksënov
   a. is a devoted husband and father.
   b. is a cheat.
   c. leaves his family for another woman.

_____ 3. Aksënov travels to the fair
   a. for fun.
   b. to sell goods and make money.
   c. for adventure.

_____ 4. Aksënov pays his bill early
   a. to escape from murder.
   b. to start in cool weather.
   c. to get away without paying.

_____ 5. Aksënov is stopped
   a. because he has killed a man.
   b. because he is suspected of killing a man.
   c. because he has seen a man killed.

_____ 6. In fact, Aksënov
   a. has killed a man.
   b. has seen a man killed.
   c. knows nothing of the murder until he is told about it.

_____ 7. Aksënov's wife
   a. questions her husband's innocence.
   b. does not know about her husband's arrest.
   c. never doubts her husband.

_____ 8. In prison, Aksënov is
   a. violent and feared.
   b. mild and respected.
   c. not described.

_____ 9. Makár
   a. is the real murderer.
   b. has stolen Aksënov's wife.
   c. both a and b.

_____ 10. In the end, Aksënov
   a. punishes Makár.
   b. seeks revenge on Makár.
   c. forgives Makár.

5 SIGNIFICANT QUOTATIONS

What is the importance of each of these quotations?

1. "I dreamt you returned from the town, and when you took off your cap I saw that your hair was quite grey."

2. "Aksënov looked, and seeing a blood-stained knife taken from his bag, he was frightened."

3. "I once really did something wrong, and ought by rights to have come here long ago, but that time I was not found out."

4. " 'Well, old man,' repeated the Governor, 'tell us the truth; who has been digging under the wall?' "

5. "For the love of God, forgive me! I will confess that it was I who killed the merchant, and you will be released and can go to your home."

2 COMPREHENSION ESSAY QUESTIONS

Use specific details and information from the story to answer these questions as completely as possible.

1. Identify at least two ironies in this story? Use specific details and information from the story to support your answer.

2. What is the relevance of the title to the story? Use specific details and information from this story to support your answer.

DISCUSSION QUESTIONS

Be prepared to discuss these questions in class.

1. What are the ironies in this story?

2. Do you think Aksënov is foolish or wise? Use specific details and information from the story to support your thinking.

WRITING

Use each of these ideas for writing an essay.

1. At one time or another, we have all been involved in an unfair situation. Tell of a time that you or someone you know has been involved in an unfair situation, and tell about the consequences of that situation.

2. In anger, people may think of seeking revenge on someone who has wronged them. Tell of a time that you or someone you know sought revenge and tell of the consequences of that revenge.

Further Writing

1. Compare and contrast Makár with Montresor in Edgar Allan Poe's "The Cask of Amontillado" (available in a library).

2. To better understand the ending and the title Tolstoy selects, read "Genesis" from the Bible (which can be found in a library). Use what you learn from this to explain both the ending and the title of "God Sees the Truth, but Waits."

NOTES

HOW *I* USE THIS BOOK

This section is *not* intended to tell anyone how to use this book, but rather it is intended to offer insight into some of the many options and possibilities in this book. I am often asked to demonstrate the comprehensive pedagogical apparatus surrounding each story and, since I cannot come out and meet with all of you, this section is an attempt to present at least one instructor's—my!—approach to this book. I truly hope, hope, hope that you use this book as you see fit. The following are simply strategies I use and are offered in response to the many enthusiastic questions I receive.

As has been continually noted, I designed this book most carefully to maximize student learning and teacher efficiency simultaneously. Every entry, every exercise, every word has been most carefully weighed. Following this list, I will explain each entry. However, to streamline this whole section, here are my steps for each story, in a nutshell:

1. First, I do the Sample Lesson with the class, step-by-step, assigning the students to complete the incomplete exercises on their own. I then review, discuss, and/or have students turn in the completed exercises so that I can assess their first journey into this book.

2. Second, with students now ready to start the actual stories, I assign the chapter introduction and the first story in each chapter, then second, and so forth. I introduce any given story via the biographical blurb. Because the blurbs are purposefully written at a more sophisticated level to initiate students into collegiate reading, encourage students to look up words, and so forth, these blurbs are a good place to start discussion. I then assign all vocabulary exercises, pre-reading exercises, and journal exercises, either individually or in groups, depending on the story and the class. Students are to pre-define, pre-think, read, and then reflect upon each story.

3. Third, after each story the students complete, I have students turn in selected pages (one page from vocabulary and one from the Journal selected at random, so that text is protected and students have to do all the work, because they never know what I will want them to pull out) and I collect the above exercises. By collecting these exercises, I gain insight into each student's progress and proficiency, necessary and consistent diagnostic and assessment instruments, and students who are well prepared, because they know they will be responsible for their work.

4. Fourth, with exercises collected, I quiz and collect the 10 Short Questions. Although seemingly simplistic, these short questions offer a very efficient measure of each student's comprehension. With students' baseline exercises and comprehension testing collected, I then discuss the story and the correct and/or acceptable answers, as well as relevant test-taking strategies, with the students. These exercises are designed for

efficient assessment, so I am then easily able to numerically grade and return all assignments by the next class.

5. Fifth, depending on the story and the class, I then assign the 5 Significant Quotations, the Comprehension Essay Questions, and/or the Discussion Questions to be completed individually, in groups, or through class-wide discussion. These are intended to be highly flexible and to be used at your discretion.

6. Sixth, for writing classes I then continue on to discuss and assign the relevant writing prompts. (Writing is intended for developmental students, while Further Writing is intended for more advanced composition courses.)

7. Seventh, as the semester progresses and some students truly start to excel, I follow the same procedures above but now may do so on an individualized basis, assigning the more demanding stories individually to the more capable students.

There it is briefly. By the time the students have completed each story, they have applied, hands-on, an entire complex of cognitive skills and I have multiple diagnostic and assessment tools. You, of course, should use this book any way you see fit and I hope the above list is merely a concise enumeration of how I use it. Should you care to read further, here are some more insights I most humbly offer.

In general, I believe that we often learn by doing and that many of our students are capable learners who simply have learned and/or adopted many counter-productive habits. Initiate and then reinforce productive habits by hands-on application and reapplication, and students prosper. To this end, the apparatus surrounding each story is consistent. Students rather rapidly learn appropriate ways to approach stories, and, because the apparatus is not only consistent but also most carefully designed to maximize learning, students are learning, prospering, and forming new and more productive habits that will improve all their reading skills and endeavors. Further, among the now several thousand students who have field-tested this book, using this book has dramatically increased performance for both reading and writing students.

Concerning **vocabulary** specifically, the very simple axiom applies that if one cannot understand the words, one cannot read. Reading is a split-second, reception-retrieval-synthesis process. Not knowing words interrupts and thereby breaks down the process. To demonstrate this, try reading this:

> Guardare the chaînon with pithecanthropus, the discovery of zinjanthropus semble démarquer a significato gradino in poursuite.

Now, we are all well-versed, well-read, and hopefully learned, yet unless one is familiar with French, Italian, and some basic cultural anthropology concepts, this is relatively unfathomable, albeit unreadable. Yet this is exactly what collegiate reading material looks like to many of our entering students—every few words have no meaning and the sum total becomes unreadable.

For this reason, each story starts with words in **Context** that are not necessarily the hardest words in the story, but rather that are the most necessary to understanding the story. Thus, in addition to applying context solution skills, each context section also presents the students with the words they will need to know to approach the story, and does so before the students read. While I do not know whether each student does the vocabulary before or after each reading, I do know that those who do a poor job or who do not do these exercises at all invariably have problems understanding the given story. These exercises, therefore, simultaneously reinforce context solving skills for each student while providing you with insight into each student's proficiency.

Similarly, the **Structural Attack** words apply attack skills for the students and also provide you with insight into each student's proficiency. These words are chosen because they best apply structural attack skills, but, unlike the words in context, these words are not necessarily essential for understanding the story. These exercises also encourage students to use the Glossary and/or a dictionary, therein applying referencing skills.

Concerning **Pre-reading Questions**, these questions are intended to be simplistic and to set the students up for reading efficiently. After using this consistent and tactile model, in time students learn to frame their own pre-reading questions.

Concerning each **biographical blurb**, I often use the blurb to introduce the story. As noted, each blurb is purposefully written at a sophisticated level to link students to collegiate vocabulary and concepts. Because of this, the blurbs often need explanation. Further, each blurb is intended to provide the students with background before reading and referrals for further readings.

Concerning the **Journal**, what can I say? This, to me, is the engine of this book. Here students record, outline, summarize, reflect upon, make sense out of, and even apply MLA documentation format to every story. This is a strenuous and tactile cognitive workout for students as they apply multiple skills, processes, and dynamics to complete it. I always collect the Journal and it is very easy for me to note those students who are having trouble; the Journal clearly demonstrates student acuity, effort, and insight.

Concerning the **Follow-up Exercises**, I quiz and collect the **10 Short Questions** while I collect the vocabulary and journal exercises and before I discuss the story. I give a few minutes in class for those who have already done the questions at home to review their answers and for those who have not done the questions to complete them. While we might assume that all students would do the work beforehand, I am regularly surprised not so much by those who do the questions ahead, as I am by those who do not. I collect this section before discussion for a very simple reason: diagnostically, I need to know what each student has gotten out of the story on her or his own and without my information and/or prompting. These seemingly simplistic questions often demonstrate real confusion and offer invaluable insight into increasing and/or static student proficiency.

With Pre-reading and Journal exercises and 10 Short Questions collected (which are, again, designed most carefully to be efficient measurement tools and which I will, therefore, easily be able to return by the next class), I now thoroughly discuss the story—and relevant test-taking strategies—with students. I also now turn to the other sections. Depending on the story and/or the class, I may assign the **5 Significant Quotations** and/or the **Comprehension Essay Questions**, or I may use them for discussion. I may assign the **Discussion Questions**, or I may use them for discussion. As noted above, this is a totally fluid area that I designed for your individual discretion. I may choose to use these for discussion in a reading class, and I may choose to assign them for writing in a writing class, or vice versa. These are truly intended to offer you many options.

Finally, the **Writing** prompts speak for themselves. Many of you have commented on how much you like them and there are, again, many options here. I have been privileged to initiate and to chair our learning community program from its very inception. In this program, I teach the same students both reading and writing curricula, and the writing prompts are a natural extension of every story. As noted above, with the now several thousand students who have field-tested this book, we have seen dramatic improvements in both reading and writing students' performances. In fact, many writing instructors are now using this book as the base text in writing courses.

So there it is. This book is designed to meet many, many student needs and to offer a great variety of teaching options. I hope, no matter what ways you choose to use this book, that your students prosper and that you enjoy the book.

Yvonne Collioud Sisko
Old Bridge, New Jersey

GLOSSARY OF PREFIXES AND SUFFIXES

Some words in the **Pre-Reading Vocabulary—Structural Attack** are simple words that have been combined or have extra syllables, which make these words look strange or difficult. When you take these words apart, they are usually quite simple to define.

When two or more words are combined to form a new word, the new word is called a **compound word.** By combining the meaning of each of the words, you can define the new word. Look at the word *everyday.* Here, two simple words—*every* and *day*—combine to mean "all the time." Look at the word *worn-whiskered. Worn* means "tired" or "old," and *whiskered* implies "old man" or "mature man." Thus, *worn-whiskered* is a word used to describe an old man.

Another way to build a new word is to add a prefix or suffix to a **root** word, or a core word. A **prefix** is a syllable added to the front of the root word that often changes the meaning of the word. A **suffix** is a syllable added to the end of the root word that may alter the use or the meaning of the word. Prefixes and suffixes are called **affixes.** As you define the words in the Pre-reading Vocabulary—Structural Attack exercises, look for and define the root word, and then define the affixes added onto the root word.

For instance, look at the word *provider. Provide* is the root word and is a verb that means "to supply." The suffix *-er* at the end means "one who." Thus, the verb *provide* becomes a noun, and the noun *provider* means "a person who supplies something." Now, look at the word *nonprovider.* The prefix *non-* at the beginning means "not" and greatly changes the meaning of the word. *Nonprovider* means "a person who does *not* supply something."

To define the words in **Pre-Reading Vocabulary—Structural Attack**, you need to know the prefixes and suffixes that are listed in Tables G-1 and G-2. Prefixes are defined and are listed in alphabetical order. Suffixes are arranged alphabetically in definition groups. Use the lists to help you in defining these words.

PREFIXES

A **prefix** is added to the beginning of a root word. A prefix usually changes the meaning of the root word. *Be especially aware of prefixes because they can greatly change the meaning of a word.* Note that some prefixes have more than one meaning and these meanings may be different.

TABLE G-1 Prefixes

Prefix	Meaning	Application
a-	full of	*Acrawl* means "creeping or spreading everywhere." The town was *acrawl* with gossip when people learned the mayor was arrested.
a-	total absence	*Amoral* means "totally unable to tell right from wrong." When a shark kills, it is *amoral* because a shark does not know right from wrong.
ante-	before	*Antedate* means "to come before." The Fourth of July *antedates* Thanksgiving.
anti-	against	*Antifreeze* means "against or stopping freezing." Vernie put *antifreeze* in her car engine before the big snowstorm.
be-	full of	*Beloved* means "very much loved." The soldier dearly missed his *beloved* wife.
counter-	against	*Counterplot* means "a plan to work against another plan." The police developed a *counterplot* to ruin the criminals' robbery plan.
de-	against, wrong	*Deform* means "to form badly or wrongly." The fire *deformed* the house and left it twisted and falling down.
de-	out of	*Deplane* means "to get off the airplane." The team claimed their luggage after they *deplaned*.
dis-	not, against	*Distrust* means "not to trust." Allison felt *distrust* toward the salesman who lied to her.
en-	within, into	*Encircle* means "to place in the middle" or "to surround." The floodwaters *encircled* the house.
il-	not	*Illegal* means "not legal." Many laws state that stealing is *illegal* and will place you in jail.
il-	more so	*Illuminate* means "to light up brightly." The fireworks *illuminated* the night sky so brightly that it looked like daylight.
im-	not	*Immeasurable* means "not able to be measured." The joy Teddy felt when he won the championship was *immeasurable*.
im-	more so	*Impoverished* means "very poor." The *impoverished* family did not even have enough money for food.
in-	not	*Incurable* means "not able to be healed." Doug caught an *incurable* disease, which he will have for the rest of his life.
in-	in, into	*Inside* means "in the side" or "through the side." Michelle walked through the door to get *inside* the room.

Prefix	Meaning	Application
inter-	between, among	*Intercollegiate* means "between two or more colleges." Michigan defeated Alabama in *intercollegiate* football.
intra-	within	*Intrastate* means "within the state." New Jersey Highway 33 is an *intrastate* road that starts at the ocean and ends at the Pennsylvania line.
kin-	relative	*Kinfolk* means "the people you are related to or your family." All my *kinfolk* will gather together at Thanksgiving for a family reunion.
non-	not	*Nonaccompanied* means "no company or alone." Bill preferred to attend the party alone, *nonaccompanied* by others.
pre-	before	*Predictable* means "able to be told beforehand." Tom's speeding ticket was *predictable* because he always drives too fast.
re-	again	*Refamiliarize* means "become familiar with again." To pass the test, Sue will *refamiliarize* herself with her notes.
self-	alone, one's own	*Self-satisfied* means "satisfied with oneself." After passing the test, Robert felt good about himself and was quite *self-satisfied*.
semi-	half	*Semiconscious* means "only half or partly aware." With all the noise at the concert, Jake was only *semiconscious* of the sirens outside.
sub-	under	*Subway* means "a road that goes underground." When there is too much traffic on the city roads, it is easier to take the *subway*.
super-	larger, above	*Superman* means "a man larger or better than other men." Bravely running into a burning building to help others is the act of a *superman*.
un-	not	*Unperceived* means "not noticed." Geri usually notices everything, but this time the dirty room went *unperceived*.
under-	below	*Underbrush* means "low shrubs and bushes that grow under the trees." Tony decided to cut the *underbrush* that was growing under his shade trees.
trans-	across	*Transoceanic* means "across the ocean." Alex will catch a *transoceanic* flight from New York to Paris.

SUFFIXES

A **suffix** is added to the end of a root word. A suffix may have very little effect on the meaning of a word, but a suffix will often change the part of speech of a root word.

What is the part of speech of a word? The part of speech of a word is, very simply, the function or use of the word. For instance, look at the word *ski*. In the sentence "Laura's *ski* was damaged," *ski* is a noun—the thing Laura had that was damaged. In "Laura and Ted *ski* downhill," *ski* is a verb—the action Laura and Ted do. In "Ted took *ski* lessons," *ski* is an adjective that describes the kind of lessons that Ted took. The word *ski* remains the same three letters, but the function it serves and the information it communicates change slightly depending on the part of speech it demonstrates. Note that although the use changes—from thing to action to description—the basic idea of a downhill sport remains the same.

In the same way, a suffix may often change the part of speech of a root word while leaving the root word's basic meaning largely unchanged. For instance, if we add *-ed* to the noun and say, "Laura *skied* down the hill," the noun becomes a verb, and the action is in the past. Thus, Laura is still involved with skiing, but now she has done it in the past.

In Table G-2, suffixes you will need to know are listed alphabetically within definition groups and with the relevant parts of speech noted. You will see several words from Pre-Reading Vocabulary—Structural Attack.

TABLE G-2 Suffixes

Suffix	Application
The following suffixes mean "one who" or "that which." Each turns a root word into a noun because the root word becomes the person or the thing that does something.	
-ant	A *servant* is "one who serves." The *servants* cleaned the mansion before the guests arrived.
-ary	A *visionary* is "one who sees clearly or into the future." Einstein was a *visionary* and saw the future uses of nuclear energy.
-ee	A *payee* is "one to whom things are paid." When Dodee owed her brother money, she wrote a check to him and made him the *payee*.
-ent	A *student* is "one who studies." College *students* are usually serious about their studies and work for good grades.
-er	A *fancier* is "one who fancies or likes something." Reid is a proven cat *fancier* and currently has four cats that he loves living in his home.
-ess	A *princess* is "a female who acts like a prince." The *princess* sat on the throne next to her husband, the prince.
-folk	*Townsfolk* are "people of the town." The *townsfolk* held a general meeting so that they could all meet the new mayor.

Suffix	Application
-ian	A *musician* is "one who plays music." Renée hired several *musicians* so that people would be able to dance at her party.
-ist	A *futurist* is "one who predicts the future on the basis of current trends." *Futurists* advise those in the government in Washington about issues on which it may someday need to enact laws.
-man	A *horseman* is "a person who is skilled at riding and driving horses." Dave is a fine *horseman* who often rides his horse around the park.
-or	A *survivor* is "one who survives or lasts." Rich lasted the longest on the deserted island and was named the *survivor*.

The following suffixes make a root word an adjective, and each changes the meaning of the root word.

-able	*Distinguishable* means "able to be told apart or distinguished." The greasy spots made the dirty clothes *distinguishable* from the clean clothes.
-er	*Lovelier* means, by comparison, "more lovely than another." Missy's garden, filled with blooms, is *lovelier* than Margaret's weed patch.
-est	*Kindliest* means, by comparison, "the most kind of all." The mother's gentle pat was the *kindliest* touch of all.
-ful	*Frightful* means "full of fright." With all its costumes and noisy bell ringing, Halloween is a *frightful* night.
-less	*Hapless* means "without happiness or luck" or "unfortunate." The *hapless* student had two flat tires and got a headache on his way to school.
-most	*Uppermost* means "most high" or "important." With a record of no accidents for two years, safety is the company's *uppermost* concern.
-ous	*Nervous* means "full of nerves" or "tense." Kirk was so *nervous* before his test that his hands were shaking.

The following suffixes mean "related to," "like," or "having the quality of" and generally change the meaning of a root word very little. Mostly, they change the parts of speech of the root word.

-al	The noun *cone* means "a form that comes to a circular point" and becomes the adjective *conical*. The tip of the space shuttle is rounded and *conical*.
-ance	The verb *repent* means "to feel sorry about" and becomes the noun *repentance*. After he broke his Mom's favorite vase, John felt awful and was filled with *repentance*.
-ant	The verb *observe* means "to see" and becomes the adjective *observant*. Carrie watches everything closely and is very *observant*.
-ed	The noun *candy* means "something sweet" and becomes the adjective *candied*. Mom used lots of sugar to sweetly coat the *candied* apples.
-ed	The noun *ink* means "writing fluid" and becomes the past-tense verb *inked*. Jefferson took pen and *inked* his signature on the Declaration of Independence that he wrote.

TABLE G-2

Suffix	Application
-en	The verb *choose* means "select" and becomes the adjective *chosen*. He had joined the Marines and became one of the *chosen* few.
-ence	The verb *depend* means "to rely on" and becomes the noun *dependence*. When Lisa paid her own bills, she knew her *dependence* on her parents would end.
-ic	The noun *metal* means "shiny element" and becomes the adjective *metallic*. Laura's silvery dress had a *metallic* shine.
-ing	The verb *terrify* means "to scare" and becomes the adjective *terrifying*. The *terrifying* thunder scared all of us as it seemed to shake the whole house.
-ish	The noun *fever* means "internal heat" and becomes the adjective *feverish*. Joel felt *feverish* from the heat of his sunburn.
-ism	The adjective *ideal* means "perfect" and becomes the noun *idealism*, which means "belief in perfection." George's *idealism* often leaves him disappointed because things are not always perfect.
-ity	The adjective *stupid* means "unthinking" and becomes the noun *stupidity*. Alice could not believe her *stupidity* when she locked her keys in the car.
-ive	The noun *feast* means "cheerful meal" and becomes the adjective *festive*. The wedding, with all its foods and colorful flowers, was a most *festive* affair.
-ly, -ily	The adjective *stealthy* means "moving quietly" and becomes the adverb *stealthily*. Bob crept so *stealthily* in the backdoor that no one knew he had entered the house.
-ment	The verb *confine* means "to restrain" and becomes the noun *confinement*. When the children misbehaved, Dad sent them to their rooms for silent *confinement*.
-ness	The adjective *nervous* means "tense" and becomes the noun *nervousness*. It was very hard for the groom to overcome his *nervousness* on his wedding day.
-tation	The adjective *ornamental* means "decorated" and becomes the noun *ornamentation*. Her diamond rings and pearl necklaces created *ornamentation* fit for a queen.
-ty	The adjective *frail* means "delicate" and becomes the noun *frailty*. At Aunt Alice's ninetieth birthday, we were all concerned about her *frailty*.
-y	The noun *stone* means "hard item" and becomes the adjective *stony*. The policeman had a *stony* look when the boy who was driving did not have a license.

CREDITS

Chapter 1: *Page 26:* "The Story of an Hour" by Kate Chopin. *Page 37:* "Snapshots of a Wedding" by Bessie Head © the Estate of Bessie Head, 1977. *Page 50:* "It Used to Be Green Once" by Patricia Grace, from The Dream Sleepers and Other Stories. Anthology Rights, Penguin Books (N.Z.). *Page 63:* "The Beautiful Soul of Don Damian", by Juan Bosch, translated by Lysander Kemp. *Page 79:* Jovita by Dinah Silveira de Queiroz, Darlene J Sadlier, ed and trans. by. One Hundred Years after Tomorrow, "Jovita", Indiana University Press.

Chapter 2: *Page 106:* "The Hockey Sweater" by Roch Carrier, from The Hockey Sweater and Other Stories. Copyright © 1979 by House of Anansi Press. *Page 117:* "Bone Girl" by Joseph Bruchac © 1993 in EARTH SONG, SKY SPIRIT. *Page 132:* "Strong Temptation—Strategic Movements—The Innocents Beguiled" by Mark Twain. *Page 146:* Excerpt from: "The Rain Came" from LAND WITHOUT THUNDER By Grace Ogot. East African Educational Publishers Ltd. *Page 163:* "What's in a Name?" by Jilian Peng, From Wild Cat: Stories of the Cultural Revolution. Copyright © 1990 with permission of the author.

Chapter 3: *Page 179:* "Cranes" by Hwang Sunwon, © 1990 University of Hawii Press. Reprinted with permission. *Page 192:* "Trail of the Green Blazer" from MALGUDI DAYS by R.K. Narayan, copyright © 1972, 1975, 1978, 1980, 1981, 1982 by R.K. Narayan. Used by permission of Viking Penguin, a division of Penguin Group (USA) Inc. *Page 205:* "Yoruba" from THE SANTERIA EXPERIENCE by Migene Gonzalez-Wippler. *Page 224:* "The Madman", from GIRLS AT WAR AND OTHER STORIES by Chinua Achebe, copyright © 1972, 1973 by Chinua Achebe. Used by permission of Doubleday, a division of Random House, Inc. *Page 239:* "Sweat" by Zora Neale Hurston.

Chapter 4: *Page 259:* "Ah Bah's Money" by Catherine Lim. *Page 272:* "The Necklace" by Guy Maupassant. *Page 288:* "The Ransom of Red Chief" by O. Henry. *Page 306:* "The Adventure of Speckled Band" by Arthur Conan Doyle. *Page 337:* "God Sees the Truth, but Waits" by Leo Tolstoy.

NOTES

INDEX OF
AUTHORS, TITLES, AND TERMS

NOTES

NOTES

NOTES

NOTES

NOTES